Perilous Voyages

NUMBER NINETY-SEVEN

Centennial Series of the Association of Former Students,
Texas A&M University

Perilous Voyages

Czech and English Immigrants
to Texas in the 1870s

LAWRENCE H. KONECNY

& CLINTON MACHANN

Texas A&M University Press COLLEGE STATION

William Kingsbury's 1877 phamplet
A Description of South-Western and Middle Texas (United States),
used with permission of General Research Division,
The New York Public Library, Astor, Lenox and Tilden Foundations.

Library of Congress Cataloging-in-Publication Data

Perilous voyages : Czech and English immigrants to Texas in the 1870s /
Lawrence H. Konecny and Clinton Machann.—1st ed.
    p. cm.—(Centennial series of the Association of Former Students,
Texas A&M University ; no. 97)
    Includes William Gilliam Kingsbury's 1877 pamphlet : A description of
south-western and middle Texas (United States)
    Includes bibliographical references (p.   ) and index.
    ISBN 1-58544-317-4 (cloth : alk. paper)
    1. Czech Americans—Texas—History—19th century. 2. British
Americans—Texas—History—19th century. 3. Czech Americans—
Texas—Biography. 4. British Americans—Texas—Biography.
5. Immigrants—Texas—History—19th century. 6. Frontier and pioneer
life—Texas. 7. Texas—Description and travel. 8. Texas—Emigration
and immigration—History—19th century. 9. Czechoslovakia—
Emigration and immigration—History—19th century. 10. England—
Emigration and immigration—History—19th century. I. Konecny,
Lawrence H., 1954– II. Machann, Clinton. III. Kingsbury, William
Gilliam, b. 1823. Description of south-western and middle Texas (United
States) IV. Series.
F395.B67P47 2004
976.4'061—dc22   2003018572

To the immigrants.

We honor you by remembering the past.

Table of Contents

List of Illustrations VIII

Acknowledgments IX

General Introduction 3

PART I

W. G. Kingsbury and His Pamphlet for the Galveston, Harrisburg, and San Antonio Railroad 13

CHAPTER 1. Introduction 15

CHAPTER 2. *A Description of South-Western and Middle Texas* (1877) 18

PART II

The Texas Diary of William Wright, February 13–July 1, 1879 71

CHAPTER 3. Introduction 73

CHAPTER 4. The Diary 79

PART III

The Wreck of the Missouri and Czech Immigration to Texas in 1873 103

CHAPTER 5. Introduction 105

CHAPTER 6. The Emigrants 109

CHAPTER 7. The Ship 118

CHAPTER 8. The Last Voyage of the *Missouri* 121

CHAPTER 9. From Shipwreck to Storm 124

CHAPTER 10. End of the Journey 137

CHAPTER 11. Excerpts from *Texas co cíl stěhování* (Texas as a Destination for Emigration, 1882) 145

Conclusion 156

Notes 159

Index 175

Illustrations

Sketch of William Wright   75
S.S. *Hammonia*   119
Central Wharf, Galveston, ca. 1873   138
Rail depot at Galveston   139
The Janča family   142
The family of Jiří and Anna Bujnoch   143

MAPS
1. Location of the Moravian villages   110
2. The Hurricanes (1873)   130

Acknowledgments

It was in the fall of 1987 when Leo Baca, the author of the series of books entitled *Czech Immigrant Passenger Lists,* prompted my research into a group of shipwrecked Moravian immigrants. We had been discussing a project of mine that eventually turned into a presentation entitled "Ship Voyage Research using Newspapers in Microform—Post Civil War Czech Immigration to Texas," and Leo related a story about a group of Moravian immigrants who had been shipwrecked on their way to Texas. Oral history claimed that this group endured the winds, rain, and tide of a hurricane while stranded on an island awaiting rescue. Being of Moravian descent myself, I was immediately interested. My interest grew stronger when Leo mentioned that Bujnoch and Olsovsky were two of the surnames of the seven Moravian families who were involved. My enthusiasm exploded when he explained that Fryčovice was one of the villages from which the families originated, because my great-grandfather Frantisek Konecny was also from Frycovice. He immigrated to Texas from Moravia in 1881. In addition to his nine-month-old son, Pavel, his wife Josefa Bujnoch-Konecny and his mother Mariana Olsovsky-Konecny traveled with him.

Several individuals had successfully documented this story through family tradition. Albert Blaha and Dorothy Bujnoch are two who made great strides in this endeavor. It was from their work that the *Liberty* passenger list was discovered: it documented the arrival of this group at New Orleans. It was from this initial document that I began. Leo was interested in discovering the name of the shipwrecked vessel, but I wanted to know everything about this wonderful story of adventure.

I received valuable assistance from several direct descendants and relatives of the shipwrecked Moravians. George and Dorothy Bujnoch were extremely helpful in supplying information, family contacts, and copies of documents received in connection with research that they commissioned in Moravia. Dorothy published the oral tradition of this story as remembered by the Lanik-Bujnoch descendants in her book *The Bujnoch Family, Our Czech-American Heritage.*

Mrs. Annie (Baros) Lanik-Wallace retained much of the oral history related to this story. Mrs. Wallace was the wife of Frank Lanik, a youthful passenger aboard the shipwrecked vessel. Mrs. Wallace shared this information with

Major Magdalene Drozd (U.S. Army, Ret.) who, in turn, shared it with Dorothy Bujnoch and later with me. Major Drozd was meticulous in keeping her notes of these items, which proved very helpful in keeping the tradition pure.

The Simek oral history was preserved by Josef, Ferdinand, and Vlasta Simek, children of Ferdinand Simek and grandchildren of Frantisek and Mariana Simek, the latter three being members of the original emigrant group. I conducted the interview with the Simeks on a Saturday in April, 1990, at their farm in Dime Box, Texas. This interview was something I normally would have done by telephone; however, the Simeks did not have a telephone. During the interview they explained that they did not have an electric washing machine either. They claimed to have bought one, but subsequently returned it because it wasted too much water. Vlasta served the best poppy seed kolaches that I have had, possibly because they were cooked in her woodburning cook-stove. Josef was present that day but was feeling poorly and did not participate in our conversation. Ferdinand and Vlasta related the Simek oral history as though it was something that had happened the day before.

Rudolph Janca contributed the Janca oral history during several phone interviews. Mr. Janca was most gracious in relaying the information as he remembered it being told by his father, Jan Janča, and his grandparents Jan and Mariana Janča—the latter three also part of the original immigrant group. Virginia Bockholt also assisted in contributing Janca oral history and photographs of the Jan and Mariana Janca family.

My thanks go to each of these individuals for their contributions, interest, and commitment to preserving the tradition of the Moravian people. If it were not for their devotion, this story surely would have passed away without making the pages of history.

I would like to extend my acknowledgments to include William L. Wright, grandson of William Wright. Mr. Wright contributed the 1879 Wright Diary and supplemental information about the William Wright family. We benefited from his diligence in maintaining a family archive and his generosity in sharing its wealth of information.

Many volunteers helped with this project and related projects along the way. I would like to thank the following organizations and their members for their assistance and devotion to preserving the history of Texas: the Czech Heritage Society of Texas; the Galveston County Genealogical Society; the Houston Genealogical Forum; and the Polish Genealogical Society of Texas.

Several individuals also deserve special thanks for their guidance, contributions, and support. These are Casey Edward Greene of the Rosenberg Library, Galveston, Texas; Adolf Hofmeister of the Staatsarchiv, Bremen, Germany;

W. M. Von-Maszewski of the George Memorial Library, Richmond, Texas; and Dorothy Pechal of the SPJST Museum, in Temple, Texas.

From the time I started this project in 1987 until today, my family has increased in some areas and has diminished in others. Grandpa is a new designation that I wear. I thank my wife Jo Ann for her love, support, dedication, and as it relates to this project, her perseverance. I also thank my late father Henry L. Konecny for my Moravian heritage.

—Lawrence H. Konecny

My research on Bohemian and Moravian immigration to Texas began in the late 1970s, following short but intensive summer study programs in Czechoslovakia, and led to the books *Krásná Amerika: A Study of the Texas Czechs, 1851–1939* (1983) and *Czech Voices: Stories from Texas in the Amerikán národní kalendář* (1991), both with co-author James W. Mendl. Among the many organizations related to Czech-American culture in which I have been active through the years, the Czechoslovak Society of Arts and Sciences (SVU) and the Czech Educational Foundation of Texas (CEFT) have been most significant in encouraging me to persevere in lines of historical and cultural scholarship begun in those early days. Currently I serve as chairman of the Board of Directors of the CEFT and I edit the journal *Kosmas,* an English-language, academic journal that focuses on Czech and Slovak studies and is sponsored by the SVU.

Ivan Dubovický has been an invaluable consultant to me in this area of study for a long time. During the many years of work on the project that finally resulted in *Perilous Voyages,* Ivan, first as Cultural Counselor at the Czech Embassy in Washington, D.C., and then as Special Advisor for Cultural and Scientific Affairs at the Ministry of Foreign Affairs of the Czech Republic in Prague, offered valuable advice and research assistance. Ivan, himself an important scholar in Czech immigration to the United States, provided us with the copy of August Siemering's rare 1882 Czech-language pamphlet *Texas co cíl stěhování* (Texas as a Destination for Emigration), which was used in the preparation of the book manuscript.

We are grateful to the staff of the Texas A&M University Press for their support and assistance as this project slowly evolved. It was at their suggestion that we decided to publish the entire text of W. G. Kingsbury's 1877 pamphlet *A Description of South-Western and Middle Texas* as part of the book. The New York Public Library kindly provided us with a copy of that publication, and the Southern Methodist University Library made available a copy of the 1878 second edition of Kingsbury's pamphlet. All along the way, the Interlibrary

Loan Services at the Sterling Evans Library at Texas A&M University offered valuable assistance in our gaining access to the research materials we needed, and librarian David Z. Chroust, with whom I work closely in editing the journal *Kosmas,* was invariably willing to help answer questions related to the Czech language and bibliographical issues in general. Deborah Pipes, who served as my research assistant in the Department of English at Texas A&M University in 1997 and 1998, was largely responsible for incorporating the text of Kingsbury's pamphlet into our manuscript. Later, Daniela Kukrechtová, a Czech graduate student and the first Hlavinka Fellow at Texas A&M in a program sponsored by the Czech Educational Foundation of Texas, translated sections of August Siemering's Czech-language pamphlet into English for our use, and subsequent CEFT Hlavinka Fellows, Martin Svoboda and Magdalena Vintrová, helped to edit portions of the manuscript that incorporated Czech words and phrases. A grant from the Texas A&M University Program to Enhance Scholarly and Creative Activities helped to fund research on Czech immigration to America at the Naprstek Museum and Library in Prague in the summers of 1997 and 1998.

In addition to thanking my mother Sophie (Matcek) Machann and all the other Czech-Moravian family relations and dear friends who have inspired and assisted my work through the years, I want to acknowledge the generous and loving cooperation of my wife Ginny, who is not of Czech descent but whose acquaintance with Czech-American culture dates back to her childhood in Nebraska, where she had several friends of Czech heritage and, in a larger sense, became aware of the various immigrant groups that have contributed so much to the development of that part of the U.S.

Finally, as a professor of English whose primary academic field of teaching and research is British Victorian literature and culture, I also have a keen interest in the diary of nineteenth-century Englishman William Wright which is incorporated into the text of our book. Working on this project has been fascinating for me as a native Texan because it brings together topics related to the history of Texas and especially the history of European immigration to Texas that I care about deeply.

—Clinton Machann

Perilous Voyages

General Introduction

In his 1877 pamphlet intended for potential English immigrants, William Gilliam Kingsbury promoted "South-Western and Middle Texas": the country developed by the Galveston, Harrisburg, and San Antonio Railroad along this route, which ran 265 miles, west and southwest, from Galveston, then a thriving commercial city and Texas's only major port, to San Antonio, the old Spanish and Mexican capital of Texas and undoubtedly destined to play a major role in the future development of the state. According to him, this corridor was not only the "garden spot" of Texas but a country "combining more natural advantages for supplying the wants of man, than almost any other portion of the Globe." The visionary Kingsbury looked forward to the further westward extension of the G.H.&S.A. by six hundred miles to El Paso, where it would link with the Southern Pacific Railroad, creating a railway route from the Gulf Coast of Texas to the Pacific Coast of California. In addition to celebrating the productivity of the Texas land, the desirability of the climate, the abundance of water, and other natural resources, he suggests a romantic image of Texas still familiar today in his descriptions of the herds of wild mustangs and the young cowboys with their riding skills, amazing rope tricks, and preference for a bracing ranch life in Texas rather than the pursuit of culture and sophistication in Europe—even when they have the choice. Kingsbury's ideas for creating vast cattle and sheep ranches and for marketing Texas beef in England on a grand scale appeal to the entrepreneurial imagination: Texas will become the "great 'Meat House' of the world." One particularly intriguing suggestion he throws out concerns possible future, unexpected wealth from mineral deposits discovered in the land bought by settlers—Kingsbury was thinking primarily of copper and silver and had no way of knowing how petroleum would one day create Texas millionaires.

However, at the center of Kingsbury's vision of Texas is something other than grandiose schemes and romantic dreams of future greatness and fabulous fortunes: it is the promise of a new start in life and practical advice about how a hard-working and resourceful Englishman with little or moderate wealth can survive and eventually thrive in this part of the world. On this level Kingsbury addresses the interests and concerns of many potential immigrants, in England and elsewhere in Europe, for whom Texas was an increasingly attractive destination in the years following the American Civil War.

The extraordinary promotional efforts made by Kingsbury and the G.H.&S.A. Railroad were to a large extent made possible by the unique history of Texas. In 1845, after a decade as an independent republic, Texas joined the United States and was allowed to keep its public lands. In additional to being used to finance Texas' educational system, much of this public land was granted to railroad companies, which in turn sold it to individual settlers (see chapter 1, note 2).

Part I of this book reproduces Kingsbury's original 1877 pamphlet, today a rare document that gives insight into the historical context and the rhetoric of Texas immigration, especially the persuasive arguments made by the representative of a Texas-based railroad that stood to profit not only from a rising demand for transportation services but also from the sale of land to immigrants. Kingsbury's *A Description of South-Western and Middle Texas* provides background to the narratives of individual immigrants and helps to illuminate the vast system of interlocking railways, steamship lines, and communication networks of which they were a part.

Part II turns to the experiences of the immigrants themselves, Kingsbury's audience. Published here for the first time is a private diary that had been kept by an Englishman named William Wright. Wright was intrigued by the claims for the American Southwest made by promoters in his country but decided to investigate for himself before committing his wife and children to immigration. His 1879 journey began with a shipwreck off the coast of Spain, but, undaunted, he continued in another ship and eventually was able to record his firsthand impressions of the land and people of Texas. His diary was made available by his grandson William L. Wright in 1992.

Offered in Part III, and also published here for the first time, is another authentic narrative of European immigration to Texas, concerning not an individual immigrant but a group, not English but Central European. In 1873 a group of thirty-six men, women, and children left their rural Moravian homeland—today part of the Czech Republic—to pursue dreams of prosperity and the good life in the far-away, exotic land of Texas. Their vision of the future dissolved into nightmarish reality when, after a grueling transatlantic crossing, their ship ran aground in the Bahamas. They were left to ride out a terrible hurricane on the little island of North Bimini before they were able to continue their trek to Galveston and, finally, to the peaceful farmlands of

Central Texas. The chief sources used in reconstructing this story are oral histories by descendants of the Láník, Šimek, and Janča families who were part of that immigrant group, along with a privately printed family history by Dorothy Bujnoch and other sources.[1]

Unlike Wright, the Moravians were not directly influenced by Kingsbury: their chief source of information about Texas was the correspondence of previous Czech immigrants. However, in the 1880s Kingsbury expanded his activities from his English base and himself became involved in promoting immigration to Texas among Germans and Czechs on the Continent. The German Texan August Siemering published a German version and a Czech-language adaptation of Kingsbury's pamphlet, portions of which serve here as a supplement to the story of the Moravian group. Included in these excerpts is an 1882 newspaper article about Czech, Polish, and Serbian immigrants that had been published by Antonin Haidušek in a Galveston newspaper, three years before he launched his Czech-language newspaper *Svoboda* (Freedom).

This collection of rare and previously unpublished documents, along with background information about the transportation and communication systems supporting European immigration to Texas in the 1870s, should be of interest to the general reader who cares about Texas history as well as to scholars in the field of immigration history. The narratives of Wright and of the Moravians are compelling stories of human adventure. As the title *Perilous Voyages* suggests, emigration from Europe to Texas at the time could be an uncertain, dangerous undertaking, apart from the anxiety and sadness associated with leaving one's homeland.

The new information presented in this book helps foster a better understanding of the role European immigrants played in the rapid expansion of the Texas population and economy in the 1870s and 1880s. In particular it casts light on the presettlement aspects of immigration, the process that drew Europeans to a part of the United States with a short but extraordinary history and an enormous potential for development.

At the top of the list of people "most needed in Texas" are, according to Kingsbury, "farmers, men who will rent or buy the land and cultivate it." And his advice concerning tenant-farming arrangements in Texas indicates that he expected at least some English immigrants to rent first, buy later. Near the end of his 1877 pamphlet Kingsbury is even more explicit about his intended audience. He is "not urging or advising any man owning his own home and well fixed [in England] to break up and go to Texas." The immigrant he has in mind is "the man who has capital at his command bringing him less than ten per cent. per annum; or he who can only look back upon a life of toil and count no gains; or he who has children approaching manhood without estate; and . . . all those who have never known the blessing there is in a place they can call their *own home.*" The basic product marketed by Kingsbury is available, relatively inexpensive agricultural land in a favorable geographic, economic, and social environment. In England population density and the price of farmland were perhaps insurmountable barriers to land and home ownership. In the Czech lands these barriers were even more formidable, and oppressive social, political, and religious institutions were additional incentives to leave one's homeland. The deeply egalitarian image of Texas social life also was attractive to Englishmen frustrated by inherited social hierarchies.

In the calculations of Kingsbury and English immigrants such as Wright, land in Texas probably figured more clearly as an economic investment—apart from other considerations—than it did to the Moravians, who were moving themselves and their families to what must have seemed a much more alien environment. Wright's greater financial assets, mobility, access to information, and ability to speak English were significant advantages. However, in spite of the cultural and economic differences between William Wright and the Moravians, they and the vast majority of potential European immigrants to Texas shared dreams about an essentially *agrarian* way of life, although the restless Wright never actually settled down on a Texas farm. Aside from ranching and hog-raising opportunities, money was to be made in cash crops—notably the ubiquitous "white gold" cotton (unintended readers of the pamphlet with real experience in the cotton fields may have laughed or cursed at Kingsbury's description of cotton picking as light, almost effortless work), the sugar cane that could be grown in more limited areas, and staple food crops such as corn, potatoes, and sweet potatoes.

Even if they arrived penniless, immigrants could work as agricultural laborers and earn money, lease farm land, and eventually buy their own land. Subsistence farming would enable the farmer and his family, once they owned their own land, to endure as an independent unit, even in hard times. When times were good, money could be saved for the purpose of buying more or better land. This simple but enormously attractive ideal really could be achieved in Texas, as Kingsbury assured his English readers, as Siemering assured his German and Czech readers, and as Antonin Haidušek confirmed in his representative newspaper article on Czech, Polish, and Serbian immigrants. Each of the nine autobiographical testimonials by Czech and German immigrant farmers included in Siemering's pamphlet describes a unique life adventure that culminates in the common goal of at least moderate farming success, as documented by the number of acres owned, inventories of livestock, and the figures for crop production and annual incomes.

Both Wright and the Moravians graphically illustrate patterns of migration that were bringing large numbers of Europeans to Texas in the decades following the Civil War. Seen in the widest context, this phenomenon was only part of the mass immigration of white populations into Texas in this era. During the years 1870–90, the total white population of the state grew from 564,700 to 1,745,935, while the black population grew only from 253,475 to 448,171.[2] The bulk of the white immigration came from internal U.S. sources, notably the states of Alabama and Tennessee.[3] Nevertheless, foreign immigrants played a significant part in this rapid growth: at the end of this period, the foreign-born population of Texas stood at 152,956.[4] Immigrants from Mexico and from the German states—including significant numbers of Slavic groups such as the Czechs from the Austrian Empire—together made up nearly two-thirds of this total; however, many emigrated from the British Isles as well: Wright and his family were among 9,441 from England.[5]

The Moravian group and Wright were part of this great migratory pattern, but there are closer links between the two stories. Both the Moravians and Wright sailed from Liverpool to New Orleans (before traveling on to the Texas port of Galveston) on vessels operated by the Mississippi and Dominion Line, a steamship line well known to Kingsbury.[6] The fact that both were wrecked en route to America is coincidental but not so unlikely as may be imagined. Late in 1879, only a month after Wright's first Mississippi and Dominion ship had run aground, another company ship on the Liverpool–New Orleans route sank en route to Havana in gale force winds a few days after embarking from La Coruña, the site of the Wright shipwreck. Unlike the other two wrecks, from which all passengers apparently were able to escape with their lives, this one cost the lives of about 169 people, including passengers and crew members.

Ironically *Borussia,* the unfortunate ship, had been manufactured in 1855 by the firm Caird and Co. of Greenock, Scotland, as sister ship to the *Hammonia,* which, after renamings and renovations, had become the *Missouri,* the vessel wrecked in 1873 with the Moravians on board. Among the lost passengers from the *Borussia* were at least two English families from the neighborhood of Newcastle-on-Tyne who were immigrating to Texas. William Todd, described in a newspaper account of the tragedy as a forty-five-year-old seedsman and gardener, was accompanied by his forty-year-old wife Elizabeth and six children, ranging in age from two to nineteen years. Along with them were William Adamson—a forty-year-old farmer who had decided to immigrate after recent losses of cattle and crop failure, his forty-one-year-old wife Elizabeth, and four children, aged nine to seventeen.[7]

It is not surprising that relatively old and battered vessels such as the *Borussia* and *Hammonia/Missouri* would be especially vulnerable to the dangers of sea travel. In their prime years, however, both had been used in the North German–New York trade. Just as sailing ships were used in the southern routes from Europe to New Orleans and Galveston after they had disappeared from the northern routes to New York and Baltimore, antiquated steamships persisted on the southern routes as well, making them relatively hazardous for immigrants.[8]

In addition to use of the Mississippi and Dominion Line, there are further connections between the story of the Moravian group and that of Wright. The Moravian families, on the way to their new home in Central Texas, rode the Galveston, Harrisburg, and San Antonio Railroad (also known as the Sunset Road) from Harrisburg to Columbus—at that time, the end of the line. This Texas railroad, then only two years old, became increasingly involved in the immigrant trade in the 1870s and set up Kingsbury in London as its European agent. Kingsbury became the foremost promoter in England of Texas as a place of immigration, and his speculative land-settlement schemes became the target of intense criticism in Wright's 1879 diary.

Finally, as Wright trekked eastward on his way back to the Texas coast after his visit to the San Antonio area, he entered Lavaca County. Passing through the countryside near Hallettsville, Moulton, and Sweet Home, he recorded some of his most flattering descriptions of the farm and ranch land that he had surveyed during his journey, and he contemplated buying land there for himself. As it happened this was the area the party of Moravian families had settled six years earlier.

Overall, the population of Texas rose from 818,579, the nineteenth largest in the United States, to 3,048,710, the sixth largest, during the thirty years from 1870 to 1900. During the 1870s, the decade of most rapid growth, the state's population nearly doubled. It is important to remember, however, that this population remained predominantly rural. The percentage of rural population stood at 93.3 in 1870 and had declined only to 82.9 by 1900. In 1870 the five most populous counties, in descending order, were Washington, Harris, Rusk, Fayette, and Caldwell, but among this group only Harris County contained one of the five largest cities—Houston, the third most populous city, behind Galveston and San Antonio, and ahead of Brownsville and Jefferson. The stories of the *Missouri* group and of Wright show us that the search for good, available farmland was the great motivator of settlers during this period of dynamic growth, when the family farm was the basic social unit. Land ownership was the common goal, and some Czech tenant farmers rented land from relatives, land that they often expected to buy or inherit. With very few exceptions, first- and second-generation Texas Czechs who became schoolteachers, clergymen, doctors, and lawyers not only owned farm land, but worked at farm labor for a significant part of their lives. The same was true of tailors, blacksmiths, and most other craftsmen.[9] The stories also detail attitudes and habits of thought associated with an agrarian life. These generalizations apply equally to Wright and to the Moravians, but there are also significant distinctions that are illuminated in these presettlement narratives.

In the end the Moravians were, in effect, absorbed into the Texas Czech communities of Central Texas. The immigration process, from start to finish, operated within a system of family and communal relationships. The original idea of immigrating specifically to Texas, rather than some other destination in the United States or elsewhere in the world, easily can be traced back to the Bergman-Lešikar connection discussed in Part III. Kinship patterns and common ties to relatively isolated and provincial localities in the European homeland are of central importance. As with the *Missouri* group, it was usual for whole families—husbands, wives, and children—within the larger group to travel together on this great life-altering adventure. This pattern in the presettlement phase is consistent with the way of life the Moravians would adopt in the Texas countryside. Even after a family was able to buy its farm, it was generally too poor to hire much, if any, labor. The success of the farm and of the family depended upon the cooperation of all family members, and this required the interdependence of individuals maintained by a code of family loyalty.[10]

Each family member functioned as part of the group rather than as an unattached individual. Family solidarity with little emphasis on individual self-interest was the dominant paradigm. The need for conformity, not only in farming practices, but in family values, attitudes, and behavioral characteristics of all kinds, was not considered to be inconsistent with the attractive American ideals of political freedom and individual liberty. Children were expected to be loyal to the family but were given much attention and open signs of affection.

Although the father was generally considered to be the unquestioned head of the family, there was the balance of masculine and feminine values characteristic of an enterprise in which both sexes were equally engaged. There was, of course, a division between male and female spheres of work. The husband supervised work in the fields and elsewhere on the farm, and he represented the family in business contacts with the outside world. The house was supervised by the wife, with emphasis on the all-important kitchen. In a large family that included children of both sexes (the dominant ideal), the daughters' tasks included housework, milking, gathering eggs, and gardening, while the sons were expected to engage in the heavier farm work. However, from approximately age ten, every able-bodied child regardless of gender was expected to contribute to the family welfare by working in the fields along with their parents. The fact that virtually all family members worked side by side in the fields contributed to a family comradery and, perhaps, a less-strict division of gender roles than that typical of various ethnic groups engaged in agriculture in Texas at this time. The husband and wife typically shared the responsibility for making important decisions, and a woman, particularly a *stařenka* (grandmother), could wield a great deal of influence both in the household and in the surrounding local community as well. Anglo-Americans sometimes thought it odd or even morally wrong that (white) women and children should work in the fields along with adult males, while Czechs sometimes considered their Anglo neighbors to be lazy and shiftless.[11]

The most obvious contrast between the Moravians and Wright is that as an Englishman he faced no major linguistic, cultural, or legal barriers as he prepared for his journey to Texas. In addition, although he was not a wealthy man, after selling his farm in England he had sufficient financial resources to explore the booming but still primitive and unfamiliar state of Texas before committing his wife and children to immigration. In the best of circumstances, however, immigration to a foreign land involves risk and uncertainty. Cautiously optimistic and intrigued by the grandiose claims of economic opportunity in Texas agriculture made by Kingsbury and others, Wright wanted to see for himself. An independent and adventurous man who had seen the world as a young sailor, Wright, as he approached the age of forty, was restless and tired of his life as a Northampton farmer. His situation was quite different from that of the Moravian men, women, and children, most of whom had never been beyond their native province, who spoke little or no English, and who would be mistaken for the better-organized and more numerous German immigrants on arrival in the United States. Wright took advantage of his mobility and access to information, while the Moravians relied on social systems of support—within their individual families and within the larger group—and on the slow but effective information network that drove "chain migration."

Wright's astute comments on the quality and value of the land, crops, and livestock he saw in Texas illustrate the expertise of an experienced, second-generation farmer. His remarks about the individual farms and farmers he met and the settlements and towns he visited—especially his critique of Kingsbury and the other immigrant agents—demonstrate shrewdness, understanding, a good sense of humor, and a positive attitude, qualities well suited for an immigrant to rural Texas in the late 1870s. And yet even after returning with his wife and children, Wright never settled down to the life of a farmer on any of the attractive locations he had surveyed. Perhaps this was because of wanderlust developed during his seafaring days; perhaps he could never find just the right farm to suit him.

It was different for the Moravians: like most of their compatriots who had already immigrated, they went about putting down roots in their new homeland as quickly as possible. This does not mean that a family would necessarily remain permanently on the first farm it established. Moving from one location to another in search of more and better farmland, especially in groups of related families, was not uncommon, but all the first-generation adult immigrants from the *Missouri* group remained in Central Texas.

These two stories, then, can be seen as paradigmatic of two related but distinctive models of European immigration. In one case a group of men, women and children, bound together by social, cultural, and familial ties, follow others like them, countrymen and relatives who had gone before. The Moravians are courageous in their determination to begin new lives as foreigners in a strange new land, but at the same time cautious and carefully focused on a limited set of goals. Wright is focused on certain goals as well—farming and ranching opportunities—but, though he intends to return with his wife, he travels as an individual explorer and entrepreneur, much more flexible and tentative in his plans for the future.

Kingsbury's career as a promoter of European immigration to Texas is interesting in itself and will be discussed further in the introduction to Part I. As will be seen, however, the actual experiences of Europeans immigrating to Texas were typically more difficult and uncertain than the rosy picture painted by Kingsbury in his pamphlet had led them to expect. Wright himself became very critical of Kingsbury's claims.

PART I

*W. G. Kingsbury
and His 1877 Pamphlet
for the Galveston, Harrisburg,
and San Antonio Railroad*

CHAPTER I

Introduction

William Gilliam Kingsbury, who was born in Booncillo, New York, on November 6, 1823, studied dentistry as a young man in Baltimore and then moved to Texas in January, 1846, to set up practice.[1] Kingsbury's taste for travel and adventure is evident in his decision to accompany his friend Samuel Hamilton Walker, a Texas Ranger, on a military campaign to Mexico during the Mexican War, and, in spite of his status as a civilian dentist, Kingsbury was wounded on several occasions. Following the war, he practiced dentistry in several West Texas towns before settling in San Antonio in 1851. During his subsequent twenty-five-year career as a dentist in that city, Kingsbury—through personal contacts, speeches, and newspaper articles—acquired the reputation of being a promoter of the state to potential immigrants. Initially appointed state commissioner of immigration and stationed in St. Louis, Kingsbury was sent to London in 1877 as the European immigration agent of the Galveston, Harrisburg, and San Antonio Railroad. (See the letters of introduction from Governor R. B. Hubbard of Texas, Secretary of State J. G. Searcy, and State Comptroller Stephen H. Darden, reprinted in Kingsbury's pamphlet [chapter 2]).

As pointed out in the General Introduction, railroad companies in Texas had a special interest in attracting immigration to the state, not only because the immigrants made use of the railroad as a mode of transportation, but also because the companies wished to sell land to the immigrants. In order to stimulate the construction of railroads in Texas during the period 1852–82, the state government made a series of massive land grants—more than 32 million acres in all—to various railroad companies.[2] Obviously the companies stood to make enormous financial profits from the resale of land to immigrants. Although several companies distributed special brochures and otherwise enticed potential immigrants, one of them in particular focused on Europe, especially Great Britain and Germany: the Galveston, Harrisburg, and San Antonio Railroad.

This ambitious company was established in 1871 by a group of investors led by Boston merchant Thomas W. Peirce, who personally advanced approximately a million dollars to finance railroad construction up to the year 1877.[3] By 1877 the road in fact stretched from Galveston to San Antonio, and the company reported 40,719 passengers and 113,426 tons of freight for the year.[4] In addition to the English, German, and Czech pamphlets associated with Kingsbury, two promotional publications, both published in St. Louis, were issued by the company for domestic consumption: an oration made by Governor Hubbard, forecasting the glorious future of Texas, at the Philadelphia Exposition of 1876; and a 278-page, hard-cover *Southern and Western Texas Guide for 1878* by James L. Rock and W. I. Smith, both published in St. Louis.[5]

In organizing and advertizing European immigration to Texas from his London office, Kingsbury made arrangements with and recommended the transatlantic steamers of the North German Lloyd Line at Bremen, Germany, and those of the Mississippi and Dominion Line at Liverpool, England. The North German Lloyd Line was widely respected, but, as already mentioned in the General Introduction, it is the Mississippi and Dominion Line that figures prominently in the stories of both Wright and the Moravians. Its fleet consisted largely of the discards of the Hamburg American Line, and, in many cases, the Mississippi and Dominion Line was the second or even third owner of the vessels in its fleet. Aside from a problematic safety record, reports from steerage passengers traveling on steamers of this company in the 1870s consistently claimed that the conditions on board were deplorable.

Most of Kingsbury's critics, however, focused on what they took to be his exaggerated claims for economic opportunities in Texas. Wright himself was one of those critics. Undeterred, Kingsbury went on to play an important role in the intensified immigration business that brought approximately 8,038 immigrants directly from Bremen or its outer seaport Bremerhaven to Galveston on two sailing vessels and fifteen steamships, all belonging to the North German Lloyd Line, during the period 1880–86.[6] All of the vessels, with the possible exception of one, were consigned to Kauffman and Runge of Galveston, Texas, and all of them were charters or special consignments. Kingsbury, still representing the Galveston, Harrisburg, and San Antonio Railroad, was primarily responsible for several charters, including that of the *America,* the first steamship of the North German Lloyd Line to travel from Bremen to Galveston during the 1880–86 era, arriving at its destination on September 29, 1880.[7] Kingsbury had traveled to Bremen in April, 1880, and signed a contract with North German Lloyd that provided for an appropriate steamship if Kingsbury could guarantee at least 500 passengers. In a letter to the *Galveston Daily News,* Kingsbury boasted that he had "placed in the hands of all licensed immigration agents throughout Germany a pamphlet descriptive of Texas, each book also containing a complete map of the United States. I printed both at Hamburg, and distributed from that place 30,000 copies during the months of April and May. . . . The Sunset road is doing all in its power, regardless of expense, and if the citizens of Texas will lend a helping hand by attentions and encouraging the new arrivals, strangers at your gates, and getting them to write good letters home, we shall make it a grand success."[8]

The pamphlet to which Kingsbury refers is the 1882 German-language version of his 1877 pamphlet mentioned in the General Introduction. Although the German pamphlet lists August Siemering as its author, it contains introductory comments by Kingsbury and is largely a reworking of the English pamphlet, from a German point of view, including testimonials from German immigrants. The Czech version of the pamphlet, excerpted in Part III, also contains introductory statements by Kingsbury and makes a special appeal to potential Czech immigrants such as those of the *Missouri* party.

A reprint of Kingsbury's 1877 pamphlet *A Description of South-Western and Middle Texas* follows. According to the original title page, it was published in London at the "Anglo-American Times" Press, 127 Strand, W.C.[9]

A Description of South-Western and Middle Texas (United States)

The Soil, Climate, and Productions; Together with Prospective Sources of Wealth. Also the Great Inducements Offered All Classes of European Immigrants. And Containing a Description and Price of the Land Belonging to and Traversed by the Galveston, Harrisburg, & San Antonio Railroad. By W. G. Kingsbury. (1877)

Preface

"Man that is born of woman is of few days and full of trouble"; there are but three short steps to his existence: dependent youth, manhood with its labours, cares, and responsibilities; old age with its aches, and pains, and helpless infirmities, and all of this earth is o'er. Woe to us! who shall reach old age in poverty.

To accumulate for this period, man measures brain and bodily strength with his fellow man in the great battle of life. The place upon the earth where this battle can best be fought, and an honest sum secured for our declining years, and for the children we may leave behind us, are momentous questions to every man. I will not say that my country is above all others the best, but I place this little pamphlet in your hands without charge, and ask you to read and compare the advantages offered by the State of Texas, with the most favoured of which the earth can boast.

The State of Texas.

The State of Texas is one of the South Western States of the American Union and the largest and most varied in soil, climate, and productions, of any of the States. Though not exactly square, its area from north-east to south-west, and from south-east to north-west does not vary but little from one thousand miles. This vast extent of territory is traversed by large and rapid flowing rivers of pure fresh water, at a distance of about sixty miles from each other for the entire distance; several of these were navigated by steam power before the era of Railroads, but only three or four are now used for that purpose. Between these rivers numerous creeks and springs, some of them of great magnitude, would furnish ample water power, and an abundant supply of water for a dense population. The eastern portion of the State for nearly two hundred miles, is covered by forests of pine, cypress, and several dense varieties of oak, said to be the finest in America, and sufficient in extent to supply all the demands of the State for a hundred years to come.

The balance of the State, is very evenly divided between timber and prairie, there being no large districts exclusively devoted to either, and individual farms generally contain nearly an equal portion of each. There is considerable agriculture carried on in all the counties within this timber belt, but the finest agricultural counties lie west of it, and extends for several hundred miles in width, and from north to south through the entire State. West of this, the country is sparsely settled, and very few efforts at farming has been made, it is however well watered and clothed with a great variety of rich and nutritious grasses, and is at the present time regarded as the great stock-raising division of the State. These divisions crossing as they do lines of latitude for such a distance, must necessarily present considerable changes of climate and productions. The northern and middle divisions (counting from north to south) is regarded as a fine farming country, but liable to more or less snow and ice in winter, giving less chances of natural pasturage, more hazard in the way of late and early frosts in spring and autumn to growing crops, and a little above the belt for successful sugar-growing, or the longest and finest lint in cotton. The southern division usually called Middle and South-Western Texas, is the country directly west and south-west of the city of Galveston, the principal sea-port town of the State, and is regarded by both Citizens and travelers as the garden spot of the State, and as combining more natural advantages for supplying the wants of man, than almost any other portion of the Globe. This section has within the last six months been opened to settlement and commerce by the building of the GALVESTON, HARRISBURG, & SAN ANTONIO RAILROAD.

This Road has its eastern terminal connection with the wharfs of Galveston, and has already penetrated the interior as far as the important and growing city of San Antonio, a distance of two hundred and sixty-five miles. From this point it is to be continued in two lines, one due west to the Mexican border, the other in a north-westerly direction, a distance of six hundred miles to El Paso, where it will be met by the Southern Pacific, now being constructed from the Pacific coast to El Paso, on the western border of Texas. The two roads when united, will form the true "Southern Pacific Railroad," and will be the shortest route across the American Continent within the territory of the United States by nearly one thousand miles. It will also have the advantage of passing through a rich agricultural and pastoral country, free from snow blockades and ice at all seasons, and for the entire distance.

It is to this line of road and the country tributary to it, that I propose to invite emigration from the United Kingdom of Great Britain, and to this end have already established an office in London. I only propose in this little paper to glance at the topography and some of the many inducements I am prepared to offer to parties who will settle in that country. These are rich and fertile lands, so cheap that the labouring man may get his board and ten acres for an honest month's work, and the rich man find large profits upon his investments. A climate so healthful that the death rate, taken from official sources, reaches but ten and a half to the thousand. An atmosphere so pure that fresh meat exposed to a free circulation will cure without tainting, and people may sleep out of doors the year round without the slightest risk of fevers.

A country in which law and order is strictly maintained and crime speedily punished; religion respected and churches supported, and a school fund that will give free education to its children for ever. A country in which the agriculturist reaches the highest returns with the least labour and the stock-raiser is furnished the food on which to rear his flocks and herds as free as the water they drink, or the air they breathe.

With these remarks I proceed to the various divisions of the subjects most likely to interest emigrants, to all of which I only ask a careful perusal, and that you note the evidence I offer coming from others not interested in any way themselves.

Letter from the Hon. James White, Ex-M.P.

I give the following extract from a letter addressed to Colonel T. W. Peirce,[1] President of the Galveston, Harrisburg, and San Antonio Railroad, by the

Hon. James White, ex-Member of the English Parliament, who represented Brighton for 17 successive years. Mr. White travelled largely over Western and South-Western Texas with his family, for his own information and looking to secure the best homes for the English Emigrant. The letter was unsolicited, and dated San Antonio, Texas, May 7, 1876: —

My Dear Mr. PEIRCE:

All my inquiries and observation more than justify the opinion you have expressed as to the merits and future prosperity of the Galveston, Harrisburg and San Antonio Railway.

Had I had the pleasure of meeting you, I should have ventured to make several suggestions, which, in my humble judgment, might conduce to the advantage of the G.H.&S.A. Railway, in connection with the British public.

I will now only glance at what I deem the most important of those suggestions. It is how best you can render available for settlement the vast territory you have for disposal, in connection with your railway.

It strikes me that you should organize a Texas Colonization Society in London, as an adjunct, or in association with, the G.H.&S. Antonio Railway. This, I think, might be done at a trifling cost.

Might you not arrange with the folks in Coleman Street [Messrs. Broom, Son, & Hay, No. 53], who pay your dividends, to appropriate a room and the services of a clerk, who could give information to intending emigrants, take passages, indeed, aid and assist in promoting the stream of emigration to your hands, from England.

With that object, I would suggest that the room used should be furnished with a government map or survey of your territory.

The character of the soil and the products should be indicated, and in illustration, specimens of the sugar, sugar cane, cotton, corn and other cereals, grass, moss, coal, and other minerals, should also be exhibited: as also the prices of lands in the various localities.

A certain amount should be expended in advertisements, and tracts or short papers should be distributed, pointing out the special advantages accruing to settlers on your lands in the various localities.

In such papers, references should be given to persons well known in England. I need not add that I should gladly be one of the referees.

You may be aware that there is great discontent existing among the ill-paid agricultural labourers of England.

Thanks to Joseph Arch (who instituted Agricultural Unions), the labourers in some parts of England were induced to strike, and thereby raised their weekly wages from 13s. to 15s.

Arch has uniformly recommended emigration of large numbers, as the only effective means of raising the wages of those that remained at home.

The government of Canada invited Arch to visit that country, promising free gifts of land to the settlers, and other facilities.

Arch went out to Canada, but the inclemency of the winter there, and the character of the lands, distance from markets, &c., led him to report that Canada was not *the country which he could venture to recommend to his fellow-labourers in England.*

It appears to me that if Joseph Arch was invited to Texas, or if he could not come, two or three persons that he might nominate (who, like him possess the confidence of English labourers), the report he or they must make, *would give a mighty impulse to emigration hither, and within five or six years, some fifty or sixty thousand of the best class of English labourers would Wnd their homes in Texas.*

Hitherto, English emigrants have had a well-grounded horror of settling in the Southern States of America. Admitting the great fertility of the soil, it has been more than counterbalanced by its incontestible unhealthiness, and inapplicability to English constitutions and habits.

In Texas, *these conditions are exactly reversed. With a healthy climate and more fertile soil, the resemblance to England is very striking, as all of us can testify.*

Having, I think, said enough to explain my views as to the best means of utilizing the magnificent property under your control, I would add that during my stay in Texas, I have taken all the pains I could to learn from books and State documents, and also from residents, all I could about this country, and I hesitate not to express my profound conviction that none of our Australian or American Colonies, nor the wide world itself, possesses a territory which can oVer anything like the equivalent advantages which Texas does to the British settler.

I should be glad—when you have leisure—to have your opinion of my suggestions. So please address me to the PALACE HOTEL, *San Francisco.*

And with all good wishes,

I remain, Yours truly,

JAMES WHITE.

The following letter from a distinguished English gentleman (the highest title that can be given to any man) now retired, and living upon his estates at Warwick, has been furnished me for publication for no other purpose than to advance the prosperity of his fellow countrymen. Such letters contain evidences "strong as proofs of Holy writ": —

Beauchamp Place, Warwick,
August 13, 1877.
W. G. *KINGSBURY, ESQ.*

Dear Sir, —I notice with Pleasure your arrival in England as a representative of the State of Texas in general, and of the Galveston, Harrisburg, and San Antonio Railroad in particular.

I do not know a man now living in Texas, who is better acquainted with, or more competent to make known the vast agricultural, commercial, and mineral resources of that great State, than yourself; and I commend the Company for their sagacity in choosing you for their Agent.

I have read with pleasure your pamphlet descriptive of South Western and Middle Texas, and can certify to all that you have said concerning the quality of the land in the counties through which your Railroad passes, having ridden on horseback over the whole extent of the road, — from its initial point to its present terminus at San Antonio; and this, too, at a time when the country was a wilderness; when railroads in Texas were not thought of; when on a portion of the route, for 60 miles, there was not a human habitation.

Most of the land lying on the route of the railroad, from Galveston to Columbus, is admirably adapted to the use of the steam plough, owing to the evenness of surface and freedom from all obstructions, being prairie land; what in England is called grazing land. From Columbus to San Antonio the country is more undulating, not hilly, and resembles much the face of the country in Warwickshire: —it is beautiful to look upon. And should the Company which you represent be willing to sell their land at Texas prices, no man can err in purchasing (although unseen), whether for the purpose of investment or of cultivation.

At the present time, Texas is to the majority of Englishmen a terra incognita, *although her shore may be reached in twenty days, and at little expense.*

Having been a citizen of Texas nearly 40 years, I think myself fully

*competent to speak as to the advantages she offers to the English emi-
grant, I do not hesitate to say, that, to the tiller of the soil, to the stock-
raiser, and particularly to the wool-grower, she is not to be surpassed, if
equalled by any country in the world. The Germans have found Texas to
be an El Dorado, and are emigrating thither in great numbers.*

    *Allow me, Sir, to again express my gratification at your advent in
England, for the purposes heretofore stated; and hope that whenever you
may find it convenient to pay a visit to Warwickshire you will not ne-
glect to call and see an old fellow-Texan.*

    I am, yours very respectfully,
LANCELOT ABBOTTS.

Middle and South-Western Texas as a Farming Country.

While the stock raiser can show large returns from his investments, the good
farmer is satisfied to maintain his position between the plough handles. It is
true that nearly all farmers are engaged more or less in raising cattle, horses,
and hogs, because these may be attended to at odd times and not interfere
with the farm work. The cereals, root crops, fruits and vegetables are cultivated
very much as in England, though with less care and labour. Corn (maize),
cotton, tobacco, and sugar are the principal crops and bring the most money
to the Texas farmer. These are all planted in rows from three and a half to four
feet apart. Corn and sugar are cultivated exclusively with the plough or cul-
tivator and require going over from two to four times, generally three times.
Cotton requires one hoeing to thin to a stand and about three ploughings.
Corn is planted from the fourteenth Feb. to first of March, and cotton about
the first of April. Sugar is planted but once in three years and is done by lay-
ing the stalks in trenches opened with the plough, and covering with the same.
On the bottom lands of the Brazos and Colorado Rivers, and their tributar-
ies in Fort Bend, Colorado, Austin, and Fayette Counties . . . and even the
rich prairies of those countries, will produce on an average of ten years, seventy-five bushels of corn, or five hundred lbs. of lint cotton to the acre. The
bottom lands of the Guadalupe River (the most beautiful in Texas) in
Gonzales, Guadalupe, and Comal Counties, will produce nearly as much, but
in the more elevated district about San Antonio and in the mountain region
just north of it, from forty to sixty bushels of corn, and about four hundred
lbs. of lint cotton to the acre, is considered a fair average crop. In competing

for a small prize offered by the "Agricultural, Stock Raising, and Industrial Association," of San Antonio, there was a dozen competitors,[2] all coming within a few pounds of each other, the premium was awarded Mr. James M. Scott, an Irishman of Boerne, Kendall County, who made three-hundred and forty-one bushels of corn, or sixty-eight and one-fifth bushels per acre, on five acres; on one acre he made sixty-nine and three-fourths bushels. One hundred ears of this corn weighed after being shelled, seventy-four lbs. and five ozs. Wheat will average about seventeen bushels to the acre, though at the Fair, above mentioned, the premium was awarded to a yield of thirty-three bushels per acre, on a field of thirty-four acres. Oats will average about fifty bushels, though seventy-five to eighty, are often made. Sugar is the most profitable of all the crops, but requires more capital to prepare it for market. Cotton-picking commences about the first of September, and lasts until Christmas, new boles of cotton keep continually putting out, so that fields can be gathered from two to three times with nearly the same results. This is light and easy work in which women and children are worth nearly as much as men, and as cotton always brings the gold at home or abroad, it is gathered with as much faith and spirit, as pennies would be picked from the ground. A good hand will pick two hundred lbs. per day. Cotton-pickers are always in demand during the fall, the price paid is a half-penny per pound. Wherever intelligent labour has been applied to the Cultivation of the ground in Middle Western and South-western Texas good results have been obtained and thousands of men can show their twenty thousand dollars for twenty years of good old-fashioned farming. I feel myself competent to speak on these subjects, as I have for twenty years owned and worked, and am still working, a farm thirty miles north of San Antonio, on which I have raised all these products, besides cattle and horse stock.

I have specimen samples of the soil, grain, and grass from all the counties along the road, to be seen at my office.

From this it will be seen that everything raised in the Northern or Western States, or in any part of England, can be successfully raised in Texas; besides these, cotton and sugar, two of the most valuable crops grown upon the earth, and always command the gold, are staple crops in Texas. It should also be noted that most of the farm work is done in winter and spring; wheat is harvested the last days of April and first days in May, and new flour is often put into New York by the 20th of that month, and commands a high price. The last ploughing is given to corn by the 20th of May, and to cotton about the 10th of June, and as cotton-picking does not commence generally before the middle of September, the farmer has three months of comparative ease in which he can give attention to his stock, or enlarging his farm. A very important feature in the country about San Antonio, is that, vegetables and fruits mature from six to eight weeks in advance of the country about the great city of St. Louis, Missouri, and now that we have railroad communication making the time within 48 hours, many vegetables and fruits are shipped at great profit. Strawberries ripen in February and last until May. Tomatoes commence ripening about the 20th of April, Irish potatoes about the 1st of May. Sweet potatoes by the 1st of July, and many kinds of vegetables such as lettuce, cabbage, beets, onions, spinach,[3] celery, parsley, and some eight or ten other varieties grow in the open air through the entire winter. The first strawberries in the St. Louis market this year brought 3s. per basket, but after the crop matured there they were a drug at 5d. The first Irish potatoes from Texas brought £1 12s. per barrel, but when the Missouri farmers potatoes are ripe they will not bring over 3s. 3d.; the same with grapes, peaches, and many other vegetable and fruit that will stand a 48 hour transportation upon cars. A very profitable crop, and one easily attended to is HONEY BEES, these little workers can come very near putting in their 365 days (and so can the farmer), in every year as there is no time when open flowers cannot be found and very few days too cold for them to be out. Mr. Sebastion Witff, living at Castroville, 25 Miles west of San Antonio, has 150 stands of bees, and during 1876 sold 8,000 lbs. of honey at 15c.(7½d.) per pound—this would be 240 pounds besides the addition to his stock, pretty fair wages if he had done nothing else.

The *Colorado Beetle* has not yet been seen in Texas, and it is not believed that the climate there will agree with him. The *Grass Hoppers* have come upon us some four or five times in the last twenty years, but they have never destroyed a crop or done any particular damage; they were never known to come in such numbers as last Fall, 1876, but our crops were never better than this. If they deposit their eggs in the Fall, a few warm days in January will hatch them out; if it turns suddenly cold with a rain and sleet they perish, if not they grow rapidly and soon get their wings, and the first hot days in March drives them to higher latitudes. They commence by flying round and round in a circle, rising a little each time until they often reach such an immense height that they can scarcely be seen even by the aid of a glass, until, as is supposed, they reach a current of wind going in their direction (north), when they take it. These pests have brought many prosperous communities in Minnesota, Nebraska, Kansas, Iowa, and other States and Territories to starvation's door, and they have had to sell their well-improved farms at less than the raw land cost them. So great has been the rush from these grasshopper regions to Texas for the last four years, teams have often had to wait as long as eight to ten days for their turn to cross the ferries on Red River; 22,073 crossed at Collibut's Ferry in 90 days; there were four others, besides which two lines of Railroads went loaded every day.

I am often asked to give some of the objections and "drawbacks" to Texas as well as all the good, and so far as I know them I will.

I will first say, however, that the land will average as good as any upon the Continent of America, and probably as good as any in Europe. It is a very healthy country; the water is first class and very abundant; the timber is good and just about sufficient for the use of the country without being a tax to clear; the climate is mild and salubrious, not necessitating expensive houses, barns, cellars, or clothing; the grass is so abundant that it furnishes food on which to raise all kinds of stock the year round; the people are intelligent, law-abiding, and hospitable; we have churches and preaching and schools, public and private, the same as here in England. These are facts that no man can dispute, and it would seem as though there could be no very serious objection to such a country. The only one I have ever experienced or heard of was that it is subject to long droughts. From 1855 to 1858, and again in 1860, there was a drought during the month of May and part of June each year that resulted in nearly a total failure to the maize and cotton crops, and gave us a terrible reputation. We had our usual quantity of rain fall, about 40 inches, every year, but it failed to come in time to save the crops. Sometimes a field of very early or very late maize would get through, but the ordinary crops dried up; sometimes rain would fall in torrents only a week too late. Captain Manchaca, a Mexican gentleman of intelligence, born in San Antonio in the year 1800, and lived there all his life, says that, with the exception of the year 1809, he never knew of a failure of crops until 1855, and since 1860 we have not had a failure. We have had, however, many droughts of from four to six weeks, but fortunately they have come in July and August after the crops were made. The soil of Texas stands a very long drought, and by deep ploughing and good tilth we can bridge over what formerly caused failures. In 1855 the country was sparsely settled, and we did not know that we could raise oats, which is now our favorite crop, for horse feed, and as it grows mostly in winter never can fail. The failure of a maize crop in Texas was never seriously felt; there is a tree (the mesquite[4]) that bears a long podded bean, which, in dry seasons especially, produces a very prolific crop; they are the equal of maize for horses, and can be gathered by waggon loads at a trifling cost. When the grass in the range gets short, as it sometimes does, the out stock—horses, cattle, and sheep— live and grow fat upon this bean. With these objections which I have treated at length, I do not believe another word can be said against Middle Western and South-Western Texas. And these objections are not half so serious as *too much rain* as in England, often destroying whole fields of grain after they are cut and before they can be got securely under shelter. There is no country on earth but has some disadvantages, and I only claim that mine has *less* than any other.

There are many other reasons, however, besides those enumerated, why English farmers should make for themselves a home in Texas. In the first place the land there is within their reach, enough for themselves and their children, while they have nothing to hope for in that direction here. There is an Imperial satisfaction in knowing that we own a piece of God's earth on which we live, and can say as we stand in front of our cottage door and look over our broad acres of waving corn, this is *my* land and *my* home, I hold the title bonds, to me and to my heirs forever. I own from the Zenith to the Nadir, the trees, the grass, the flowers, and everything upon its surface above, the minerals, the water and earth below, are all conveyed in this title bond. If I set a post, drive a nail, or plant a tree or flower, the fruits thereof are all mine, and no lord of the manor, or agent can cross my gates and demand an annual rental; this farm is mine, I cultivate it without conditions, and I sell the hay and straw and droppings from my own cattle to whom I please. 'Tis true you may have to work hard there as here, but the tread-mill, and wine-press are all your own, and what comes from them are not taxed nor tythed, that others may live in opulence and ease. There is another important reason. In this over crowded country the sons and daughters when grown, must of necessity strike out to some foreign lands; some go to India, some to Australia, New Zealand, Canada, the United States; in short, they are scattered over the broad earth, and the poor father and heart-stricken mother eat their bread in sorrow, knowing that their places can never again be filled at their table, or they behold their faces more. In Texas there is nothing easier than to secure land enough for all your children, if not exactly adjacent, at least within five or ten miles, so that the entire group, with all *their* children can assemble at the old family mansion to eat the Christmas Turkey, and when the last great and final struggle comes, what a satisfaction to have your children, and children's children assemble round your bed, to bid them all an eternal farewell, and leave your blessing with them, knowing they will follow you in tears to the grave. I had a letter from a gentleman only yesterday saying, "I am going to Texas, not on my own account, but on account of my children, I wish to secure them all homes that I may keep them about me."

There are many other cogent reasons that will suggest themselves to the reader, but my space will not allow me to pursue the subject farther; I refer with pride to the letters of the Hon. Mr. White, Mr. Lancelot Abbotts and other distinguished English gentlemen; men of such high moral character, they would not endorse my descriptions of Texas for the State itself, did they not know them to be true. There is no very glittering prospect for the farmer or middle-class men here in England, with the present value and rate of taxes the lands cannot be rented cheaper; and Philanthropists and even the Government itself is encouraging emigration abroad. The acreage planted to wheat is continually decreasing, while the population is perpetually increasing.

Mr. Stephen Bourne, of the Custom House Statistical Office, says half the bread eaten in England is made from foreign wheat; that of the 33 million inhabitants of the United Kingdom, 15 millions live upon food received from abroad. A failure of crops in England accompanied by a failure abroad, would bring ruin to thousands of farmers and middle class men. With high food comes less work; the workman has more to pay and less to pay it with. The prudent man should consider well these momentous problems and increasing complications, and while he has yet the means, determine to get upon a farm of his own and place himself above this highly artificial existence.

In concluding this article upon farming, I must in justice say that England is a beautiful country; and that I have been treated with great kindness and hospitality by the people during the time I have been here, and I am only advising people to leave it and go to Texas simply because they do not own the land nor never can.

What it Costs to Start a Farm in Texas.

Everything depends upon the scale and amount of money one has to start upon. I have known many instances of men starting with nothing but a team, and buying their land entirely upon a credit, and within five years have a nice large farm all paid for, with plenty of farm tools and farm improvements, with fruit, orchard, and some stock. Such men were not only hard-workers, but were thrifty, and had frugal and industrious wives, who, with their little garden, chickens, pigs, butter, and eggs, helped wonderfully. To get provisions, lumber, nails, farm tools, and clothing, the men would have to cut hay upon the prairie and sell it in town, cut and haul firewood, plough for a neighbour, and do anything he could with his team to make money to live and improve his farm.

In that mild climate any kind of a house that will keep the rain out will do for a while, and it can afterwards be used for an outhouse of some kind.

I will suppose a man to have £150, and that he does not wish to buy land on a credit, and has his choice fixed upon a certain tract held at three dollars per acre, or say: —

100 acres of land	£ 60	0	0
A fair team of mules or horses	16	0	0
Waggon and harness	15	0	0
Farm Tools	5	0	0
Lumber and nails for door, windows, and floor for small house	6	0	0
Two milch cows and calves	6	0	0
One horse, saddle and bridle	7	0	0
Stock of pigs and chickens	2	0	0
Hire of land for three months	12	0	0
One year's provision	20	0	
For oats or maize to feed team while working	1	0	0
	£ 150	0	0

The above is a liberal calculation and every item can be had for the money, but it implies that the emigrant shall with the aid of a hired man for three months, build his own house, and fence in a portion of his land, and should with ordinary industry be ready to plant a field of thirty acres the next year, and have made enough with his team and labour to buy seed wheat, fruit trees, and many little comforts and articles of furniture for his house. A Texas farmhouse where a man is starting poor, is built very quickly and cheap; we cut poles about the size of telegraph poles to the proper length, dig a slight trench to hold the lower ends, fasten at the top with a strip of lumber, the rafters are made of poles, and the house thatched with a long coarse grass well adapted to the purpose, a little lumber for window shutters, doors, and floor, and the family can be kept dry. By burning some lime and hauling a few loads of sand, the sides can be plastered and whitewashed so as to make it quite sightly and comfortable. There may be some English ladies that would object to following even their husband into such a house, but I think when they come to consider that it is *their own* little home, and that in a few years they will be able to have a much better, most of them will stand it.

There is a large settlement of Poles in Wilson County, who came there so poor, they had to dig holes in the hill sides for houses, but these same families now have large fine stone houses upon the hills, and their settlement in point of cultivation, fruits and adornments generally, are equal to any in any country. The German colony, who settled in Gillespie county twenty-nine years ago, were so poor, they lived the first winter on wild game and parched acorns. Now, their county town contains over 5,000 inhabitants; they have some thirty thrashing machines, five steam grist and saw mills, and the farmers are all rich. An eye witness described the scene at their celebration of the first quarter of a century of their settlement. They concentrated upon the road a couple of miles from Fredericksburg, dressed in their old German garments, wooden shoes, old break-down waggons and poverty-stricken beasts; often cow harnessed in with a mule, or an ox or an ass with a horse. Their old waggons were filled with boxes and trumpery on which rode the women and children. A party of men went ahead with axes to clear the road and prepare the crossing of creeks, while others with little old German bird guns walked beside the waggons to keep the Indians at a proper distance from their house-hold goods. The train, when started, presented a most ludicrous appearance. The young fellows, the "boys of the period," born and raised in Texas, wanted no better fun than to play the *role* of Indians in such a scene, and dressed in buck-skin, bedecked with feathers, coon-skins, cow tails, paint, bows and ar-rows, shield and lance, and riding the fleetest of steeds, they made oft and repeated charges upon this immigrant train. The guard aforesaid, with their little shot guns would pour volley after volley into them, and many of the would be Indians galloped away playing wounded, hanging upon the side of their horses, while others invariably captured some of the fair daughters of the train. Occasionally a halt would be called, the curtain lowered, and a glass of lager beer all round, when wigs would be adjusted, daughters restored, and perhaps a guard would change places with an Indian. When the grand ball opened that night, there was a thousand couples upon the floor, and the old man and his wife who first crossed the creek nearest to Fredericksburg and entered upon the lands of the Colony, led off the dance, waltzing down the whole length of the great hall amid the shouts and applause of the multitude; then the next couple, and the next, until all of the *original* men had passed when the ball was fairly opened. It lasted with feasting and drinking for four days and nights, during which time the music never ceased, and the amount of lager beer destroyed could only be known to the man who could count the leaves of the forest, or sands upon the shore; but neither Englishmen or Americans, in fact, no people except Germans could successfully get up such an anniversary celebration.

As fence building is an important item in opening a farm, I will give an idea of its cost. In the vicinity and north of San Antonio, good cedar rails (the most durable of all) can be had at £12 per 1,000 delivered upon the place, and post oak rails at £8. When the timber is growing upon one's own land, the cost for making the rails when we hire it done is 4s. per 100; a fair chopper can make from 100 to 200 per day; ten 8 foot rails will make a first-class worm fence six lineal feet. From this it is plain that a man fencing his own land from his own timber could get along at the rate of fully 60 feet per day, or 520 yards in a month. When short of money or time a very good fence can be made by setting posts at 5 to 6 feet apart and wattling in brush; this makes a good fence for five or six years with occasional repairing, and can be made at about £10 per mile.

Now, where and in what country where a civilized man can live, can a man take £150 and his own labour for a year and make for himself such a home and have this number of stock upon it. It could not be thought of in the Northern States or Territories or in Canada, the climate there is so rigorous and the winters so long the man could not work upon his farm for more than six months in the year; and this small pittance would be eaten up long before any returns could be expected. In Texas the climate is so mild and generous a man may work at any kind of farm work every day during the winter, while his stock make their living upon natural grasses. As to what a man can make from a farm after he gets it improved depends upon the seasons and his mode of culture, the same as in all other countries.

Supposing he got in the 30 acres he would ordinarily get, say

From 10 acres in wheat,	170 bushels, at 7s.	£ 59	10	0
" 15 acres in maize,	750 bushels, at 2s.	75	0	0
" 5 acres in cotton,	4 bales, £10	40	0	0
A total of		£174	10	0

How much better this result than paying £3 per acre merely for the *use* of the land one year.

I have often known men to buy land wholly upon a credit, and pay for it from the first crop, besides having their improvements. The above calculation is rather below the average yield, and I think will cover the cost of a thrashing machine to clean the wheat and bagging for the cotton. The State of Texas last year produced 800,000 bales of cotton, which brought the State £8,000,000 in money, and not one acre in a thousand of her best cotton lands are in cultivation.

Large tracts of land are purchased cheaper in Texas than small ones, and a man with £500 could easily buy 1,000 acres and commence improvements upon it. I have made this calculation for a family of five and with £150. Should a man have more money he could build a finer house, or, what would be much better, buy a small flock of sheep, or a few more cows, or expend it in larger fields. The man having less than £150 can take up school land or buy either from the Railroad Company or individuals upon a credit; in fact, no man with a strong arm and willing heart need fear to take his family to Texas, if he can make a living for them here he can make them wealthy there; and he will soon make as good kind friends there as he will leave behind. The lands, however, are advancing rapidly in price; those that sold at a shilling two years ago are worth eight now, and still advancing, and the sooner parties make a purchase the less money will be required. This is also an important feature in estimating the returns of an investment as above, this 12 s. land, with tile improvements the man would put upon it in one or two years, would be cheap at £3 per acre, and in five or six years it would take double that sum to buy it.

Cattle Raising in Texas.

This has ever been a favourite pursuit with the old Texan, not because it brought any very large returns in old times, but because starting with a few head of cows and calves large herds would grow up about them incurring no money cost and very little trouble. In 1848 I sold 108 as fine fat beeves as I have ever seen at 112 s. per head.

Previous to about 1868–69, hundreds of thousands were killed annually for their hides and tallow alone. While this looked almost a sin, it was also a necessity, for the natural increase was so great that the settled portion of the country was being over-run, with cattle there being at one time over five million head to a population, of less than 800,000. About this time, however, some enterprising Yankee, with perhaps a little less enterprise than Columbus, brought his money to Texas, invested it in cattle, and drove them overland to Kansas, and shipped them from there by rail to the Eastern Cities, when they realized from 10 to 12 pounds per head. This ball once in motion, everybody was anxious to "make a drive," and at one time it was feared all the cattle would be driven out of the country. In 1873 there was about 800,000 head driven from Texas to Kansas; but a financial panic that year caused many of the purchasers to fail to meet their obligations, and put a check to the exodus. Cattle now have a market value, and a beef that does not cost four shillings to raise will command three pounds at the farm, and even this is not a third of his value if properly handled and put into the proper markets of the

world. In former years the cattle of Texas were allowed to go at random over
the prairies, the owners driving them to pens once a year to mark and brand
the calves, which is done by cutting the ears in a certain way and burning with
a hot iron some letter or device upon some part of the body, generally upon
the hip or side. Except gathering up the beeves for market, this is really the
only expense the raiser is ever put to. This mode, however, is being rapidly
changed since cattle are assuming some value, and large pastures are being
constructed and improved bulls brought from the Northern States, and great
improvement is shown as the result. Still not one acre in fifty thousand of
Western Texas is under fence, and the importation of finer breeds is still limited to a few individuals, but the work has commenced and will go on. The
raising of cattle in pastures will enhance the value of lands and quality and
price of beef. We estimate that four acres of good grass land in Western Texas
will raise an animal from a calf to a four or five year old beef, and to show the
profits of this business over money at interest, even at ten per cent. per annum, will take, say 400 acres of land   £ 80
Expense of fence for same   80
100 head of calves, say   100
Interest on 260 pounds, four years at ten per cent.   104
                                                                        £ 364

By sale of 100 beeves at £4—£400.

From this it is plain that we should not only have the ten per cent. interest,
but at the end of four years we should have our land and fence and forty
pounds in money besides. Four hundred acres of land at £80 implies that it
shall be upon the border of the settlements; but for large tracts it can be fenced
at about one shilling per acre, and Englishmen know the value of beef too well
to even sell one for the paltry sum of £4; they will soon devise ways and means
of putting them into this country, where they are worth from six to eight times
that sum; nor would he buy his calves at £1 per head when he can raise them
for a quarter of that sum. Nothing is allowed for care and attention, nor is any
needed; one hundred head of cattle put into a 400 acre pasture, or a thousand
into a 4,000 acre fence, and the expense and trouble is not greater than looking after money at interest—a little salt is needed in the one case and com-
missions, brokerage, and the drawing up of papers in the other. It takes more
money to start in cattle than in sheep; but if the cattle raiser can get anything
like an approximation to what the beef sells for in this country, less a fair
amount for the transfer, it will be found to be more profitable by a large per
cent. As before remarked, the opening up of the Overland Route from Texas

to Kansas; and now the completion of a line of Railroad to the City of San Antonio connecting with the entire system of Roads throughout the United States has already raised the price of beeves from one pound to four; and I now propose to show how they can just as easily be raised to eight or even ten pounds, by showing

How to Transfer Beef Cattle from Texas to England.

In the first place, the beeves should be raised in pastures South-west, West, or North-west of San Antonio; and for three reasons, because it has the best climate, the best grass, and the best water, producing a healthier and larger animal. Arrangements having been made for shipping either from New Orleans or Galveston, whichever offers the cheapest and best rates, and a plan of the deck and stalls in which the beeves are to be carried obtained, pens with sheds containing similar stalls should be erected at some point on the Railroad either upon the Colorado or Brazos Rivers. These arrangements complete, the beeves, say 200 in number, should be brought to San Antonio and placed upon the cars and carried to the preparatory pens; this will gentle them to some extent. They should now be placed in the stalls and numbered, and fastened with the same fixtures as will be used on the ship, and the process of gentling and feeding, hay, maize, millet, oil cake, or whatever may be best, commenced. They should be numbered, because animals become attached to each other and are fretful and nervous if separated. At first they will refuse to eat anything you can offer them, and for the first ten or fifteen days will fall off rapidly; but in three or four days they will begin to eat, and within fifteen or twenty days they will begin to improve and have a great relish for their new food, and from this time until their arrival in London they will take on flesh every day. The cattle would likely be required to remain in their preparatory pens from forty to sixty days; four men would be sufficient to feed, water, clean the stalls, curry and gentle the animals so that they could be handled as tractably as unbroken cattle in England, or as there is any necessity for. At the proper time they would be again placed upon the cars and taken to the steamer, and there placed in exactly the same position and fed upon the same food as in the preparatory pens. I mention the Colorado and Brazos Rivers for the reason that maize, millet, hay, and every thing that cattle will eat is raised there in the greatest abundance and at trifling cost, and if cattle be stalled and fed any where in America at a profit, these rivers certainly afford the best chances. There is also cotton seed enough raised in the vicinity, now thrown away, to fatten thousands of head, by feeding either raw or converted into oil cake. Of course the stock-raiser can, if he thinks best, build these preparatory pens upon his own farm and raise his own feed; but generally, I think the handling and shipping of the cattle will be done by speculators and merchants; and my only object in this paper is to show that these men can and shortly will pay the stock-raiser from eight to ten pounds for each animal.

Texas beeves are now transferred either by rail or on foot from Texas to Kansas, thence to Illinois, where they are fed and gentled; thence to Boston by rail, and from that point to England by steamer, and sell here at from twenty-eight to thirty-six pounds per head. I will, therefore, take an average and say a good beef is worth thirty-two pounds, and estimate on 200 head, which will be about a cargo.

Value of 200 beeves in England at £32		£ 6,400
From which deduct railroad transportation from		
San Antonio to Columbus	£ 88	
To feed animal, 15 bushels of maize	240	
" " " hay or millet say	80	
Hire of four men	32	
Transportation from Columbus to Galveston		
& shipping	88	
Transportation thence to England	1,600	
Feed and attendance on voyage	150	
Insurance, accidents and incidentals	122	2,400
		£ 4,000

Now suppose this was done by a speculator, and he paid	
the stock-raiser £10 each for his beeves	2,000
He would still have a net profit of	£ 2,000

I have made this calculation, estimating the sea voyage at £8 per head; and as these vessels are anxious to get adult passengers and feed them all they can eat upon good and wholesome food at £6, 6s. I believe that when assured of a full cargo of good gentle cattle that they can manage that will meet them *sixteen hundred pounds* sure every trip, for this one item alone, plenty of suitable vessels will be found glad to make such a contract. In addition to this, they could bring cotton, wool, hides, wheat, maize, pecans, and Texas istle,[5] which in some localities grows so profusely that I believe four men could gather a ton per day. On the voyage out they could carry settlers for Texas and their effects, salt, manufactured goods, fine stock, horses, cattle, and sheep, for the improvement of the herds in that country, and railroad iron, for railroads are building there in every direction.

But if we were to allow ten pounds instead of eight, it would still leave a margin of sixteen hundred pounds as profit. I have made no allowance for loss, because if the cattle have been made accustomed to the food and are placed in good stalls and properly attended to, not one in a thousand, will die on the trip. Cattle are not affected by the motion of the ship; they will eat all the way, and there will be just as little risk as in carrying so many human beings.

Now, when the day shall come, and come it soon will, that the Texas stock-raiser can get ten pounds per head for a four-year-old beef steer, delivered at San Antonio, the lands in Western Texas, that can now be bought at from twelve shillings to £1 per acre, will *rent* for that much every year, simply for the grass that grows upon its surface. Texas has millions and millions of acres that as yet has hardly been explored, and millions of men will find profitable employment and fortunes in cattle raising, and fleets of steamships will fill her harbours for cattle, not alone for England, but for all the nations of Europe, and she will soon become the great "Meat House" of the world.

I am not writing on this subject as a novice. I have been raising cattle for twenty-five years, and I have dealt in them and handled them in every possible way; and at one time, in connection with a partner, slaughtered on an average one hundred per day for over six months; salted the meat in barrels, and sent it to the principal markets in America, and to a few in Europe. I give it as the result of my experience that beeves should be slaughtered at points where every portion of the animal can be utilized. In a large city like London, the head, the horns, heart, liver, tripe, melt, hoofs, shanks, casings, glue-stock, hair, and everything pertaining, will bring the money and go far towards reducing the passage. There are some peculiarities about cattle that take years to learn; but the length of this paper will not permit me to extend the subject. I shall, however, be pleased to see parties at my office for further details.

Horse Raising and Ranch Life in South-Western Texas.

That Texas is well adapted to the raising of horses as well as cattle, sheep, and hogs, is amply proved by the fact, that upon the first settlement of the country by Americans and for thirty years thereafter, there were more or less "wild horses" in all sections, and in the unsettled portions they were numbered by hundreds of thousands, if not by millions. The wild horses, or "mustangs," as they are called there, were a very serious objection to the country in some respects, for it was always dangerous to turn your gentle stock loose either night or day for fear the mustangs would come along and take them away. Many and many a time have citizens and travellers been left on foot, and many a settler has lost all his stock of horses by their getting a sight of, or mingling with, the mustangs. If the oldest, most jaded, lame, halt, and broken down horse or mule just gets a sight of these wild horses, they instantly become as wild themselves, and dash away as though the "speed of thought were in their limbs."

When I first went to Texas in the winter of 1845–46, the whole country from the Guadalupe River to the Rio Grande seemed covered with them; they went in immense herds, and when frightened by the approach of man, they would go thundering away as though the whole earth was moving as far as the eye could reach. Sometimes if not fired upon, the old stallions, after starting their harem, would linger behind, and finally commence circling round and round a party of travellers until finally, with wild snorts, head and tail high in air, they would dash in and cut off the pack animals of the party. Under such circumstances, it would be all a good rider could do to keep his seat or prevent his own horse from becoming a "mustang" upon the spot. It is a deplorable, but nevertheless an amusing sight, to see three or four pack mules, on which you would have to wear out a raw hide every day to make them go three miles an hour, get with the mustangs; new life, wind, and limbs are in them in a moment, and with a bound they are off, filling the air with your tin cups, coffee pots, plates, knives, forks, bread, wine, or whatever you may have had in their packs. Many times have I had to live upon wild game without salt until a Salt Lake or settlement could be reached.

The wild horse of Texas sprang from escaped gentle stock first introduced by the Spaniards in their conquest of Mexico, of which Texas was then an integral part. They were the true Andalusian horse with more or less Arabic blood, and as beautiful specimens of that noble animal as could be found in the world.

As the settlements progressed and the demand for horses increased, hundreds of men, mostly Mexicans, found profitable employment in catching and gentling the wild horse. Pens with wings a half mile long in some instances were built so strong that nothing short of the great Trojan Horse of Virgil could break them down. Once in the pen, the old studs were killed simply to get them out of the way; the mares and young stock were "toed"—*i.e.* a portion of the front part of the hoof was cut away until it would bleed, which would soon make the animal too lame to run and in this way they were soon gentled and brought into the settlements and sold for whatever they would bring. I have seen 1,000 gentle mustang mares offered in San Antonio at 4s. per head without being taken. While upon this subject I should say that the wild cattle of the country were killed for their hides, which were sold at 2s. each. Deer, antelopes, bear, hogs, buffalo, turkeys, partridges, prairie-chickens, and hares were to be seen in every direction; besides these herbivorous animals, the wild cat or spotted leopard, the Mexican lion and tiger, the civet cat, and three or four species of wolves and other smaller flesh-eating animals made sporting with a good pack of hounds a great luxury. These last named animals of course preyed continually upon the young calves and colts of the wild cattle and mustangs. I mention these things only to show the capabilities of the country, even in a state of nature, for the raising of stock, notwithstanding these last named natural enemies. There are no mustangs or wild cattle in the settled portion of Texas now, and the sheep men have put a *quietus* upon the wolf; but by going a little beyond the line of settlements the finest sporting and fishing grounds in America are found, and especially in winter, when the ducks, geese, brant, swans, and all water fowl from the north come in by millions. Horse raising in Texas is a most alluring and attractive pursuit, and especially to young men; if the boys of Texas could have their avocations in life left to them, every one would become a horse raiser. I am well acquainted with a wealthy gentleman in San Antonio who sent his son to Paris to be educated, giving orders to spare no expense in his education. After about six months, the door of his father's house opened without warning, and in walked the boy. "Why, Dunc (short for Duncan), what on earth has brought you home?" "I don't like to live in Europe, and I don't want to go to school no-how." "What, don't want an education, and become a lawyer, and perhaps a great man?" "No, I don't." "Well, what on earth do you want?" "I want a horse ranch."

That settled it; arrangements were soon made for a stock of horses and the young man, though only fifteen or sixteen years old, managed his stock with the judgment and prudence of an old man; and I have often seen him selling his young horses in the San Antonio market at from five to eight pounds per head, and even at these figures he made money fast. He is now a man some 25 or 26 years old, and has sold his horses and has a large flock of sheep; and within ten or fifteen years will have an income that will enable him to make a tour to Europe every year if so inclined.

The people of England would be surprised to see the Texas boys ride their horses, and the skill with which they use the lasso. I have seen them pick up a silver dollar from the ground with the horse at full speed, vault from the saddle to the ground, run for a rod or so with one hand on the pommel of the saddle, and with a spring, swing themselves into it again—throw their hats up in the air, and so maneuver the horse as to have it light upon the head. With the lasso they are experts, and can catch any animal upon the full run, either by the head or foot, and as a general thing will name the foot, and succeed nine times out of ten. A wager was once made in San Antonio, that a certain skillful hand with the rope could catch the wildest horse by the tail with a rope, and hold him. This would seem to be impossible, but the horse or horses to be run are first penned, and their tails in part covered with mud, just enough to keep the rope from slipping, when the man would catch and hold them nearly every time. An amusing incident occurred during our little family unpleasantness; an Englishman came out to Brownsville, Texas, to buy cotton, and falling in with Captain Henry Newton, expressed a great curiosity to see men throw the lasso. Accordingly the Captain took eight of his men, and rode out to a herd of cattle upon the prairie; but before any of them would throw, they informed the Englishman, that there was a war going on accompanied by a blockade on ropes, and that such things were very hard to get, and very high in price, and sometimes the animal would get away with a rope round his neck. The gentleman declared that no one should lose a rope on his account; if such an accident happened he would make it good: it being understood that each rope cost ten shillings. In about five minutes four of the boys had thrown their ropes on a steer, and after a pretended struggle which the Englishman would have sworn was genuine, the animal got away with all the ropes. A consultation was held, and the Captain charged the other four to be sure and catch the steer and get the ropes; the steer had got off a half mile by this time, but a charge was made, and four more ropes were put over his neck in no time with the same result; he got away with now eight ropes, and only one more left in the party. In reply to the question, "Shall we try him with this last rope?" the Englishman said, "No, I'll shoot the blasted thing, pay for him, and take the ropes off myself." Finally, the man with the rope decided to take the risk himself, and ask the Englishman which foot he would have him caught by. "By the right fore foot," was the reply; and coming up with the steer again, upon the full run, he not only threw the rope over the foot mentioned, but threw the beef heels over head upon the ground, and long before he could get up, the man, this time single handed, was upon his head, and held him to the ground until he had taken off all the ropes.

The boys now informed the Englishman that they would show him how to rope cattle, and, coming up to a herd, they yelled and moved their hats until they frightened them into a furious run, when each one with a rope caught an animal and threw him to the ground and took off the rope in less than a minute's time. The Englishman was astonished, and declared if such an exhibition could take place upon any of the race-courses near London from three to five thousand people would go to see it at four shillings admittance. The Lasso is a common rope, or one made of raw hide or hair, with a common slipping noose at one end. This is held by the right hand, the slack in the left, and whirling the noose round and round over the head it is thrown with great precision over an animal at full speed and at distance of from twenty to forty feet. It looks difficult, but it is easily learned with a few months practice.

Our present stock of horses in Texas are grades upon the mustangs, but, except a little gained in size, no great improvement upon them in my opinion. Our best Texas raised horses stand about 15 hands high, but the majority of them will not go over 13 hands. They are, however, very strong, active, and enduring; a good one will carry a man upon his back sixty miles in a day, or as long as any man can sit upon him. The price at this time may be said to range from four to fifteen pounds, and for mules from six to nine pounds, with no great demand. The business, however, can be made equally profitable with sheep or cattle, and with a good European market, with direct steam communication, it may be found to excel them both. The stock of horses are large enough, but the trouble is they are nearly always stunted while they are colts. The mare weans the colt, say in November or December, while the grass is poor and more or less dry, and while the little fellow will make his living and come out all right in the spring, he will get poor and does not grow for three or four months at the very time nature intended him to grow the fastest. All that is needed to overcome this is to have a pasture, and when the colts are taken from the mares in the Fall, feed them with a little corn and hay, or have a wheat field for them to feed upon; anything that will keep them in flesh and growing. I tried this upon a common scrub colt, and made an animal sixteen hands high, worth in Texas £20. From experiments made by myself and others, it is calculated that ten bushels of maize or oats, with some millet and hay, that would not cost besides attention over two pounds per head, fed to the colts the two first winters, would produce animals 16 hands high and add to their weight when grown nearly or quite 500 lbs. A beef will grow to his standard size if it takes him a year longer to do it, but a horse will only grow while in a certain condition, and at a certain age will stop altogether.

The reason more attention is not given to horses at this time is, we have such vast quantities of them, and having but a poor market we find it best to let them make their own living, spend no money on them, and get what we can for them. With this exception it costs no more to raise a horse to be five years old than it does a beef, while he is worth in the markets of Europe about double. Even the class of horses that are now raised there entirely upon the grass, and well sold at £8, readily command £25 to £30 here in London.

It seems strange that with the broad ocean extending from shore to shore, that some arrangement cannot be made to bring the producer and consumer into direct commercial relations. From all I see and hear since my arrival in England, I feel satisfied that this will soon be accomplished; and when accomplished my mission here will have ended, for when the people of Great Britain come to know for a certainty, what kind of a country Texas is, they will flock to it by thousands, and without invitation from anyone. And when it is demonstrated to certainty that horses, cattle, sheep, and hogs, can be successfully and cheaply transferred, the lands we are now offering at such nominal rates, will sell themselves at ten times the present prices; wealthy Englishmen will buy immense tracts, and if not themselves, will settle their sons or sons-in-law upon the same, for no other purpose than to raise live stock to ship to England.

Fortunate and far-sighted is he who shall in advance of the era of direct steam navigation to Texas secure to himself land that will return to him tenfold when that day shall come, for come it surely will.

Sheep Raising in Texas.

This seems to be the favourite pursuit of Englishmen and Scotchmen in Texas, and several millions of dollars, heretofore invested in California and Australia, has within the last five years been brought to Texas; they seem to take to the business naturally, and I have never known one of them to fail. Within a circle of 80 miles of San Antonio south-west, west, and north-west there are hundreds of young Englishmen who have been sent there and started in the sheep business by their parents in this country, and all are succeeding and on the high road to fortune. One young Englishman of my acquaintance, who reached the country without a dollar in money took a flock upon shares, receiving one-half the wool, and one-half the increase for attending to them, the owner furnishing the house and pens, and giving him a credit for provisions. In three years he had thirteen hundred fine merino sheep for his share, had bought and paid for 200 acres of land, and had 75 acres in cultivation. The young man had some experience with sheep in England, but would pay any young man who had a taste for the business, to work on a sheep ranch six months or even a year, for his board and clothes, to learn the business, but this would not be necessary, as wages to faithful hands can always be had.

I give the following data from which, parties may figure the profits of this business as carried on in Texas: —

A flock of Mexican ewes are worth in the San Antonio market from four to six shillings per head. (Messrs. Leal and Brothers, San Antonio, are importers, and will answer letters on the subject.) Good grade merinoes cost from fourteen to seventeen shillings per head. A full blood buck from eight to twenty pounds. Full blooded ewes from five to eight pounds. The average clip from a flock of grade merinoes is from five to five and a half pounds, though often reaching seven, and worth in the San Antonio market, in coin, from one and a half to twopence per pound less than in Liverpool. One man or boy can herd from one thousand to one thousand five hundred head. The average increase from a flock of ewes is about eight per cent. of lambs at a year old. The total cost of herding, salting, shearing, loss, and attention, would be from fourteen to sixteen pence, according to the size of the flock. Mexican ewes will only shear from one to two pounds of wool of an inferior quality, but they are good mothers and produce a healthy grade, and it is an easy way to get into business, where time is not an object and capital limited. During our Civil War, the sheep business flagged in Texas, owing to the prevalence of a disease known as the scab, but we now have a law known as "the Scab Law," copied mainly from the Australian law, which forces every man to cure his sheep, under a heavy penalty, and I do not believe there is a diseased flock in the State at this time.

I give the names of a few flock masters in the vicinity of San Antonio, and although engaged in their private affairs most of them will find time to answer short and pertinent letters on the subject. John James, of San Antonio, Bexar Co., Texas; Geo. H. Judson, P.O. the same; W. D. Parrish, Leon Springs, Bexar Co.; Samuel Lytle, Castroville, Medina Co.; David Brown, Pleasanton, Atascosa Co.; Messrs. Morryce and Brother, Brackettville, Kinney Co. (Englishmen from Australia); Judge Wm. Stone, Eagle Pass, Maverick Co.; Hulet Griner, Uvalde, Uvalde Co.;[6] F. E. Burr, Beeville, Bee Co. (an Englishman).

The following article prepared by Colonel John James and addressed to the Hon. J. B. Robertson, late General Superintendent of the Bureau of Immigration for the State of Texas, goes fully into many details of sheep raising in Texas. Colonel James is the son of an English army officer, and went from

Nova Scotia to San Antonio about 1838, where he has accumulated a splendid fortune, and is the peer of any man in the State in all the walks of life. He says: —

Ten years ago, there were very few sheep in the country west of this city. Further south, towards the Rio Grande, there were many flocks, principally of the coarse wooled sheep introduced from Mexico. In cases where they were owned by Americans, the rule was to procure good rams to get a finer and more valuable grade of wool. Since that time we have found that the country embracing the counties of Uvalde, Kinney, Maverick, Frio, Zavala, Dimmit and LaSalle are well adapted for the Merino sheep.

We know of no other diseases among them except the scab, which is not hard to cure, nor is the expense heavy to do so. We think that the scab will not originate in that country, if the sheep are properly cared for and kept out of dirty pens. We have now an excellent scab law, and that disease will be so generally controlled that we will not hear much of it from this time forward. We run our sheep in flocks of from ten to fifteen hundred, generally as high as the last named figure, and we use Mexicans for shepherds, and pay them $12 (£2 10 s.) a month and rations, which cost six dollars a month more. The cost of living on a ranch may be rated somewhat as to the taste and habits of each ranchero.[7] If persons can economize labor, the outlay for food is not a serious item. Meat is abundant and cheap, and is generally produced on the ranch. The people live generally upon fresh meat, cattle, hogs, mutton, chickens and game. Coffee, sugar and flour cost higher than where there are railroads. Corn is either raised on the ranch, or purchased at about $1 per bushel, and there are mills within reach to grind it.

Sheep and cattle men care very little for farming, their attention in the spring of the year being devoted to their stock, which then requires more attention than at any other times. We find that the finer wooled sheep pay the best, but we do not want pampered sheep.

We have not tried fairly to raise the finer and heavier mutton sheep. We know they do not herd well, or as well as the merinos. A great deal of expense is saved by being able to run them in large flocks.

We put the rams October 1st, therefore our lambs begin to drop by the 1st of March. We run the rams with the ewes for a month or two months, after which we separate them and keep apart until October. Two rams for one hundred ewes will do, but three are better. It is doing well to raise 800 lambs a year old from 1000 ewes. Probably 900 will be born, and generally nearly all are raised. The merino sheep seldom brings more than one lamb. Shearing is done in May. A good hand at that work will shear and tie up 50 fleeces in a day. If the labor is employed off the ranch, the cost of shearing, tieing up the wool and sacking it, is five cents a fleece. We do not wash our sheep, and we sell our wool in San Antonio for gold. Often the agents of the manufacturers come here and buy the best clips. There is generally a fair competition for the purchase of it.

My sales of wool within the last six years have averaged for each sheep from $1 to $1.25. The lowest price, per pound, received, was nineteen cents; the highest price, forty-two cents.

I have my flocks about sixty-five miles southwest of this city, which point is about the eastern limit of the best sheep country, so far as now tried and known.

We do not always pen our flocks at night; our shepherds often sleep out on the ridges at night with the sheep—the flocks, at night, being near to each other, nor do we put up any feed for winter use. The grasses and other food they get upon the average, is as good in January as in June. Nor do we have any shelter for them during stormy weather except what we find in the ranges in the way of thickets and undergrowth—the object then being to break off the force of the wind.

Our grasses, we think, are as nutritious and valuable as the best cultivated grasses. But the grasses are not all that sheep require. Herbs, shrubs, nopal, and saline grasses and plants contribute more to fatten these animals than the grasses. These last named are peculiar to that country, and which we Americans know the names of, in some instances by the designation given to them by the Mexicans, in their own language but not otherwise.

The climate in the sheep country referred to is generally warm, but very healthful—being tempered by the breezes from the Gulf, in summer, while our coldest weather comes as northers—sometimes wet, but oftener dry. For a considerable part of the year, the atmosphere has but little moisture in it, and this is one of the reasons why it is so good a sheep country. Often in the best ranges, the sheep have to be driven two to four miles to water, and this is another reason why the sheep thrive so well— for sheep do not require much water. In the hottest weather water once a day is plenty for them and they will drink it, when it is better that they should not. It is true that a dry climate is the best for sheep.

In selecting a sheep ranch, the black land is to be avoided, and it takes an expert to make a good selection of a point for these animals before actually testing it by using the sheep upon it.

The value of breeding sheep is regulated by their quality and age. The finer flocks can hardly be purchased, as those who have them, are satisfied with them, and would purchase more rather than sell, if they could do so; the value may be stated at one dollar and a half for coarse-wooled Mexican ewes, up to five dollars for the fine sheep in flocks. Good and fine rams sell at from twenty-five to a hundred dollars or more. I purchased thirty yearling bucks in June, selected out of one hundred and fifty brought here from Illinois, and I paid sixty dollars a head for them, as we are breeding for a larger sheep, and a longer staple.

There are plenty of four year old mutton sheep upon the ranches now in Uvalde and Frio counties, which will net sixty pounds, and will yield twenty pounds of tallow, and this is a good weight for merino sheep to reach.

Last January I sold my four year old wethers at the ranches for three dollars and seventy-five cents per head, in gold, and they were fine and fat when they were slaughtered in Chicago.

David Brown sold six hundred a few days since, at Uvalde, at three dollars and fifty cents a head.

It is true that this business will be an important one in this country. I think it will be second only to the great cotton interests of Texas, but it will take time to get the breeding stock to occupy the country. Sheep for breeding purposes can be got from Mexico, but they are very indifferent in quality, and size and wool very coarse, otherwise they have to come from the Western States.

By selling our mutton in January or February, when animals for food are often on the decline in more Northern countries generally, and so in other parts of Texas we are enabled to get fair prices, which compensates us for the distance we are from our market; this we will call the first crop. The second crop is the wool which comes into the market about the last of May, and I regard each crop as more certain than by cultivating the soil.

The labour to attend to sheep is not hard work, but a lazy man does not suit the business, as these animals require good and regular attention, and never should be neglected, if you would be prosperous.

When a wool-grower has sheep enough to supply a flock master, say five thousand head or more, fifty cents a year will keep and care for the each sheep, including taxes and all other expenditures, and will also enable a man to procure and pay more reliable labor than we have now.

You will also note that this country is outside of what is generally known as the best agricultural country of Texas, as the grain raised in it is generally raised upon irrigable lands, where such lands can be found, and there is enough of it to be found to keep grain down to a reasonable price, to supply the wool and cattle men at present and in the future. There being one irrigable farm in Uvalde county which produces some twenty thousand bushels of grain, besides other farms of like character in cultivation, or being brought into cultivation. This country will also raise its own sugar, and probably rice, to supply their wants after a year or two. Cane has proven to be a success in Kinney County. A large quantity of sugar has been made there the present year, so you may also note that a country which can raise its own food of a fine quality, and have for exportation wool and mutton, and a great deal of it, besides its immense cattle interest, with its desirable climate, cannot long remain without attracting special attention to it.

To conclude, I will say that wool-growers, using several thousand acres of land each (regulated of course, by the number of sheep each grower has), are not likely to have many neighbours. Therefore, men having families, used to society, must have a residence in a village as near to his business as he can find a suitable location. Otherwise the females in the family are lonesome, being often left alone, while the men are attending to the flocks.

The business suits single men better at the present time—but upon the general occupation of the country that difficulty will be less felt.

Lands for sheep have been purchased generally during the past year at about four to six shillings per acre, but values are increasing.

Wool-growers may begin upon a small tract of land, but the time is at hand when they will be required to own or rent the land they graze upon.

All prudent wool-growers buy lands adjoining to them as fast as their means will permit them to do so.

Very respectfully,

JOHN JAMES.

Figures and tables upon sheep raising are apt to be deceptive documents, and if some I have seen were carried out for 100 years the world would not hold the sheep. I give the following table and assure my readers it is below rather than above the experience of Flock Masters in Texas. That very reliable paper, the *Anglo-American Times,* published in London, in its issue of September 7, 1877, gave the name and address of one with whom I am well acquainted, that has done much better than these figures show. The man who does not realize these profits in ten years will either have met with some great misfortune, or proved himself incapable of managing such a property. To estimate this in English money, it will be near enough to call the American dollar the equivalent of four shillings. . . .[8]

Letter from an English Sheep Raiser in Texas.

I have not had the pleasure of meeting the writer of the following letter, but have heard him well spoken of, and know he has made a host of good friends in his new home: —

Beeville, Bee Co., Texas.
May 5, 1877.
w. g. KINGSBURY, *Esq.*

   Sir, —I notice in the Galveston News, *of 23rd ult., your letter relative to your intended trip to England for the purpose of directing emigration to Western Texas, as well as to make known the great natural advantages of this portion of the State.*
   I consider this a scheme of the most beneficial character to the country and wish to do as much as lies in my power towards furthering its objects, being convinced, that the principal thing required is British labour to develop the vast resources of this Western Texas.
   I am an Englishman, and left London nearly three years ago, with representatives of a company formed for the purpose of exporting live stock from Texas direct to English markets; a vessel called the "Finisterne" was fitted out for the experiment, and landed the first cargo of Texan cattle and horses at Southampton with but slight loss, the undertaking being quite a success. The two gentlemen most active

in this scheme, and who having been out here, have the interests of this country at heart, are Mr. F. H. Ralph and Mr. R. Jacob, to whom I have much pleasure in enclosing cards of introduction, should you be disposed to see or communicate with them.

As regards my experience, I may say that I have travelled over much of this western country, and know casually several localities on the G.H. and S.A.R.R., which are highly recommended for rich and productive soil most suited to agricultural interests, the culture of cotton, Indian corn, sorghum, oats, &c.; but my object now is to give you and those who required some little information relative to this county (Bee) its advantages, industries, and progress as far as my observation goes.

The county consists of fine rolling prairies with a good proportion of timber, principally live-oak, post-oak, and mesquit; it is amply provided with water courses, of which the Aransas River, Paesta, Rapalote, Medio and Blanco creeks are the chief.

This country is unequalled for its splendid grazing, and sufficient proof of this is that one hundred thousand head of sheep are scattered over this county alone. Sheep farming is rapidly becoming the chief occupation and industry of the people being the most remunerative investment for small capital. For the benefit of the wool-grower there is an association organized at the county-seat, Beeville, for the purpose of bringing together sheep-owners with the object of providing in every possible manner the general welfare of this important industry in this section.

Cattle, though abundant, are not so numerous on the prairies as formerly. This cannot be wondered at, considering the thousands taken away from here annually to distant markets.

The cattle interests are gradually but surely getting into the hands of a few large capitalists and stock-raisers, and large pastures are built and building for their purpose. The demand for cattle and horses has raised their value and lands accordingly; at a recent sale of county lands in Beeville, by public auction, several thousand acres brought six shillings per acre on five years time with 8 per cent. interest. Local competition caused these prices by parties wanting the lands to enlarge their pastures; excellent lands suited to all purposes, well watered and timbered, can be bought for four shillings per acre, and it will not be long, judging from the present, that these name lands will as readily bring £1. There is an instance of increased value of land: —Two years ago I bought a league of land, two miles distant from Beeville, for three shillings per acre, for which I have refused five shillings. I bought last month at the sale 2,000 adjoining acres at ten shillings, and expect shortly to enclose in all about 16,000 acres in a pasture for stock-raising purposes; hitherto I have given my entire attention to sheep breeding, and so far have had success, having commenced with 1,000 head, my flocks numbering now about 2,000 and the young sheep showing marked improvement of breed, shearing a fraction over 5 lbs. on average a year.

Sheep-raisers here are taking great pains to improve the breed, and the pure blood Spanish Merino Ram, Vermont and Kentucky have proved to be the cross suited to this climate. Sheep can be bought from four shillings to ten shillings according to grade, and the rams referred to from 5 to 10 per head. I shall be glad to give those seeking particulars about sheep-raising in Western Texas, any information on the subject, my opinion is there is not a country better adapted to this purpose. The farming interests are comparatively neglected, and it is a pity that with such unsurpassed soil and climate it should be so; it is here the immigrants are required to show the natives what their land will produce if only cultivated; here a man can sell to good advantage all he can raise; corn all winter brought five and six shillings per bushel, because it was grown at a distance.

Beeville is very pretty, situated in the valley of the Paesta, it consists of a court-house, hotel, livery stable, two stores, post-office, saddler, boot-maker, and two blacksmiths; the amount of business done in this little place is surprising. Here is also an Episcopal and Baptist Church, good school, and the law and medical professions are represented, and, let it be remarked in connection with these latter, that this country has the reputation of being among the most quiet and settled; an instance of the popular desire to have order, and the law enforced occurred last week when the full penalty was inflicted for the only murder committed in the county for many years. The intoxicating liquor prohibition law is in force. Doctors are not over-worked; people live to a good old age. I had in England very indifferent health, but have not been laid up a day here, and I attribute this to the healthy climate and the prevailing gulf breeze.

St. Mary's, Refugio Co., is the nearest coast town, and is distant about 45 miles from here; we have communication with Galveston both by schooner and telegraph, and have also a good market for produce.

I beg to enclose you, with the other names mentioned, cards of introduction to Mr. B. J. Scott and Mr. George Startin, of London, and my father, Mr. Charles Burr, of Brighton, England, who, besides being men of some influence, are very much interested in Texas.

Mr. R. Jacob has now five sons in Western Texas, and another on the way out with my brother.

Yours truly, F. E. BURR.

P.S.—In reading over the above-respecting lands, I am reminded of the splendid tracts destitute of water which can be bought under four shillings per acre, where it becomes necessary to dig wells, and some sheep men find it pay to put up wind-mill pumps at a cost of £100; this secures plenty of water through the entire year."

Letter from an English Farmer in Texas.

The following letter is from the pen of a young English Farmer, who makes no pretensions to getting his bread in any other way than by the sweat of his face; but he is a sterling young man of sober industrious habits, is highly respected among the people of his new home, and will shortly (I learn) lead to the hymeneal altar one of the most accomplished and beautiful young American ladies of his county. I am well acquainted with this family, and know that when they reached San Antonio, they had less than two pounds of money in the world, no furniture, house, or home. I point with pride to what they have got now, and know that within ten years more, by the gains of their labour and the increased value of their lands which they will constantly improve, and the stock that will grow up about them, they will be wealthy people, living upon *their own lands* and masters of their own domain: —

Boerne, Kendall Co., Texas, May 10th, 1877.
Dr. W. G. KINGSBURY.

Dear Sir, —Complying with your request to give you a short statement of my experience in this country, and how I like it, I would most respectfully say that I come from Nant Head, Cumberland co. Eng., arriving here in the month of June, 1873. I came with my parents, who have seven children in family, all younger than myself. A few days after our arrival, we obtained work at building rock fence, and although this is the hardest kind of work and the weather the hottest of the year, we felt no inconvenience, the heat being tempered by a cool S.E. breeze from the sea, about one hundred and eighty miles distant, and we worked all the day through as we did in England. Our family has enjoyed good health all the time, and we are well pleased with our new homes here in Texas. So far we have rented land each year and have not had a failure of crops yet. For two years I worked for my father, who is getting old and has a large family of mostly small children to support, for which I, of course received nothing, but, in the two years I have worked for myself, I have bought and paid for one hundred and six acres of good land, every acre, being fit to plant, and have got a fence round seventy-five acres of it; it is within two miles of Boerne, our county town, in a good neighbourhood, and I got it at four dollars per acre (16s. 8d.), and paid for it in work, making fence at forty cents (1s. 8d.) a yard. I have also got a pair of good horses, a yoke of oxen, farm tools, and cow and calf all paid for. Considerable part of my time has been taken up in making the fence round the seventy-five acres. My father has also done very well, has now one hundred and sixty acres of land, a good rock house, six head of horses, three yoke cattle, two waggons, farm tools, five head of cows and calves, fifteen head of hogs, and his year's provisions. We are pleased with Texas, soil, climate, and people, and hope you will succeed in getting thousands of my countrymen to come to this country, where, with ordinary industry and economy, they can soon become the owners of land, and have a home of their own. From what I have seen, I believe Texas is as good a farming country as England, and here the land can be bought out and out for less than half what we used to pay for rent for each year; there are many profitable crops raised here that cannot be raised in England at all, such as Indian corn (maize), cotton, sugar, and many kinds of fruits, and the climate is so mild farmers can work in their fields every month in the year, and sheep, horses, cattle, and hogs live the year round without feeding except upon the natural grasses that grows spontaneous all over the country. I will answer any letters addressed to me from England, and wishing you a safe, pleasant, and prosperous journey,

   I am, very truly yours,

JAMES D. STEPHENSON.

Letter from the Rev. W. R. Richardson.

The following practical and interesting letter, is from the pen of one of the most learned and profound thinkers of our State, an Episcopal Clergyman: —

Cathedral of St. Mark's, San Antonio, Texas,
May 18, 1877.

Rev. and Dear Brother,

At the request of my friend Dr. W. G. Kingsbury, who is about to visit England in connection with some immigration agency, I venture to address you a line to bespeak your kindly courtesy to Dr. K., in case circumstances should bring you together. At the Dr.'s request, I also add a few words relative to the scheme he has in hand, and the induce-ments he holds out to those who may wish to found themselves homes in this new world of ours. I have been living in San Antonio, the chief town in South-Western Texas, for the past nine years, and so am prepared to speak with some certainty as to its climate, &c., &c.

Dr. Kingsbury's representations as far as I have seen them, I think very correct and reliable. This is one of the most healthful climates in the world—Mortality will actually not reach over one per cent. per annum, except in this city where it is as high as one one-eighth to one one-twelfth per cent., of which a large number are strangers, and invalids who have come here too late to be benefited by the change. We have three months of what we call winter, the thermometer sometimes but rarely falls as low as 15 deg., or even 10 deg. Far., though ranging mostly from 60 deg. to 75 deg., it is not uncommon for us to have our churches decorated with flowers grown in the open garden. We have three months of actual summer, ranging from 80 deg. to 90 deg. Far. in the shade sometimes though rarely touching 100 degrees. This heat is tempered by an almost constant south-east trade wind.

Labourers work all day here in the open air on their farms, or in other out of door occupations all through the summer, though it would not be prudent for strangers and unacclimated persons to do this. Lands are abundant and excellent, and are to be had at from one to five dollars per acre unimproved, improved lands at propor-tionately higher rates. These lands are adapted to the culture of all the small grains, Indian corn, and cotton. I can see daily on the farms

*near the city, oats, rye, barley, wheat, Indian corn, and cotton all
growing side by side, and with equal luxuriance and success. We are,
however, subject to severe droughts, although in nine years residence
here I have known no entire failure of crops, early planting and deep
thorough tilth will generally secure against that. Still with all its
advantages for agricultural and sheep husbandry and the raising of
cattle and horses, this is not an Eldorado or land of promise for the
indolent and thriftless; there must be investment of capital or
intelligent labour to yield return. Even the skilled mechanic should
not be entirely empty handed. To put it briefly, I believe that those
who can do well at home, can do better here. While the thriftless,
wasteful "ne'er do well" at home, cannot succeed here. With regard to
religious and educational privileges. The Episcopal Church which is
the same as the Church of England, has in South-Western Texas one
Bishop who resides in San Antonio, about a dozen clergy who by a
sort of itinerary[9] reach most of the larger towns and villages say once a
month. In this city we are the strongest Protestant denomination,
have a beautiful and commodious church which we call a cathedral,
because of the special rights and privileges we have given the Bishop
in connection with it. We have a membership of about one hundred
families, and between one hundred and fifty and two hundred
communicants.*

*Most of the so-called orthodox denominations are well represented
throughout the country. Schools are to be found in every neighbourhood, public and free.*

*Trusting you will kindly excuse the liberty I have taken in address-
ing you, although personally a stranger, and thinking you may be
interested in knowing somewhat of the region which is attracting so
many of your people to its shores.*

*I am very truly, your most obedient servant in Christ and for his
Church,*

W. R. RICHARDSON,
Dean of the Cathedral of St. Mark's.
Rev. HENRY LONSDELL,
Eyer Cottage, The Grove, Blackheath, London, S.E.

Letter from the Rev. Father Johnson.

The following letter from the Rev. Father Johnson, one of the most talented and popular clergymen in Texas speaks for itself: —

San Antonio, Texas, United States,
May 15th, 1877.
To the members of our Holy Church wherever found.

It having become known to me that Dr. W. G. Kingsbury is about to establish an office in London for the purpose of encouraging immigration from England, Scotland, and Ireland to this State, I take pleasure in stating that I have resided here for fifteen years, and I consider this climate superior to any known to me.

The land is rich, easily cultivated, and produces all the cereals, corn, cotton, sugar, tobacco, garden vegetables, fruit and flowers.

The water is good and in great abundance, and is had from wells, springs, creeks, and rivers. The timber is ample for all purposes of agriculture, and in great variety. The south-western portion of the State is unequalled for health, chills and fevers are unknown, and thousands come here from other sections of the United States to be cured of consumption and pulmonary complaints, by simply breathing the pure air of this region, and there has never been a case of yellow fever or sunstroke in this city containing over twenty thousand inhabitants.

The moral condition of the people of this section of the State is good, law and order is well maintained and crime as promptly punished as in the other States: there are Catholic churches in all the towns of any size and others are being established in country neighbourhoods, as fast as Catholic immigrants enter the country, and I can safely say that no Catholics will be without church and school privileges. The church in this city has eight hundred members, and one thousand pupils attend our schools.

Of Dr. Kingsbury, I can say that he has been a resident of this city for over thirty years; he is regarded as a man of honor and probity of character and entirely responsible for everything he promises. His written description of Texas, which I think falls short of the reality, is as near the truth as any man can convey a description of a country to the mind of another by writing.

The cheap lands, mild and beautiful climate of this region, make it in my opinion a most inviting field for immigration for all classes, and

*especially for the landless and homeless of Europe, who with industry
and economy soon become proprietors here and for whose sake I make
this statement, only adding that the clergy and people of this State will
give you a hospitable welcome.*

THOS. J. JOHNSON,
*Pastor of St. Mary's Church, and Chancellor of the Diocese of San
Antonio, Texas*

Letter from Gov. R. B. Hubbard.

As I am a stranger in England desiring to command the confidence of the
people with whom I may do business, I shall be pardoned for introducing the
three following letters from the three highest officers of my State, —the Governor, Secretary of State, and Comptroller of public accounts. They are given
under the broad seal of the State, and the originals can be seen at my office
at any time: —

*Executive Office, State of Texas, Austin,
May 21st, 1877.*

To whom it may concern.
    *The bearer Dr. W. G. Kingsbury, a citizen of Texas, has been ap-
pointed immigration agent for Great Britain and other European
Nations, to represent especially the "Galveston, Harrisburg, and San
Antonio Railroad Company" of Texas. I have to say that Dr. Kingsbury
has been for several years an immigration agent, appointed by the State
of Texas, to represent her interests, her capacities, resources, wealth, and
progress; her present power and prospective greatness in the Southern and
Western American States, with head quarters at the city of St. Louis,
Mo., and since 1875 has continued such agency on account and by
employment of some of the wealthiest and most influential R. R.
corporations of the South-West.*
    *As the executive of this State, I acknowledge with great pleasure the
success and faithful zeal and unquestionable ability which have
characterised his labors in these important positions. He is honest and
capable; no immigrant who through his representations, sought the
shores of Texas, has ever been deceived. What he may say orally, or in
writing, or in the press about Texas may be relied upon. In conclusion*

I commend him as a citizen of Texas, honoured and respected at home
as I trust be—may be honoured and respected abroad.
Very respectfully,
R. B. HUBBARD.

*I take great pleasure in endorsing the foregoing statement touching
the qualifications of, and eminent services rendered the State of Texas,
by Dr. Kingsbury as her trusted agent, and commend him as trustwor-
thy, and reliable in every sense of the word.*
Very respectfully,
J. G. SEARCY,
Secretary of State.

Comptroller's Office, State of Texas, Austin.
May 21st, 1877.

To whom it may concern.
*Having observed from notices in the public press that Dr. W. G.
Kingsbury has accepted the land and immigration agency from the
"Galveston, Harrisburg, and San Antonio Railroad Company," to
visit Europe in that capacity, it affords me pleasure to say that Dr.
Kingsbury's long residence in Texas (31 years), and his intimate
acquaintance with the climate, health, and varied resources of the
State eminently qualify him for the place of usefulness he has accepted,
and from a personal acquaintance of nearly thirty years I feel war-
ranted in commending him to those who may desire information upon
all subjects relating to this great State. Articles heretofore published by
him, descriptive of the various sections and resources of the State, are in
the main correct.*
STEPHEN H. DARDEN.
Comptroller Public Accounts,
State of Texas.

I have also letters of endorsement from the Hon. A. M. Hobby, President
of the Chamber of Commerce at Galveston; from W. R. Allen, Acting President; A. W. Soper, General Superintendent; and E. A. Ford, General Passenger Agent of the St. Louis Iron Mountain and Southern Railroad, the great
through route from St. Louis Mo. to Texas; also from Col. T. W. Peirce,
President of the Galveston, Harrisburg, and San Antonio Railroad, to

Messrs. W. B. Huggins and Co., Glasgow, Scotland, Messrs. Pothonier, Hall, and Co., 9, Cornhill, London; Messrs. Cooper and Brother, 2, Talbot Court, Gracechurch Street, London; Messrs. J. S. Morgan, and Co., 22, Old Broad Street, London; from Edward P. Curtis, cashier of the National Bank of the State of Mo., to Messrs. Baring, Brothers, and Co., London; from the English house of Walthew and Co., Cotton Factors, of Galveston, to Messrs, Tapscott, Smith, and Co., Liverpool; from the Hon. F. R. Lubbock, Ex-Governor of Texas, to Messrs. C. Grinshaw and Co., Liverpool, to Hon. J. P. Benjamin, London, to Lancelot Abbotts, Esq., Beauchamp Place, Warwick, to Mr. Jarnes Smith, Gower Hill, Glasgow, Scotland; from Messrs. Ball, Hutchins, and Co,, Bankers at Galveston, to Messrs. Lemonias and Co., Liverpool, and Messrs. McCulloch and Co., Bankers of London.

I have many other letters (not all of which have been delivered), from distinguished individuals in Texas, many of whom are Englishmen who are prospering in that country, to their friends in this, but my space will not permit a further mention. These letters have in some instances been furnished me from personal considerations of long friendship no doubt, but in many instances, and especially those from the clergy, above quoted, they are given more in the interest of humanity, than to benefit the State of Texas, themselves, or any class of men in it. They are well advised as to the condition of the working classes in the over crowded countries of Europe, and seeing the millions of acres of rich lands about them that only need the vitalizing hand of the Agriculturist to make them the peaceful and happy abodes of men and women, now landless and homeless, they are willing to devote a portion of their time for the sole purpose of benefiting their fellow-men; they work as did the labourers upon the Temple, "without the hope of fee or reward." It may not be in good taste for me to make comparisons between my country and this, or any other, but I have often heard intelligent Englishmen declare that the lands of South-Western Texas were as good and as easily cultivated as any in England, and with the same tilth would produce as much per acre of *any crop,* and many of the most profitable that cannot be raised here at all, and yet these lands can be bought with good title in fee simple *forever,* for less than one half what the farmer pays here in rent for one year. The labouring man in Texas receives just about double the wages he gets here and his board besides, and yet the farmer makes more money. The farm labourer as indeed all classes have good wholesome meat set before them, three times a day, the year round. Good fresh beef and mutton can be had throughout the country at two pence per pound, and the producer makes twice the money the English producer can make and sell it at a shilling. Bread, butter, poultry, eggs, and vegetables are much cheaper than in England, and yet the producer realizes a larger profit. Tea and coffee not being subject to import duties are much cheaper and all classes use them freely. Our people speak the same language and have nearly the same customs as here, and Englishmen, being considered more like "kinfolks" than foreigners, are welcomed with generous hospitality.

Raising Hogs in Texas.

Strange as it may appear, there are hundreds of men in Texas who contend that there is more money in raising hogs than in any other kind of stock. Certain it is that a good breeding sow will bring from five to ten pigs in a year, and often twice, and that these pigs generally weigh from 175 to 225 lbs. at from twelve to eighteen months old, fed upon nothing but grass and mast from the many varieties of oak timber. I have never known men to acquire any great wealth in the business; but up to last spring we have never had any Railroad or means of getting live hogs to any market, and the climate of South-Western Texas is too warm to make the saving of meat a certainty, and especially on anything like a large scale. Farmers can always save meat for their own use and as much more for sale, but they have to have everything in readiness, so that when the wind changes round to the north, known in Texas as a "norther" they can commence killing at once in order to get the animal heat from the meat before the weather gets warm again. The "northers" in the Fall are of but short duration; but in January and a part of February they extend over a period of three days, which give a fair chance to cure from eight to twelve hogs, and by taking advantage of several "northers" quite a supply can be saved. This is of course attended with some loss (little thought of there), as no family can make way with such a quantity of spare ribs, back-bone, heads, and feet in so short a time. Sometimes one "norther" will succeed another so quickly as to enable us to save all the bone-meat, but this cannot be depended on. We are now, however, in direct Railroad communication with all the great markets of the United States, and live hogs can be shipped from San Antonio to St. Louis at about four shillings per head, where they always bring from three to four pence per pound. The best range for hogs is open post oaks, as it furnishes an abundance of grass in summer and nuts during Fall and winter. Hogs left to themselves soon get wild, and to make the business pay must either be confined in pastures or some one must go among them every day or two, call them together and feed a little corn, a very little to each hog keeps them gentle. We sometimes plant patches of sorghum in different places through the range; this not only keeps them gentle, but makes them grow finely in summer. I believe the large English pea I see growing here in England would be an admirable thing for hogs in Texas, and where land is so cheap they could be raised in great quantities, and after the regular crop is taken off. An English gentleman once gave me a dozen or so, which I planted in my garden in October; they grew finely and ripened well, but a calf got in one night and eat them all up. The experiment satisfied me they would grow, and I would advise parties going out to take such seeds with them. There is excellent hog ranges in some portions of Gonzales, Guadalupe, Caldwell-Wilson, and Atascosa Counties: the latter has been famous for its hog product, supplying the City of San Antonio and shipping considerable quantities to other markets in the way of bacon. There is no doubt but with our Railroad a good business will be done this winter; and it is a business that can be started with very little capital, as common stock hogs are only worth from four to eight shillings per head, though fine bloods are scarce and bring from two to six pounds each. A pair of fine English pigs would be a good thing for settlers to take out with them.

The Geology and Mineralogy of Texas.

In a publication such as the present intended for the general reader, it would be obviously out of place to enter upon any extended description of the geological features of Texas. All that can be done here is to point out the prospective advantages that will at no distant day be derived by the owners and occupiers of Texas lands by the development of its mineral resources. Although the geological investigation of the State is only in its infancy, yet sufficient is already known to warrant the belief that Texas has a mineral wealth second to none of its sister States, and destined in the near future to be a commanding element in the great future of this highly favoured State. Iron, Coal, Copper, Lead and Silver, together with a variety of other useful minerals are already known to exist in Sections, and when immigration has proceeded a little further and the country has been still further opened up by railroad, there cannot be a question but that large industries will be developed from this source. It has been well and wisely said that the twin minerals, Coal and Iron have produced more beneficial results to mankind than all the Gold and Silver that have ever been discovered. Texas has a superabundance of these useful minerals, and in addition thereto has limestone in close proximity to both, thus enabling the iron smelter to convert the ore into the metal at a minimum of cost. It is a well-known fact that in Pennsylvania and several of the Eastern States, the Iron and Coal have to be carried to each other for hundreds of miles, thus greatly enhancing the cost of manufacture; but in Texas, the Iron, the Coal, and limestone from their nearness to each other, will enable the Pig-iron to be produced at two-thirds, what it usually costs in the East. All countries thrive best with varied industries, and while it is undeniable that Texas for generations to come will be principally distinguished for its magnificent agricultural advantages and developments, yet it is well to assure intending immigrants that there will be abundant opportunity for other pursuits should their tastes or habits lead them to their adoption. In several of the Western Counties of the State, Copper Ore in considerable quantities lies scattered over the surface, and wagon loads of that valuable mineral could be collected without the use of pick or spade by hand alone. Lead is also found cropping out in several localities, and only waits the skill and industry of the miner to render it a most important branch of mining wealth. Specimens of Silver Ore are also found in various portions of the State, warranting the belief that this valuable mineral will be found in considerable quantity when properly explored. Under these circumstances, it is surely not too much to expect that a closer and more systematic examination of the mineral regions of the State will show a largely increased development entirely unknown at present. It is unnecessary to point out to the people of this country the value of mineral lands. The richest men in Great Britain today are the owners of mineral lands—Coal, iron, and Copper. Many an immigrant who purchases Texas lands will, in addition to the agricultural value, find himself also the possessor of mineral wealth, of which he had little idea when he made the purchase. This is no fancy picture, as it is daily occurring in the Western States and Territories of the Union. Specimens of the minerals already discovered, can be seen at my office and the localities will be pointed out where discovered.

Sugar Growing in Texas.

COLUMBUS, COLORADO CO., TEXAS,
February 8, 1875.
HON. J. B. ROBERTSON, SUPERINTENDENT BUREAU OF IMMIGRATION
AUSTIN, TEXAS:

Sir, —*I requested Mr. Baker, editor of the Colorado* Citizen, *to send you Mr. Jarvis Brune's report on the culture, costs and profits of*

the ribbon cane and sorghum. It is not only the most profitable of field
crops, but the most healthy and pleasant. The ribbon cane harvest
comes off in the last of November, after the heat of summer is over, and
Dr. Cartwright, of New Orleans, held and proved, in his lifetime, that
it was the Materia Medica for the cure of all lung diseases.

Mr. Wolsey, in a diversification of crops, is getting rich in this county
on his own labour. He plants corn, cotton, oats, sweet and Irish potatoes,
sugar cane and sorghum. He has work the year round, and harvest from
May until December; his sorghum is ready in June; his oats and Irish
potatoes in May; picks cotton in September and October; cuts and works
up his ribbon cane in November, and gathers corn and sweet potatoes in
December. In July and August he is comparatively idle.

The following is the result of six acres in ribbon cane:—

Rent of six acres of land at $5 per acre	$ 30 00
To plant one acre costs per year $17.50	105 00
Three ploughings, $27; two hoeings, $20	47 00
Stripping and cutting cane	40 00
Transportation to mill	60 00
Six men's wages at mill for manufacture	20 00
Forty empty barrels	50 00
Twenty cords of firewood	30 00
Use of machinery	20 00
Transportation of molasses to Columbus	40 00
Total cost	$ 542 00
The six acres produced 1680 gallons of molasses, and sold at 70 cts	$1176 00
Leaving a net profit of	$ 634 00

This cane only needs to be planted once in four years, and the facts
and figures show a net profit of $105 66⅔ per acre—116 per cent. upon
labour and capital; and as a good hand can work fifteen acres easily
(for its culture is about the same as corn), $1,470 in gold can be made
in one year, by one hand, and upon one crop; and as river land sells
here at from $10 to $12 per acre, one crop will pay nine times the
purchase money.

The same party kept an accurate account of one acre in sorghum: —

The whole cost of cultivating and converting was	$ 33 75
It produced 100 gallons of molasses at	_62 50_
Net profits	$ 28 75
Profits in favour of ribbon cane per acre,	$ 76 91⅔.

But as sorghum can be handled in June, when there is little else to do, and the second crop makes fine feed for hogs and all kinds of stock, its culture is nevertheless profitable.

   Very respectfully,   R. K. GAY.

The Lay of the Land in South-Western Texas

is beyond the descriptive powers of any man, it must be seen by one's own eye to be fully appreciated. What I have seen of England, cultivated, adorned, and beautified as it is, reminds me very much of South-Western Texas in a state of nature, and parties who have visited that country will bear me out in my assertion that one may travel for hundreds of miles passing continually through a country as beautiful as Regent's or Hyde Parks in London, and very closely resembling them; broad open prairies gently swelling and falling, skirted by large open timber, the whole covered with a rich green carpet of luxuriant grass and dotted here and there by immense beds of variegated flowers. It is a sightly country to the eye, and there are whole counties along the line of this road in which not so much as one acre of uncultivatable land can be found.

How They Rent Lands in Texas.

The owner of the land will furnish the Tenant with a house for himself and family; all necessary teams and feed for the same; all harness, wagons, and farm implements, seed, fire wood, a garden and potato plot, and the use of one or more cows sufficient to furnish milk for the family. The Tenant to cultivate the land (already fenced and in cultivation) and divide the crop equally after it is gathered. The owner will also furnish provisions at the lowest market price to be paid for without interest after a sale of the Tenant's portion of the crop. To parties who can get to the country but would not have means to buy land, this is an excellent opportunity, for after one or at the most two years renting they will be able to buy land and start on their own account. I have good places along the line of the H.G. and S.A. Railroad for over three thousand families as renters and will give the best of reference in England that every word and letter of the above terms will be fairly and faithfully complied with to all who will arrive in the country any time from the 15th of November to the 1st of March, about the 1st of January or a little earlier being the best time. I will furnish the name and address of Texan farmers wishing to rent their lands, to any and all who may desire to enter into a direct correspondence with them.

The Health of South-Western Texas.

As this subject is favorably mentioned in the letter of the Hon. James White, and several clergymen, whose letters will be found in this pamphlet, I think the evidence quite complete; but as all such things are only relative or to be judged by comparison, I will state that Rutland County is the healthiest in England by three per cent., and yet the death rates are 19 per annum for each 1,000 inhabitants, while in San Antonio, the largest inland city of Texas, and with no sanitary precautions, the death rate is only a fraction over ten to the thousand, while in the country, outside the city, it will not amount to five. I have noticed one thing in this connection in England, that while the cemeteries prove that men and women live to a good old age, there is an atmospheric or climatic condition here that makes people old and stiff even before they reach middle age, and especially those who live an out-door life. There is a flexibility of joints, lightness of limbs, and buoyancy of spirit in both old and young in Texas, not observable here; school boys turn summersaults, young men perform astonishing feats of horsemanship, and old men of sixty to seventy years, think nothing of mounting a horse and riding forty miles a day. This is accounted for by the pure dry atmosphere and the clear limestone water, which gives great strength of bone and bodily physique. The children of the Germans who settled in the region about San Antonio, thirty years ago, are a head taller, and every way larger than their parents.[10]

How to Get to Texas.

There are several routes, but the cheapest is the direct water route from Liverpool to Galveston, changing at New Orleans, from which place the trip for 88 miles is made by rail, passing through the orange groves and sugar plantations of Louisiana; thence down Berwick's Bay and by the inside channel to Galveston, occupying 20 hours from New Orleans. From Galveston to San Antonio by rail, starting at 6 A.M. and arriving about 9 P.M., through a beautiful and most interesting country the entire distance; for a full description see article on the back of map "Sunset Route.". . . [11]

Questions Answered.

The following are a few of the Questions I am often asked by letter:

Question.—If Texas is such a good country, why has it not settled up long ago?

Answer.—Before the war people did not wish to settle in a Slave State, and for four or five years after there was supposed to be a sectional prejudice; besides there were no Railroads and no effort made to make the country known; but in the last ten years about 2,000 miles of Railroads have been built, and in the last three years over two million of people have settled there. At this ratio it will equal New York in less than ten years.

Q. Tell us about the snakes and poisonous insects?

A. There are snakes there, and you may or may not see one in five years. I have never known any one to be killed or injured by them or any other insect; but when we go hunting or fishing, we generally take a little good whisky for fear of snake bites.

Q. Do men carry arms in Texas and shoot and kill for every supposed insult?

A. No man carries arms in Texas except in a few frontier counties where there was danger from Indian raids at the time the law was passed. The law imposes a fine of £5 and costs, amounting to not less than £4 for each offence; one half of the fine goes to the informer. Men do not fight there more than here.

Q. What newspapers are published in Western Texas?

A. Every town of any size has a paper. The "Galveston News," published at Galveston; "San Antonio Express" and "San Antonio Herald," San Antonio; "The Inquirer," published at Gonzales; "Union Land Register," published at Boerne, Kendall County (full of information); "Seguin Times," published at Seguin; "Fayette County Record" and "La Grange New Era," both published at La Grange, Fayette County; "Castroville Era," Castroville, Medina County; "San Marcos Free Press," San Marcos, Hays County; "Colorado Citizen," Colorado County; "Wilson County Chronicle," Sutherland Springs,

Wilson County; "San Saba News," San Saba. Four penny stamps sent in a letter to any of them (not me) will secure you a copy or two by return post.

Q. Have you Freemasons and Odd Fellows?

A. Yes, in every town.

Q. What are the wages of house servants?

A. From £2 to £2 10s. per month and board.

Q. What is the price of board?

A. From £4 to £7 per month, according to the room and accommodations.

Q. What are labourers' wages by the day or month?

A. Without board 6s., with board 4s.; from £3 to £4 by the month with board.

Q. On what Line do you send passengers direct?

A. By Mississippi and Dominion Steamships. See card.[12]

Q. If labour is in demand and land so cheap in Texas, why don't the Railroad men who are so often on strikes in the more Northern States go to Texas and get work and homes of their own?

A. These men are not farmers and would not work a farm if one were given them. Strikes are no evidence of *want* of work; on the contrary, they are proof that labour is in demand. No man or combination of men would voluntarily quit their work unless pretty sure that they can do better some where else, or get an advance upon their present wages. I asked some railroad men here why *they* did not strike and thus get better wages; the reply was, "If we were to do that our places would be filled before morning at the same wages, and we would have nothing to do." Still these American strikers get about double the wages and buy their provisions at about half the price.

Q. Would the dairy business pay in Texas?

A. I think it would pay splendidly; the cattle raisers would give (to parties not able to buy) the use of their cows, beyond what is required for the calves, and pastures for one-half the proceeds, and butter and cheese can be made there the same as in England. The Texas cows are fair milkers when properly handled, and by planting a field of these English turnips, 40 tons to the acre, and feeding 50 or 60 cows during the Fall a deal of money could be made.

Q. Has Texas a good free School Law and a fund to maintain it?

A. A very good law, and the money on hand and the value of the land belonging to the fund makes a total of $27,810,553 as per official reports.

Q. Are Englishmen subject to a climatic fever in going to Texas?

A. No; never heard of such a thing.

Q. Are stock subject to disease?

A. No, except the scab among the sheep, which is easily managed. (See article on sheep.)

Q. Is it safe to take live stock from England to Texas?

A. Perfectly so, for all kinds except grown cattle, calves not over 12 to 18 months can be taken over with some risk; they will all have a fever, but if fed on bran not over three or four per cent. will die.

Q. What can a man do in Texas with from £50 to £100?

A. Buy a piece of land in the post Oaks and start a long ranch, and keep honey-bees.

Q. Which do you think the best part of Texas?

A. It would not be becoming in me to say; but if you will travel up the valley of the Guadalupe River from Gonzales to Kerrville you will see the most fertile and beautiful country you have ever seen.

Q. Which kinds of stock pays the best in Western Texas?

A. With a suitable location and the same money invested, hogs would no doubt pay the best; there is so little difference between horses, cattle, and sheep men had better choose that which they like the best.

Q. What does it cost to take live stock to Texas from Liverpool?

A. Horses £15; calves £5; sheep £5; a coop of chickens £1; a box 2 feet by 3 feet, containing pigs, about £3: the owner to furnish feed and attendance, the ship to furnish water; this takes them to New Orleans, and from there the price will be but a trifle.

Q. Can seeds or fruit trees be taken to advantage?

A. Yes, the English walnut, gooseberry, currant, plum, and pear, and the different varieties of turnips, carrots, and parsnips, and the large English pea.

Q. In which counties are the lands of your Company, and the School lands to be bought on the ten years credit, and who shows them to immigrants?

A. The lands are in Colorado, Wharton, Kimble, Edwards, and other counties, and shown by our Agents at San Antonio.

Q. What is the rate of taxation?

A. For State and county all told a little less than 2s. upon £20 valuation.

Q. Is any property exempt from forced sales if a man gets in debt?

A. Yes, a large amount: a lot in town to the value of £500, and all the improvements and household furniture upon it, no difference what the value; £200 acres of land in the country with all the improvements, tools, implements, and furniture; private and public libraries; five milch cows and calves; two yoke of work oxen; two horses and one waggon; one carriage or buggy; one gin for seeding cotton; twenty hogs; twenty sheep; all provisions on hand for home consumption; all saddles, bridles, and harness necessary for the use of the family; the shop fixtures and all tools of mechanics—none of the above described property can be sold for debt. All property accumulated after marriage belongs equally to the man and wife—the husband has the management, but cannot sell the home-stead without the free consent of the wife. These are most just and righteous laws. A home-stead in Texas is easily obtained, and when once obtained can never be taken from the family as long as an individual member remains.

Q. Have you any reduction of Railroad fare in England?

A. Yes, from London to Liverpool I have a reduction of 3s. 6d., and hope to have it from other principal points.

Q. Do Englishmen generally like Texas?

A. Yes, I never knew one to dislike it, and they appear to have more sense in adapting themselves to the requirements of a new country than any other class of immigrants. The Hon. James White, ex-M.P. for Brighton, says of South-Western Texas: —

"I hesitate not to express my profound conviction that none of our Australian or American Colonies, nor the wide world itself, possesses a territory which can offer anything like the equivalent advantages which Texas does to the British settler."

The Class of People Most Needed in Texas

are farmers, men who will rent or buy the land and cultivate it; labouring men and women who will work for monthly wages; mechanics of nearly every trade; men with capital who will engage in the stock business, build mills and manufactories: develop the immense mineral resources of the country and enter into commercial pursuits generally. There is a limited demand for teachers, male and female, especially in the rural districts. Professional men, bookkeepers, clerks, and indoor men generally would, if out of a situation here, probably do better there, but there is no pressing demand for that class. The men most needed are those that can turn the virgin soil and produce something from the ground.

Our country is too accessible and has too many natural advantages for us to pay the passage of any or invite the masses of unproductive people upon us, we only want those who with their capital or labour will not only be self-supporting but add to their own and the wealth of the country, and become good and law-abiding citizens amongst us.

The best time of year to enter Texas from Europe would be from September to the middle of May, the three summer months being the most inactive in the way of farming or business.

IN CONCLUSION, I beg to say that I have come to England to do business so nearly *on the square* that every man dealing with me will ever after be my friend. I am not particular about selling lands before they are seen, but should parties wish to make purchase as an investment I will give reference in England that my representations will be correct. I am not urging or advising any man owning his own home and well fixed here to break up and go to Texas; but to the man who has capital at his command bringing him less than ten per cent. per annum; or he who can only look back upon a life of toil and count no gains; or he who has children approaching manhood without estate; and to all those who have never known the blessing there is in a place they can call their *own home*, I ask all such to place a map of the world before you, and if upon its broad surface you can find another country so easily reached and with so much present and future promise as South-Western Texas, then I say go to it, and Heaven bless you!

Address all communications to

W. G. KINGSBURY,

5, Euston Grove, Euston Station, London.[13]

A Last Word to Texas Immigrants.

I have written this little book in a plain, practical way confining myself to *facts* as I *know* them from a long residence in the country, and just as near the truth as an honest man can convey a description of a country to paper. I have no personal interest in any man's going, charge him nothing, and get nothing myself. There is nothing easier, however, than for Immigrants to find fault, and profess to have been deceived: I therefore as a last word, wish to say that while every word I have written pertaining to Texas is the very truth, still money does not grow upon trees, and a man must have money of his own, or he must work for his bread there as well as here. The mere fact of your entering the State and becoming a Citizen does not imply that the State or people will support you in idleness.

You can buy lands cheap for cash or upon a credit, but you must cultivate it yourself. If you are poor, a neighbour might loan you the use of a cow, but he would not milk her for you. Might give you a bushel of corn, but would not shell and grind it for you. Might rent you land upon the shares, furnishing you with houses and teams, but he will expect you to do the work as agreed. We are not inviting a class of people who must be assisted to the country, or supported after they get there; Texas has too many natural advantages to make that necessary; and your becoming a citizen places you under as much obligation as it does the country, or any citizen of it, *i.e.,* the country will benefit you as much as you can the country. To men of capital, large or small, and to the honest, industrious, poor, who are able and willing to do something for themselves, there is not a more generous country on the earth; but to the lazy shiftless drone, the man who thinks the "world owes me a living," or he who expects to make money by being superior in intellect, or more shrewd than other people, will find it is a barren field. I want no man to go under any misconception whatever.

W. G. KINGSBURY

5, Euston Grove, Euston Station,
London, N.W.

PART II

*The Texas Diary
of William Wright,
February 13–July 1, 1879*

CHAPTER 3

Introduction

The Texas Diary of William Wright, February 13–July 1, 1879 is a revealing document in the history of European immigration—and, specifically, English immigration—to Texas in the late nineteenth century. Englishmen had been among the first colonists led into Texas by Moses Austin in 1821, but, as Thomas Cutrer points out, English immigrants at this time were assimilated so quickly and thoroughly into the American cultural mainstream "that it is now impossible to determine just how many Americans who came to Texas prior to its revolt against Mexico were native English."[1] Nevertheless, throughout the nineteenth century English-born Texans actually lagged behind other European immigrant groups in seeking United States citizenship, and in particular those claiming a hereditary rank within the English class system tended to resist the strongly egalitarian aspects of Texas culture and politics. Despite this the English in Texas were quite influential, especially in introducing innovative ranching and farming practices, such as growing wheat and cotton on West Texas prairie land for the first time.[2] The insistent curiosity and analytical frame of mind exhibited by Wright in his diary entries is consistent with this innovative spirit.

Wright's commentary focuses on the burgeoning but controversial "immigration business" of the time, as illustrated by Kingsbury's efforts. Rebounding in 1879 from five years of economic depression, Texas' immigration businesses in general, and Kingsbury in particular, aggressively promoted the state abroad. As previously noted, Texas land and railroad agents portrayed Texas as a region of inexpensive but fertile land in an attempt to attract the farming and ranching classes. At the same time, they solicited small tradesmen and laborers in Europe to augment the labor pool in Texas.

In 1879 Kingsbury and the Galveston, Harrisburg, and San Antonio Railroad expanded these activities by making an agreement with the Texas Farm and Freehold Union of England, an organization dedicated to English immigration to Texas as a means of alleviating labor unrest caused by unemployment and low wages at home.[3] The railroad company would furnish land to immigrants brought to Texas by the Union under its joint stock company and lottery system. In addition to the G.H.&S.A. pamphlets, Kingsbury and his associate J. C. Coyle, whose pen name was "Lone Star," published many letters in newspapers promoting their business and many of their claims about opportunities in Texas were even more extravagant than the ones made in the 1877 pamphlet.[4]

Frequent counterclaims by dissatisfied immigrants were also published in some of the same newspapers; however, the immigrants often were not considered credible because of their relative lack of status and education. The following report concerning a disgruntled English immigrant to Texas originally appeared in the New Orleans *Daily Picayune* before it was reprinted in the London *Times*:

> One of the English farmers who went to Texas last month intending to settle on a farm has returned to this city (New York) in disgust. He was induced to emigrate from Yorkshire through the representations of a London agent who represented that the land in the neighbourhood of New Philadelphia and Eagle Lake was good for agricultural purposes and that each emigrant was to receive one hundred acres of land at $3 per acre, and pay for it at his pleasure. He found, on the contrary, that the land was suitable only for cattle raising, and there was no prospect of supporting his family. Out of 92 farmers who left Yorkshire for the same locality just previous to this departure he says not more than 12 remain in Texas, the rest having come north threatening vengeance against the English agent who misled them. Personally he has applied to the Superintendent of Castle Garden to locate him where there is good farm land or assist him in finding employment. He has a wife and five children, and brought enough money with him to keep his family a year.
>
> Nor is this the only case of misrepresentation. It would be well if intending emigrants would consult the reports of Her Majesty's Consuls before they decide upon casting their lot in this part of the world.[5]

In his diary William Wright, an interested and careful observer, offers considerable support to this and other critics. Wright was highly critical of Kingsbury as well as G.H.&S.A. Railroad officials, notably President T. W. Peirce, for making false or misleading claims about opportunities for English immigrants and others in Texas, and he reports widespread dissatisfaction among the settlers lured to Texas by the propaganda of Kingsbury and the

Sketch of William Wright (1839–1916), by Shawn McMillan, based on a
photo reproduction submitted by Wright's grandson, William L. Wright.

railroad. Among the disappointed individuals whom Wright met in Texas was
the sheep rancher David Brown, who lived near Pleasanton and who is mentioned in Kingsbury's 1877 pamphlet.

Wright was born November 11, 1839, in the English village of Grendon.[6]
Located near the city of Northampton, at that time the village consisted of
about twelve houses, a pub, and a church. Wright's father was a farmer and
grazier. When Wright was fifteen years old, his father took him to London and

apprenticed him to a ship captain. After five years' apprenticeship, in 1860 Wright signed on as third mate on the *Agincourt* under the command of his mentor. He traveled to India and China on a ten-month voyage. In 1862 Wright traveled to Australia.

Apparently he had sailed to New Zealand in 1867 (see the entry for 29 March) prior to marrying Ann Agnes Harris in that year and abandoning his life on the seas. Back in England, Wright followed his father's profession on a farm near Grendon. His wife was from a well-established though not wealthy family. She attended a young ladies' finishing school in Belgium prior to her marriage to Wright.

In 1878 Wright sold his farm, his house, and most of his household furnishings in anticipation of immigrating to the United States.[7] He moved his family to the home of William Harris, his wife's father. He corresponded with acquaintances who had already moved to America, seeking information about land and business opportunities. By November of that year, Wright had deposited more than twenty-five hundred pounds in the Northamptonshire Union Bank and was planning a trip to Texas in order to investigate the claims made by Kingsbury and the other promoters.

Wright departed from the home of William Harris on February 13, 1879, at the age of forty. He sailed from Liverpool on the morning of February 22 on board the Mississippi and Dominion steamship *Memphis*. Unfortunately the *Memphis* ran aground at Animas Rocks at the entrance to the harbor at La Coruña, Spain, on the morning of February 25. The *Memphis* was a complete wreck; nevertheless, after a twenty-two-day layover, Wright departed La Coruña on March 19, on board the Mississippi and Dominion steamship *Teutonia*. He arrived at New Orleans on April 11. Wright traveled by train from Algiers, Louisiana, located on the south side of the Mississippi River from New Orleans, to Morgan City, Louisiana, then by coastal steamer to Galveston, Texas, and then to the town of Clinton and on by other means to Houston.

Wright began his trek through Texas at Houston on April 14 and ended it back in Galveston on May 31. During the forty-eight days that he traveled through Texas by train and on horseback, he maintained a descriptive account of the towns, the countryside—especially developed or potential farm and ranch property—and the people he met.

Although Wright was largely disillusioned by what he discovered to be the unfounded claims of the Texas land promoters, his impression of Texas was sufficiently positive to reinforce his resolve to emigrate. On October 9, 1879, Wright once more departed Liverpool on the *Teutonia,* this time with his wife and children.[8] According to family tradition, William wanted his wife and children to sail first class while he made the voyage in steerage, but his wife insisted that they all keep together, so the entire family sailed in steerage. The Wrights arrived at New Orleans on November 3 and remained on board the *Teutonia* several days before crossing the Mississippi River to the rail station at Algiers. From there they traveled by train to Morgan City, also known as Brashear, Louisiana. At Morgan City they boarded the Morgan steamer *Whitney* and traveled to Galveston, arriving November 10, 1879.

Tragedy marked the beginnings of the Wrights' life in Texas. They were still rooming at the Washington Hotel in Galveston when their son Percy Walker Wright, who had contracted pneumonia and diarrhea, died on November 11. He was four years and ten months old.[9] He was buried in an unmarked potter's grave. Agnes Wright must have been dismayed—she had already lost three young children in England.

Although the history of the Wrights' life in Texas is uncertain after this point, family tradition indicates that they lived near Houston for a time. After their home burned down, they moved to Waco, Texas, settling in a location that is now part of the Baylor University campus. In spite of his numerous diary entries relating to farm and ranch land, Wright evidently did little farming or ranching after he settled in Texas. In Waco he worked as a landscape gardener. Apparently he and a son-in-law were involved in the Oklahoma Land Rush of 1889. Eventually the Wrights moved to the Canadian province of British Columbia, where they operated a small rural grocery store.

A Note on the Text

William Wright's handwriting in his original diary (in pencil, on both sides of the pages) is generally clear and legible, but he did not observe standard conventions of punctuation or capitalization. The text has been lightly edited to supply these conventions, but there has been no addition of words, rearrangement of word order, or other structural changes of this kind. A few misspellings of place-names and other words and instances of eccentric usage have been quietly corrected, but British or archaic forms such as "centre" and "under weigh" have been left intact in order to preserve, as far as possible, the flavor of the original. Underlined words and phrases are preserved in that format rather then being italicized. Some of Wright's abbreviations have been spelled out, such as "Agnes" for "A" and "Spring Creek" for "Spring Cr.," while others, more standard or obvious, have been allowed to stand.

Following the opening block, Wright's chronological diary format has been altered slightly in order to provide a uniform left-hand column of abbreviated dates for the convenience of the reader. Occasionally Wright divided the entry for a single date into two or more sections by drawing horizontal lines between them, indicated here by double-spacing.

CHAPTER 4

The Diary

William Wright

Wollaston

N. Wellingboro', England

Left February 13, 1879.[1]

Sailed from Liverpool, February 22, 12 noon (Saturday). Ran on shore at Coruña, 4 A.M. (Tuesday) 25th.[2] Left ship 3 P.M. same day. Telegraphed news to William Harris.[3]

26 Feb	Wednesday. Wrote Agnes.[4]
06 Mar	Received letter from Agnes and Frank.[5] Wrote to Agnes, sent photographs.[6]
10 Mar	Went on board the P.S.N.C. or S.S. Magellan—Newspaper from Frank.
11 Mar	Received letter from Agnes.
13 Mar	Wrote to Frank. Sent by Captain of Schooner "Onward."
15 Mar	Wrote to Agnes. "Teutonia" arrived and we went on board.
16 Mar	Sunday. Went on board Teutonia for good.
19 Mar	Wednesday. Teutonia left Coruña at 5 A.M.—splendid morning.
20 Mar	Thursday. Strong breeze, ship rolling very much, going 12½ knots. Most of the passengers sick. 264 miles.[7]
21 Mar	Friday. Ditto. Ditto. Passed several ships. 276 miles.
22 Mar	Saturday. Fine day, wind moderate, everybody on deck, passed several vessels. 250 miles.
23 Mar	Sunday. Fine day, moderate breeze, nearly ahead, going 11 knots—all well.

24 Mar   Monday. Steady breeze, made sail, going 10 knots. 1376 miles from
          Coruña.

25 Mar   Tuesday. Light wind, under steam only. Lat. 32°N, Long. 39°W.

26 Mar   Wednesday. Light wind, fine and very warm.

27 Mar   Thursday. Light wind and fine. Concert on deck in evening in
          aid of the Sailor's Bethel at New Orleans, Collection £6.19.6,
          very slow.

28 Mar   Thomas Hawkins Wright 41.[8] Steady breeze from the south and
          fine weather. The boatswain was well thrashed by his mate
          (McMahon) last night for using abusive terms with him and is
          laid up today. Lat. 31°N, Long. 53°W.

29 Mar   Saturday. Fresh breeze and squalls of heavy rain. Twelve years
          today since my return from New Zealand. Murdered an ox
          today. Passed a vessel.

30 Mar   Sunday. Fine, wind ahead. Service read by Dr. Norman. Passed 3
          ships. Lat 29°12'N, Long. 61°52'W.

31 Mar   Fresh gale ahead with heavy squalls and rain, heavy sea. Ship
          making very bad weather of it. Beds all wet from leaks in upper
          deck and water washing about below the beds, steerage not fit
          for pigs to live in. Two vessels in sight. 115 miles.

01 Apr   Tuesday. Moderate gale and fine. Very rough last night, ship
          pitching very much; good deal of sickness. passed several vessels
          today. Lat. 28°N, Long. 67°15. 114 miles.

02 Apr   Wednesday. Moderate breeze ahead and fine. Passed 3 vessels.
          Lat. 27°57N, 72°54W. 208 miles.

03 Apr   Thursday. Ditto. Ditto. Passed 5 vessels. Passed Hole in the Wall
          light at 10 P.M. Lat. 26°57N, Long. 77°54W. 226 miles.

04 Apr   Friday. Light wind and fine, passing through the Bahama
          islands. Land very low and barren—passed several fine light
          houses.

05 Apr   Saturday. Anchored in Havana harbour at 3 P.M. Fine and hot. A
          good harbor but small—seems to be some fine buildings on
          shore.

06 Apr[9]

07 Apr   Monday. Went on shore at 9 A.M. and walked through the
          market, a very poor one. Sailed for New Orleans 4 P.M. Light
          wind and fine.

08 Apr   Head wind and fine. Passed many vessels.

09 Apr   Wednesday. Ditto. Ditto. Ditto. Made the lights at entrance to the Mississippi River at 7 P.M. Pilot came on board at 11.30 P.M. Ship standing off and on till daylight.

10 Apr   Thursday. Entered the river at 6 A.M.—put in quarantine and ship fumigated. Started up river at 4 P.M. and made fast to wharf at 8.30 A.M. Got our luggage examined and wrote to Agnes, expecting to go on immediately, but being Good Friday find we must stay until tomorrow. Put up at a Swiss house at $1 per day.

12 Apr   Saturday. Left New Orleans at 8.30 A.M. by rail, arriving at Morgan City 12.30. Went straight on board steam boat and got to Galveston at 8.30 A.M.

13 Apr   Left again at 1 P.M. Got to Clinton 5.15 P.M., thence 7 miles by rail to Houston, arriving at 6.30 P.M.

14 Apr   14th [Mon.] Left Houston 10 A.M. by train for San Antonio, Kingsbury's Luling agent traveling with us. The agent is a man totally unfitted for the position as he has only been here a few months. A native of Yorkshire and knows nothing of farming. A great many of the former arrivals are still at Luling, out of employment. The country between Richmond on the Brazos and Eagle Lake is much as Dr Kingsbury states in his pamphlets—allowing for gross exaggeration.[10] The Galveston, Harrisburg, and San Antonio Railroad passes through the center of a vast prairie for about sixty miles—timber on both sides the line at about 5 miles distance. Upon arrival at New Philadelphia we expected to see a rising little place but no such thing. Three or four rough shanties and a refreshment room at the station composed the rising <u>City</u> of New Philadelphia. I had intended getting out but returned to the train, quite disgusted, to go on to Eagle Lake. This place consists of about 12 small houses and a few small trees—so much for Kingsbury's description of it. Did not stop here though we dropped several families who had bought land. I do not think Eagle Lake will be healthy as there seemed to be a good many water holes and some swampy ground near the railroad. Going on from Eagle Lake we came to Borden, where the first signs of cultivation and settlement appear. The soil near the line looked very rich and the crops healthy, though the wheat crop is a total failure this year on account of the drouth. From Borden to Luling the country

north of the line is very pretty, being well interspersed with timber and plenty of land in cultivation. At Luling we dropped about 20 more to swell the number already there with nothing to do. After leaving Luling it soon got dark and we arrived in San Antonio at 9 P.M. and put up at the Central Hotel at $1.00 per day.

15 Apr   I have had a good walk about San Antonio today and am very pleased with the city (better than I expected). The shops, plazas, etc.—things are as cheap and some things cheaper than in England. Trade is very dull here at present time, though the wool is coming in now and storekeepers expect to have a busy time in about a week from this. Mr. John Williams[11] is staying here with his wife (the man who entertained John Chapman) and he has kindly invited Smith,[12] Harley, and myself to go and stay with him at Williamsburg in Lavaca County as long as we like so that we can look about the country. The climate here is magnificent. As there is nothing doing here we have engaged a wagon (3 of us—Smith, Harley, and myself) to go to Dr. Brown's[13] 18 miles south of Pleasanton, Atascosa County, tomorrow at $4 per day.[14]

16 Apr   Started this morning at 5 o'clock for Pleasanton. Passed through mesquite brush to the Medina river (12 miles)—from thence through about 23 miles of very sandy country covered with live oak, post oak, black jack and walnut timber to Pleasanton, arriving at 3:30 P.M. Fed the horses and went on about 6 miles and camped for the night. The country through which we have passed today is completely burnt up. The rivers all dry and not a vestige of grass. There has been no rain in this section (barring light showers) since October. The people unite in saying that this is the most terrible drouth they have suffered from for 40 years, and cattle, horses, sheep and pigs are dying in great numbers. Pleasanton consists of 3 or 4 good stores, a doctor's shop (Dr. Johnson from Edinburgh[15]), school, etc., etc., and contains about 200 inhabitants. The country round is very sandy and the water bad.

17 Apr   Got under weigh again at daylight and entered upon Musgrove's ranch, calling at the house for water. Shot some rabbits, partridges, hares and California quail. Arrived at Brown's at 9 A.M. and found him busy shearing. The country here is thickly

covered with low brush and cactus, all of which is very prickly.
Brown had ten Mexicans shearing for him. He owns about 3000
sheep (Merinos) and tells us they averaged 6½ lbs. wool last year
but does not expect more than 4 lbs. this year, as the sheep are
very poor. In fact they are starving, he says. Kingsbury is taking
a great responsibility upon himself in sending people to him as
he does not want them, and in fact is quite sick of Dr. Kingsbury.
We stayed and had dinner and as we could not get anything for
the horses decided upon going back, leaving Harley[16] with his
brothers at Brown's. Fortunately we brought some oats with us
for the horses. Camped at 7 P.M. at the same place as last night.

18 Apr   Started at daylight and fed the horses at Pleasanton and took a
different road to see F. Londonge's collection of Texas Animals
and Birds. Got out of the track and did not get to 2 [illegible]
till 5 o'clock. He seemed very pleased to show us his museum
and he certainly has a good collection, all shot and stuffed by
himself. He told us he had served an apprenticeship to an
animal stuffer in Paris (he is a Frenchman). He has a large ranch
(about 40 square miles), also a store on the Medina river about a
mile below his house where he has founded a colony of Mexicans. Crossed the Medina, having watered the nags and finished
our provisions, and arrived at the Central Hotel[17] 11.20 P.M., the
horses completely done. The brush was on fire in many places
on our return journey—passed through one fire.

19 Apr   Saturday. Went to the post office and found a letter from Agnes
and was pleased to find that all were well. I find a lot of English
men in town with their wool from the northwest counties. They
say there is plenty of grass and water there, so Smith and myself
have bought a horse each at $19 and $20 and are going to lead
a gipsy life for two or three weeks, traveling through Bandera,
Kendal, Kerr, Gillespie, Blanco, Hays, Caldwell, Gonzales
and then to Williams' in Lavaca Co. We start on Monday.
[Hutchison?], McCall, Plant and S. Richardson[18] came in
tonight.

All the people here (not interested in the railway) with whom I
have spoken, and they are not a few, condemn Kingsbury in no
measured terms, and d—d swindler is quite a common name
for him. They say he is doing Texas a great harm by his exaggeration and misrepresentation and promising men work and

good pay upon arrival. There is no work to be had as the crops have nearly all failed.

20 Apr   Sunday. Went to the Roman Catholic Church.

21 Apr   Monday. Find cannot start today as Charles Smith is going with me, so am spending today in buying another horse, saddle, etc., etc.

22 Apr   Left San Antonio for Boerne at 10:30 this morning, passing through about 10 miles of great mesquite country. Afterwards 8 miles thin post oak to Leon Springs—there are a few houses here and a good hotel, this being a summer resort for the people of San Antonio. The country around here is very pretty and park like, with small hills and valleys. Had a tremendous storm of thunder and lightning on our way here, the rain and hail coming down in torrents. Went in to camp about six miles further on, on the Salado Creek.

23 Apr   Wednesday. Rose at 4 A.M. and shot a wild duck. Had a rather uncomfortable night as it rained several times. Got under weigh at 6 A.M. but had not gone far when the rain came down in torrents. Tried to push on to Boerne but the wind blew so strong in our faces and so bitterly cold we were glad to take shelter at a German's. Stayed under a shed there 5 hours when, the rain ceasing, came on to Boerne and intend staying here for the night as the ground is so wet to camp on.

Boerne is or will be a nice place—has three good hotels and several large stores and a brewery. The land seems good black loam, but the drouth has caused a failure in the wheat crop. The people, most of whom are Germans, seem to think this rain will save the corn and cotton crop. Bought six yards of calico to make a fly,[19] 13¢ a yard.

24 Apr   Left Boerne this morning at 7 A.M. but it soon began to rain, and we traveled but slowly, taking shelter under the trees during the worst storms. Only did 10 miles and went into camp to dry our blankets, as it had cleared up a bit. Got the fly up and made ourselves as comfortable as we could under the circumstances. A fine valley on the Guadalupe river under cultivation by Germans to the north of us.

25 Apr   We were glad of the fly as it rained all night. Did not start until eleven o'clock as our trap had to be dried. Heard some wild

turkeys but could not get a shot at them. Camped early as Smith's leg is bad from prickly pear pricks.

26 Apr   Started at 5 A.M. and traveled over the hills to Verde Creek, passing through some good valleys, the soil being black loam. There are three families on Verde Creek, one of whom is Goldie, the man who wrote the letter published by Kingsbury—"A Swansea Trade[s]man"[20] His brother came out in the Teutonia. Had dinner with them, then went and camped up the creek. I do not think much of Verde Creek. The land is useful black loam, but there is only a poor stock range. Saw here the first crop of wheat—a very poor one owing to the drouth—belonging to "Cling," a German.

27 Apr   Sunday. Walked up the creek but did not see anything worthy of notice. The valleys here are heavily wooded, so the land must be cleared for cultivation. Have given up going to Bandera as we hear there is no grass and very little water.

28 Apr   Started at 6 A.M. for Kerrville, passing through an uninteresting country of stony hills and small valleys and arriving at 11 A.M. Bought some fishing gear. Camped on a creek a few miles out and caught 2 turtles and some catfish, which are good eating. Kerrville is a poor little place, about 30 families living there. There are 3 stores and 1 barroom. The country is pretty but a good deal settled up.

29 Apr   Started over the hills into Gillespie Co. These hills are very stony and covered with dense scrub—in fact, the roughest bit of country in southwest Texas, as we found to our cost. The sun going in and it coming [out?], I think we were five hours in the scrub, scarcely able to drag our horses through. The sun came out in the afternoon and we got out into some open post oak country. Good stock range in the spring, but as it is all sage grass, the stock don't do so well on it in the summer. The country looked beautifully green as the grass was burned last winter. Saw here the best horses I have seen since I have been in Texas. Most of them about 15 [hds. ?] and strong. Camped near to a ranch, the man supplying us with water.

30 Apr   Started for a new settlement this morning on the Pedernales Creek, making it about noon. Found here a German and 3 American families. It seems good land and will grow (or they told us so) 1¼ bales of cotton to the acre. They were busy

planting. Obliged to camp here as Smith's horse is taken bad and we cannot get him any further—think it must be some Texas complaint. He runs at the nose by the quart and will not eat—hope he will not knock under. Went shooting this afternoon. Result—3 couple ducks and a wild sow pig about 6 months old. And this evening I caught about 8 lbs. of catfish in the creek, so our larder is full of meat, but we are out of flour and coffee.

01 May   Thursday. Smith's horse a little better so we are stopping here to-day to let him get his strength up. Have had a good look round and find there is some good cultivatable land and tolerably good run for stock and plenty of water. Grand wash this afternoon.

02 May   Started this morning for Llano County, but Smith's horse could not carry him, so he had to walk. Met "Old Man Taylor" and his wife. They are nearly 80 years of age. He told us he was a preacher and was going to the Guadalupe[21] and advised us to see Spring Creek about five miles from where we met him. And as we must have some flour, came here, and I rode into Fredericksburg 12 miles and got provisions. Shot a turkey. There are 5 or 6 families settled here—most of them cultivate a little land and raise stock.

03 May   Stayed here today to have a good look round and find this is just the place to suit me. Rode to the Pedernales about six miles over some excellent land—black loam sparsely timbered on the hills and the valleys nearly clear and covered with mesquite grass. This is the best agricultural and stock country I have seen— plenty of water and the stock looking fresh and healthy. Very little stock upon it at present—it is a beautiful track of country and only two or three squatters on it. Saw a small flock of sheep near the mouth of Spring Creek looking healthy and in good condition. There is an unlimited range for stock on the low hills, which afford excellent feed and shelter in winter. Called upon Captain Temple—he has been here some time and says sheep do well here. Shall go into Fredericksburg on Monday to see the county surveyor.

04 May   Sunday. Walked around and both Smith and self are more in love with this country than ever. Find there is 640 acres—about 200 of which is flat valley land and good—for sale by a man at Castroville. It joins the settlement and is good land though not

so good as 3 miles lower <u>down</u>. The wild grapes grow in abundance all over this country and are very full of fruit—the wild flowers are beautiful.

05 May   Came into Fredericksburg this morning and saw the County surveyor. He says the Castroville land is held for a thousand dollars and that the next 3 miles of water frontage belongs to Peter Hayden, Brooklyn, New York, and the rest, to mouth of Creek, to Francis Morris, Box 3090, New York, who also owns some more good land on the Pedernales adjoining. Neither of these owners will sell or let. The Castroville estate is owned by Dan Wurzbach of Castroville, Medina County, who was asking $1000 for the section 3 years since, but surveyor does not know how much now—must see him on my return to San Antonio. The surveyor also showed us on the map 2 sections on Coal Creek—2 miles south of the border of Llano County—which he has for sale. He says it is good sheep country, open but hilly and plenty of mesquite grass and water good. Would take $1 per acre. There is also west of this 3 or 4 sections which could be located at (surveyor would undertake to do so at the price) $90 per section. There is no running water in this tract.[22] Taxes on all located lands $25 per section per annum.

Left Frederickburg at 4 P.M. for Blanco, which is about 35 miles going part of the way (18 miles) by the Austin road. Three miles out we got a tremendous thunder storm. The rain came down in torrents and it blew a hurricane. Fortunately we managed to take shelter in an old tumble down hovel, so did not get very wet. Were kept there till 7 o'clock, when we made another start—but after going about 4 miles, the storm commenced again and we had to pull up for an hour under some trees and kept things as dry as we could. The country we are traveling through is flat and densely timbered in most parts. The effect of the rain is to turn it into a lake. The moon coming out, we travelled along through the mud until 11 P.M., when the horses "giving out," we halted in a clear place and pulled the saddles off. Very little grass for the horses. Managed after several attempts to get a good fire and sat down to wait for daylight, but soon fell asleep and nearly into the fire—so, as it seemed likely to be fine, we cut some bushes and laid down on them in our blankets and were soon in the arms of Morpheus.

Fredericksburg is nicely situated on a fertile plain with hills all round. Most of the plain is in cultivation and supports 3 flouring mills and 1 cotton gin. The land is a rich chocolate loam with red sandstone subsoil. I am told this is the best kind of land in this part of the country, as it holds the moisture. Wheat is about half a crop this year, owing to the drouth, but corn and cotton is expected to be a good crop, as the rains have come in time. The corn looks splendid and the cotton is nearly ready to thin out. There are about 800 inhabitants in Fredericksburgh, nearly all Germans. They have some good stone houses, stores, etc., a fine Roman Catholic Church, also two Methodist and one Baptist Chapels, besides a little round Lutheran Church in the centre of the plaza built by the first settlers and about the size of the market house at Harold Wells.[23] The mills have steam power and run 4 pairs stones each.

06 May   Tuesday. Got started this morning at 7 A.M. after a good breakfast of fish which I caught in the river. Still dull and cloudy and looking like rain. Came to grass and water about ten [A.M.], 18 miles from Fredericksburg so stopped to feed the horses. Hope to reach Blanco County tonight.

1 P.M.—the sun has just made his appearance. There is plenty of rich land between here and Fredericksburg but it is heavily timbered.

Started again at 3 P.M. and went 7 miles through heavily timbered post oak country, leaving the Austin road and striking across for the Blanco road, passing several ranches. Struck Blanco road in 3 miles. The land between the two roads is a deep black loam and where cultivated the corn looks excellent. Entered an elevated table land in Blanco County surrounded by low grassy hills. Very little timber and no living water so far as I could see. The land is rich at the north end but poor to the south. Passed several good ranches. Camped at dark near a water hole.

07 May   Wednesday. Started at 8 A.M. as I had to bake for breakfast and made Blanco about 1 P.M., passing through a rocky valley with coarse grasses on it and the hills. Not suited for sheep though the cattle look well. Blanco is a rising little town and there are some pretty houses in it. I should think about 200 inhabitants,

one mill and a saw mill. There is some good black land, timbered, round Blanco. Traveled on up the mountains and
camped at a spring, having shot another wild pig which we
proceeded to singe—had liver for supper.

08 May   Thursday. Rose at 4 A.M. Got under weigh at 6 for Curry's Creek.
Passed through the mountains for 4 miles and then opened on a
large plain dotted here and there with settlements, across to the
creek, leaving which we crossed more mountains in centre of
which is a small valley about 6 miles by ¾—the most lovely spot
I have yet seen in Texas. The grass as level as a lawn and a settler's
house in the centre. On reaching the top of the hills we de-
scended into another plain partly settled. We are now on the road
to Boerne. Had to travel till nine o'clock last night to find
water—at last we struck the Guadalupe river and camped for the
night.

09 May   Friday. Started early this morning and made the Cibolo Creek,
where we stayed four hours to feed the horses as they had no
grass last night. Have been passing through a rather thickly
timbered post oak country—some good land in the valleys.
Leaving the Cibolo Creek, we came upon a beautiful valley
about 8 miles long, looking more like our English meadows,
covered with good grasses and lightly timbered with post oak
and live oak. I think, for the size, one of the prettiest valleys I
have seen in this state. Arrived at Leon Springs, 18 miles from
San Antonio, at 7.20 P.M., and upon making enquiries found
that the valley above mentioned with a good stone residence in
the centre is owned by a widow, Mrs. —[24], who is anxious to
sell. It contains about 7,000 acres and the price with all improvements 8 to 10 thousand dollars. There is good water
generally but last season the stock suffered from the long drouth.
This is a good horse or cattle ranch and I should think at least
one-half good cultivatable land. I shall try to get the widow to
sell 100 acres as there is excellent stock range and only 20 miles
from San Antonio. Camped 2 miles below Leon Springs on the
Saluda Creek. Very little grass for the horses, but that little good
mesquite.

10 May   Saturday. Started this morning at six but had only gone 200
yards when Smith's horse fell and we could not get him up
again. Stayed with him some time and got him on his legs, but

finding him too weak to proceed, left Smith with him and came on into San Antonio. Lost my last knife at this camp (the one Sophie gave me). Met a Dr. Nelson on the road as I was feeding my mare and having a pipe. He comes from Lavaca County and invited me to go and see him. He also recommends me to go to Nueces County. Says it is a fine stock country and gave me introduction to Gen. John Baylor, now in San Antonio. He says I shall not like Lavaca County. Arrived in San Antonio for dinner. Went to post and got two letters from Agnes with photographs of [Chicks?]. Expect Smith in tomorrow. Found Daniel and Cantor here.[25]

11 May   Sunday. Wrote to Agnes Wright last night and to Tom today. Very warm. Smith not arrived.

12 May   Monday. Posted letters to Agnes and Tom, also papers, and wrote to Wurzbach about land on Spring Creek. Rode 8 miles on road to meet Smith but failed to do so—if he does not turn up tonight must go out and see what's the matter.
            A good many sheep in the market just now. The sheep men seem turning their attention to goats as being more profitable. They can be bought at 50¢ to $1 and require 4 crosses to make wool of any value. A pure bred Angora buck costs $80.

13 May   Went out to see what had become of Smith. On arriving at Leon Springs found he had gone to Tom Green County with Scott's herd at $45 per month. Found a letter for me at San Antonio on return explaining. Glad he has got something at last. Had a very hot ride, leaving here 9 A.M. and getting back at 4 p.m—nearly 40 miles—pretty good with the thermometer at 90° in the shade!! Received a letter from THW.[26]

14 May   Wednesday. Waiting to hear from Castroville. Shall then start for the coast. The sheep men are congratulating themselves on the price of wool. C. Brown told me he made 23¢ per lb., top price, and says it will pay at 20¢ per lb. Since the rains the prospects have wonderfully brightened—most of the English who came out with me have engaged to go herding at $12 to $15 per month and board. Got samples of wool from C. Brown of different grades. Thermometer 92° in shade. Mean to leave here tomorrow. Sent papers to Tom and Frank. Wrote Smith.

15 May   Thursday. Got a note this morning from Alsop asking me to call upon Mr. Caldwell[27] if I went to San Marcos. Was just preparing

to start for there and then to Luling. No news from Castroville. Left San Antonio at 3.30 P.M. and took the Austin road to New Braunfels, passing through the village of Selma. The country for 12 miles out of San Antonio is flat and densely covered with mesquite bush. Here and there patches in cultivation and some fine residences to the west of the road, about ½ mile, where there seems to be a creek and some cedars. After passing Selma at 16 miles, got into an open country—sort of rolling prairie—very little timber and pretty well settled. Rode on to within 3 or 4 miles of New Braunfels when, it being dark, camped under a live oak.

16 May   Friday. Started at daybreak and passed through a well settled and cultivated country to New Braunfels. The corn crop looking remarkably good, cotton also—wheat and oats moderately good. Wheat harvest is just commencing. New Braunfels is a brisk little town with some good buildings, flour and saw mills, and a woolen manufactory just started by a German banker at San Antonio. Altogether it looks like a thriving place, is on the Guadalupe River, and is a good farming district. Went into camp at nine, as the sun was very powerful, and had breakfast. Also did some washing and mending. Was joined by a Mr. Gullet of San Marcos just before leaving and travelled on here with him. The last 14 miles up a rich valley (undulating), covered with settlements, and nearly the whole in cultivation. The corn and cotton crops are magnificent and wheat and oats very fair, some very good. By the bye this Mr. Gullet has ten sections to sell in the heart of Edwards County at 50¢ per acre—good land and plenty of spring water. Passed several improved farms for sale at $20 per acre and one unimproved at $5 per acre, but the latter is cut up with roads. Arrived at the pretty little town of San Marcos at 3 P.M. and have walked all through the place and am now writing this at the head of the river, which gushes out of the foot of a mountain as clear as crystal and cool as ice (<u>almost</u>) and forms itself into a river at once, 100 yards below the springs. It is 6 feet deep and 80 yards across and runs rapidly just below. The stream flows out of the mountain about 15 yards wide, or rather there are ten streams running out, covering that width. San Marcos is the prettiest place I have seen in Texas, situated about ½ mile down the river,

with high hills covered with cedars for a background. There are some good business houses; a small mill; several churches; a college, which Mr. Gullet speaks very highly of—especially the female division; and substantial and pretty residences. Am staying here the night to have a good look round, and then on to Luling. I forgot to mention a fine court house built centre of a large plaza—also several good hotels. Here the sale of beer and spirits is prohibited except as a medical comfort, and one has to get a prescription from a doctor. Of course every one that drinks beer carries a prescription in his pocket. What a farce!! I wanted a glass of beer, having had a very hot and dusty ride but was told I couldn't be served as I hadn't a prescription, but a man was pointed out to me sitting in the back room who had one, so I walked up to him and he ordered the beer and I paid—another farce.

I am quite in love with this place and believe a very good living can be made here farming, as the crops are pretty certain and the land only wants good tillage and early planting to make it produce handsomely. Evidences of prosperity everywhere abound in large houses the settlers are putting up. A good flour and saw mill with cotton gin would enhance this prosperity very much, and there is ample water power, as the river has a good fall. All that is needed is <u>capital</u>.

17 May | Saturday. Started early for Luling via Prairie Lea through a well settled country with good farms and crops until near Luling, where the crops were not so good. Luling is getting to be a good sized place with some fine buildings in it. Found Richardson and Godden[28] here, the latter looking very bad. (He was laid up for three weeks after arrival). He has gone to work for a farmer but doesn't seem to like it much—the work is too heavy for him. A lot more English just arrived. Left Luling and travelled through a very sandy country, densely covered with timber and brush, the timber consisting of post oak, black jack, white oak, walnut, etc. Not many settlements, but crossed the head of two valleys waving with corn for several miles down, the whole of them seemingly in cultivation. Three miles from Gonzales the country gets more open, and I passed many nice farms with good houses upon them. Some of them built of brick—several seemed deserted.

18 May   Sunday. Remained here last night and went to the Methodist
           church this morning, a nice looking place outside, but very
           rough and unfinished inside. Didn't think much of the parson;
           in his discourse he said we should all be asked to take a seat
           when we got to heaven. There are some very good buildings in
           this old town, including 3 large blocks of business premises built
           of brick, and most of the houses have gardens and orchards.
           Moved out of here in the evening and camped 4 miles on the
           road to Hallettsville. <u>I am sorry to say</u> my mare has a very sore
           back.

19 May   Monday. Passed through a flat country on which were numer-
           ous settlements of Negroes. Should say it is unhealthy, there
           being many swamps and a dense growth of fine timber consist-
           ing of the various kinds of oak and some immense pecans—the
           latter denoting a wet soil. Seventeen miles from Gonzales,
           entered upon the most lovely prairie country I have yet seen.
           Met an American gentleman here who informed me I had
           missed taking a road in coming out of Gonzales. Consequently,
           I was near Moulton on the Flatonia Road instead of being, as I
           thought, on the road to Hallettsville. Travelled with him to
           Moulton, when he kindly put me in the right road. He tells me
           the land about here is very good, and I can easily believe him,
           for I have passed finer crops of corn, cotton, wheat, and oats
           than any I have seen elsewhere—some of the corn being 12 feet
           high and thick as my wrist. He tells me this country is very
           healthy, has been here 25 years and never required a doctor in
           his family. As I was coming through Moulton, which is a pretty
           town situated on a hill with extensive view amidst park-like
           farms and well cultivated fields, the girls (about 40) were
           coming out of school and they certainly looked the picture of
           health. Mr. Allis tells me the rainfall here is ample and that
           where ever in Texas you can draw a line due South to enter the
           Gulf of Mexico, there is ample rainfall, the prevailing winds
           being from that quarter. Crossed a beautiful rolling prairie,
           sufficiently wooded with post oak to make it very pretty, the
           land very good and where cultivated showing fine crops,
           sufficiently watered and covered with grass up to my pony's
           knees, the stock looking well, some nice farms and good houses
           scattered about. To the west it is gently rolling prairie as far as

the eye can see, with motts of timber here and there, and occasionally a belt ½ a mile wide. Missed my road again and camped on Rocky Creek[29] ½ mile from Sweet Home. Seems some nice places to settle on near here but I don't like it so well as nearer Moulton. Mr. Allis tells me there is a farm for sale between Moulton and Flatonia—about 200 acres, 40 in cultivation, good house and all fenced. The man would sell cheap as he wants to leave. Mr. Allis thinks 12 to $15 per acre [good?]. Shall have a look at it if I go back that way.

20 May   Tuesday. Didn't get started until 8 o'clock, as my mare had very little grass last night. Entered Sweet Home about 8.30 and found I was 8 miles from Mr. Williams'—so, getting directions, proceeded, and after sundry mistakes in the road, arrived at Mr. Williams' for dinner at noon. Both gave me a <u>hearty</u> welcome and seemed pleased to see me. There is a Mr. and Mrs. Bradfield here from Hampshire. He has been here 3 years (in Texas) but returned to England last July and married his second wife and returned in November. Is now with Mr. Williams, as his business has grown too large for his own management. They seem very nice people—he was a farmer in England and, like many more, lost his money. He says he likes Texas very much. The country round here and to the South of this is bush country; therefore, though there are farms for sale—improved and (Mr Williams tells me) to be had cheap—I should not care to live here. Mr. Williams also tells me there are some farms for sale at Sweet Home on reasonable terms and that it and Moulton are the two best communities in the county. Have been helping Mr. Bradfield with his house this afternoon. It will be very comfortable when finished—30 ft. x 28 ft.—plenty large enough as they have no family. His father lives at Wolferton, Norfolk. I am to call upon him should I go to Norfolk.

21 May   Wednesday. Drove with Mr. Williams and a Mr. Bright to Hallettsville, which is a nice little town but not very enterprising. Mr. Williams introduced me to a Mr. Crane, lawyer who has an estate of 2000 acres for sale 3½ miles from Hallettsville. From there we drove on the Schulenburg road to Mr. Williams' near Hackberry, where we had dinner—from there to Mr. McGowans to look at a small steam engine, that being the object of our drive, Mr. Bright requiring one to work his cotton

gin. Left Mr. Bright there and returned about 10 P.M., having driven 40 miles. This has been a very hot day. The thermometer 98° in the shade and no wind. I did not feel it very much, and they seldom have it so hot even in July, as there is always a breeze in the hottest months. One of the horses set to kicking and broke the double tree. Mr. Williams had hard work to prevent them smashing the whole concern amongst the timber but fortunately succeeded and, after repairing damages as well as we could in the dark, we got into the road again and arrived home without further accident.

22 May   Thursday. Left Mr. Williams' this morning at 7 A.M. They pressed me very much to stay over Sunday, but I must get away to the coast. Called at Mr. Crane's office but found he had not come in to Hallettsville so went on hoping to find him at home as I wanted to see more of his estate, Mr. Williams having given me very good accounts of it. Found Mr. Crane had gone to Schulenburg, but Mrs. Crane kindly sent the foreman Mr. [Edie ?] round with me and I spent six hours thoroughly examining the estate. I found it a very desirable one and in every particular answering the printed description given me by Mr. Crane yesterday, having which [the printed description] I need not enlarge upon it here more than to say that this is a most eligible estate for six or eight to join and buy to work on the cooperative principle, and I believe it would pay handsomely, as the country round is settling thickly and the value of the land increasing fast. Must think this over at leisure and see what I can do on my return to England. Mrs. Crane kindly invited me to dinner and, as I was very hungry, did not decline. She is a very nice lady—true American—and born on this place, her father, a Mr. Mitchell, having settled here many years ago. But he lost all his property after the [American Civil] War, having 200 Negroes taken from him. Left here at 4 P.M. and rode on, passing Hackberry, Oakland and Content—passing which latter place I camped, it being dark. I passed many good farms and some fine open country before getting to Hackberry—since then have been in the bush.

23 May   Friday. Did not start until eight this morning, there being so little grass for my mare. Travelled through bush country, (though there are many clearings and neat farms) on the road to

Columbus. Camped for three hours, 8 miles from Columbus. Passed through Columbus, which seemed a very quiet place, and on through the bush to Alleyton, 4 miles from the latter place, it being nearly dark and on the edge of the great prairie. Camped under the last trees for the night, lost my feed bag.

24 May   Saturday. Got to Eagle Lake for breakfast. Found here several English people who say the place is not so unhealthy as people think but that the bottom lands 2 to 6 miles off on the lake and Colorado River are considered very unhealthy. Mr. Rodgers from Wiltshire arrived here in January last and is keeping an hotel and says he is doing very well. I also found here a Mr. Andrews who has been amid [illegible] in Green's employ and since then seven years in South America, a very nice fellow—has two boys with him. Went this afternoon with a Mr. Wilkinson from Bradford, York, to look at a farm five miles west of here, belonging to a man named Wilson. He seems to have some good crops and the best peach orchard I have yet seen and magnificent grapes and melons. He is working part of his farm as a market garden and says it pays very well. This is the only attempt I have seen at gardening on a large scale. He wants 8# [£8 or $8?] an acre for his farm, but the houses are old and badly built, so I think it is dear at 5# [£5 or $5?]. Mr. Wilkinson bid him five for it.

25 May   Sunday. Am staying at Eagle Lake today to rest my mare and have been walking about on the prairie. I find but little in cultivation and, on that little, nothing worth calling a crop. The railway lands here are very poor and fit only for stock raising purposes. The soil is something like the chalky soils of Sussex and is either too wet when it rains, being devoid of drainage, or set like a brick, a vast contrast to the rich black sandy loam and hog wallow of Lavaca County. Went to the nigger church tonight. Did not go in, the scent being too strong, and well I didn't, for I fear I should have offended by laughing at them, for of all the services I ever saw, this beats them for ridiculousness. They call themselves "Baptist Episcopalians." I need not write more about it here, as I am not likely to forget it in a hurry.

26 May   Monday. Have been trying to sell my mare and saddle this morning, but, as I can only get a customer for the mare, am going on to New Philadelphia. Had hard work to get away from

Eagle Lake, they wanting me to stay another day or two, but managed to do so at last and arrived at New Philadelphia in time to get some fried bacon and coffee with Alsop. Found about 20 of Kingsbury's people here, all of them thoroughly disgusted with the place. They are living in a shed dignified with the name of Immigration Depot and have to find a living the best way they can. And I don't suppose they get more than one day's work a week—for which they receive $1.10, just enough to keep them alive. They are all very discontented. I heard as I was leaving Eagle Lake that T. W. Peirce had been mobbed at Luling a few days ago and, with a pistol to each ear, made to write to Kingsbury to stop sending any more men out who have not means to start in some business. I think if the Dr. [Kingsbury] were to appear on the scene just now, some of them would hang him. I would not give much for the lives of his agents here, for the men are getting desperate and the agents don't trouble themselves in the least about them. Indeed, they are worse than useless to the immigrants. After dinner, rode down to see the Pontefract family, Pontefract[30] having bought land about 3 miles lower down. He is trying to get his money back again but I don't think he will succeed. Cooke (the agent here) came in whilst I was there. He comes from Sheffield and I think a more thorough ruffian and bully I never saw. I told him I was pleased to make his acquaintance as I wished to see his fine crops of corn, cotton, etc. that we heard so much about in England and which we read of in his letters to Dr. Kingsbury. By jove I never saw a man get into such a rage and I thought once or twice it would be a case of fight; however, I kept my temper and played with him 'till I got tired of hearing his curses. He says his letters to Dr. Kingsbury were privileged communications and ought not to have been published—one way of getting out of it. I think he is having a roughish time of it here, as there are constantly fresh arrivals and he gets nothing but curses from them. A man said he had seen a man hanging to a tree in the bush 7 miles off, kicking about, and on being asked why he did not cut him down, said he thought it looked like Cooke, so he just let him hang. This shows the estimation in which the Company's agents are held. I have been trying to sell my outfit here but cannot get on to sell the lot. The station master bid me

$25 for the mare, but no one wants the rest so am going on after staying the night with the Pontefracts.

27 May   Tuesday. Rode up to Cooke's this morning to try and sell my horse, etc. to a man named Moore staying there, but he didn't mean business, says Cooke, who was rather more civil and even asked me to have some breakfast—which I declined. He evidently saw he made a mistake yesterday and tried to justify himself by throwing all the blame on Kingsbury. The model farm is a perfect wilderness—the corn will never come to anything and cotton cannot be seen for rubbish and the Colorado beetle is eating all the potatoes. Eleven Welshmen came here, I am told, a few days since and just looked at this farm and went off again, saying that if that was a specimen of the products of New Philadelphia, they wouldn't stop there. They had been led to expect that houses had been erected and land broken, all ready for them to go to work. In fact, they came to take possession of Kingsbury's improved farms. Cooke showed me a letter printed [in a newspaper] by Kingsbury from Cooke, saying that eight of their farms were ready for settlers and he had orders to get more ready. The fact is that 2 small houses have been put up and fenced, but no land has been broke—in fact nothing is or will be done to help the immigrants by the railway company. All they think of is getting him here so as to get cheap labor on their line, and the fare back is so expensive that few have the means to go (5¢ @ mile). Left this place at 8 A.M. and travelled over a dreary flat prairie to Richmond on the Brazos River. The prairie all through covered with coarse grass fit only for store stock. Everything in Richmond is very quiet and very dear. Tried again to dispose of my outfit but to no good. A planter bid me a good price for saddle but didn't want mare, but I mean to sell all together.

28 May   Wednesday. Left here this morning at 7 A.M. and travelled through the bottom lands for 7 miles. They are heavily timbered but very rich, of a red sandy loam, and produce good sugar cane, corn, and cotton, but are very unhealthy. At 7 miles from Richmond, entered upon the prairie and traveled 'till noon, when it being intensely hot and finding a few trees for shade, I rested the mare 'till 3:20 and arrived at Houston 7 P.M.

29 May	Thursday. Went to the post this morning and was pleased to get 2 letters from Agnes but sorry to learn of her illness, though thankful she is going on all right. Could I have got these letters in San Antonio they would have made a great difference in my plans, but now I shall adhere to my first intentions and return to England. P.M. Have been trying all day to sell my outfit but without success. It is very hot here and makes one feel very enervated. Have suffered with looseness since I entered on the flat country. My mare is standing at Hudson's stables. He wishes me to tell Woodhams to come out again, as he wants to leave him in charge of his business whilst he comes over to England.
30 May	Friday. Went to the post this morning—no letters. Expect one from Smith also from Agnes. Trust no news is <u>good</u> news. Find the steamer for New Orleans leaves on Saturday morning at ten o'clock. Must sell my pony today if possible.
31 May	Saturday. Sold the mare last night for $25 but the man didn't show up with the money, so have been obliged to sell my outfit to Hudson's for $30, as the train leaves at 10 A.M. Arrived at Galveston 12:30 P.M.[31] and went immediately on board the S.S. "Hutchinson" and sailed for New Orleans, arriving there at 4 P.M. on June 1st, Sunday, and put up at the Henry Clay house @ $1 per day. Find there is only one ship for England, the Mississippi & Dominion S.S. "St. Louis." Capt. Reid expects to sail on Thursday.
01 Jun	
02 Jun	
03 Jun	
04 Jun	Wrote to Agnes, having arranged for my passage in the St. Louis yesterday.
05 Jun	Thursday. Wrote a short note to Agnes, as I found I had made a mistake in Fluier [spelling of Fluier is uncertain] and Company's address in yesterday's [letter]. Sailed for Havana at 8.30 P.M.
06 Jun	Friday. Left the river this morning at 7 A.M., head wind and wet. Accommodations on board the "St. Louis" very bad, a queer set of passengers and lots of children, so hot and crowded below. Am obliged to sleep on deck. We are promised more room when we get to Havana. Left one of the passengers named Clarke,

alias Monroe, alias Morgan, etc., etc. (who came in the "Hutchinson" from Galveston and went to the same house as myself in New Orleans) in jail for smuggling, carrying concealed weapons, etc. The landlord of Henry Clay House has promised to send me papers when his trial comes on, I having left him money and stamps for that purpose.

07 Jun   Saturday. Head wind and fine. Ship taking in a good deal of water, being very deep in the water, but expect she will make better weather of it after leaving Havana, part of the cargo being for that port.

08 Jun   Sunday. Head wind and fine, sighted the Island of Cuba at 9 A.M. and anchored in Havana harbor at 3 P.M. Expect to stay here 3 or 4 days. Very hot and the mosquitoes very troublesome.

09 Jun   Monday. Fine and very hot. Discharging cargo.

10 Jun   Tuesday. Took 60 Spanish passengers on board for Vigo[32] and sailed at 5 P.M.

11 Jun   Wednesday. Head wind and fine.

12 Jun   Thursday. Calm, in sight of the American coast. 304 miles in the last 24 hours.

13 Jun   Friday. Fair wind and squalls of rain. 306 miles. Everybody drenched by a current ripple coming on board.

14 Jun   Saturday. Calm and fine.

15 Jun   Sunday. Fair wind and fine, steering east, ½ north, 11 knots. Lat. 39°N, Long. 67°W.

16 Jun   Monday. Strong southwest winds and fine. Ship making very good weather of it. Signalled large steamer, passengers, 6 P.M.

17 Jun   Tuesday. Fresh breeze and fine. Lat. 41°N, Long. 56½°W. 2168 miles from Vigo at noon.

18 Jun   Light winds and rainy. Passed several vessels. 242 miles.[33]

19 Jun   Thursday. Strong winds from north with rain. Very cold. Engines stopped last light at 7 P.M. but got going again at 10 P.M. 238 miles.

20 Jun   Friday. Light winds and fine. Passed several vessels. 202 miles.

21 Jun   Saturday. Light winds and fine. 220 miles. Passed the Norwegian Barque Suwa.

22 Jun   Sunday. Light winds and fine. 226 miles.

23 Jun   Light winds and fine. Passed the ship Blue Jacket. 227 miles.

[Two lines illegible.]

24 Jun	Tuesday. Light winds and fine. 217 miles.
25 Jun	Wednesday. Light winds and fine. Passed several vessels. 228 miles.
26 Jun	Thursday. Ditto. Ditto. 227 miles. 11 A.M. the old man died. Passed 6 vessels going south.
27 Jun	Friday. Agnes' birthday. Anchored in Vigo, 7 A.M. Steamed up to the Quarantine ground and sent Spanish passengers ashore. Left for Liverpool 12 o'clock. Fuertes and family[34] going with us; landed one of the Spaniards in a dying state.
28 Jun	Saturday. Fresh breeze and squally, heavy swell.
29 Jun	Sunday. Fresh breeze and fine, cold; passed the Scilly Isles at 6 P.M.
30 Jun	Monday. 6 A.M. passed the Tuskar light house. Moderate breeze and showery, very cold. 6 P.M. signalled the light house at Holyhead. 7 P.M. pilot came on board. 11 P.M. anchored. Blowing very hard with rain, bitterly cold.
01 Jul	Arrived off the Huskisson dock at 7 A.M. Not allowed to enter this morning on account of the Spaniard that died. Landed at 4 P.M. Telegraphed to Agnes and Frank. Got clear of the ship at 9:20 P.M. and slept at North Western Hotel.[35]

PART III

The Wreck of the Missouri
*and Czech Immigration
to Texas in 1873*

CHAPTER 5

Introduction

On the eastern section of the Gingerbread Ground, part of the Great Bahama Bank, about 40 miles east-northeast of the Biminis and approximately 160 miles northwest of Nassau, lie the remains of an old wrecked ship, one of many claimed over the years by this treacherous stretch of reefs that marks the southern border of the Northwest Providence Channel.[1] Not much is left—some old wooden ribs of a ship half-buried in the sand, a quantity of chain strewn about the area—but these may very well be the final traces of the steamship *Missouri*.[2] The *Missouri* is almost certainly the "mystery ship" that sometimes appears in a popular legend about Czech immigration to Texas in the nineteenth century, a story about families from northeastern Moravia who were shipwrecked somewhere in the Bahamas en route to Galveston, Texas, in 1873.[3] The story of the Bujnoch, Olšovský, Moris, Láník, Janča, Polášek, and Žárský families—36 individuals in all—of the *Missouri* party constitutes a remarkable chapter in the history of Czech immigration to Texas in the nineteenth century, and it is fully told here for the first time.

Emigration from the Czech lands to the United States in the second half of the nineteenth century was only part of a great exodus from the Austrian Empire,[4] but the Czechs were one of the earliest groups to become involved in this movement. For example, the 6,426 Czechs who came to the United States in 1854 represented a full 90 percent of the Austrian total for that year. In 1871 they still accounted for over 75 percent of the total, but by the end of the century this figure had dropped to under 10 percent.

The first groups of Czechs who came to Texas played a small part in this early pattern of immigration.[5] In 1849 Rev. Josef Ernst Bergman, Evangelical pastor of a Czech congregation in Stroužný, Silesia, decided to bring his family to Texas. He settled in the little German community of Cat Spring in Austin County, where he served as pastor and teacher. Almost immediately he began to write letters to his Czech friends in Europe, describing Central Texas as a land of economic opportunity. His letters were circulated among groups in the towns and villages of northeastern Bohemia and across the border in

Moravia who were interested in emigration, and one was printed in the news-paper *Moravské noviny.* They were directly responsible for inspiring Josef L. Lešikar to organize potential emigrants in the area around Nepomuky and Čermna in northeastern Bohemia. The first group, under the leadership of Josef Šilar, set out in late 1851 on a circuitous route that took them from the German port of Hamburg to Liverpool, New Orleans, and, finally, Galveston. By the time they reached Cat Spring in the spring of 1852, about half of the original party of 70 had died of illness along the way. The second group, under the leadership of Lešikar himself, fared much better. They sailed directly from the German port of Bremen to Galveston, landing a few days before Christ-mas in 1853. This direct Bremen to Galveston route was preferred by most subsequent groups, which, from the mid-1850s on, were dominated by Moravians rather than Bohemians.

It is no accident that the first groups of Czechs migrating to Texas came soon after the completion of certain railroad lines in the Czech lands.[6] The lack of adequate transportation links between potential Czech emigrants and the north German ports of Bremen and Hamburg helps to explain why Czech group immigration to Texas began about seven years after that of the Ger-mans.[7] As soon as it became feasible for the Czechs to travel by rail from their native regions to these ports, they followed routes—across the Atlantic to the port of Galveston and thence to Central Texas—that had been established by the Germans.

Construction of the first steam-powered railroad in the Czech lands began as early as 1836, under the direction of Franz Riepl. By May, 1847, one line of the Northern Railroad of Emperor Ferdinand (KFNB) ran from Břeclav to Brno, while another ran from Břeclav to Přerov, with a branch line to Olomouc, and on to Bohumín, on the present-day Polish border. At the same time the Northern State Railroad ran from Prague to Olomouc, where it con-nected with the KFNB. In April, 1851, a railroad north from Prague to Děčín was opened, also by the Northern State Railroad. At about the same time, a track between Děčín and the Saxony border was opened by the Czecho-Saxonian Railroad Company. This last link provided Bohemian and Moravian emigrants with access to the railroads of the German states and, finally, to the seaports of Hamburg and Bremen.

Bremen was the port used by the North German Lloyd Line, and, begin-ning in the late 1850s, that was the main steamship line that carried Moravian immigrants to Texas. Because of business connections and political ties devel-oped since the early 1840s, Bremen had won out over Hamburg and Antwerp for this portion of the immigration business.

In Galveston the immigration business was dominated by the Kauffman House, agents of the North German Lloyd Line and of other shipping companies. This firm had been founded in Galveston in 1842 as Edward Kauffman and Co. by Edward and Julius Kauffman, who had begun to conduct business in the city two years earlier. In subsequent years the name of the firm was changed to Julius Kauffman and Co., Kauffman and Klainer, Kauffman and Wagner, and finally Kauffman and Runge in 1873.

Julius Kauffman was the dominant force in the company until his death in January, 1880.[8] He had considerable skills as a merchant, importer, and shipping agent. A native of Bremen, he used his contacts there to develop and strengthen the Bremen-Galveston connection over the years.[9] Through arrangements made by the Kauffman House, Germans or Czechs already living in Texas could prepay the transatlantic passage for relatives and friends, either by paying in full or by taking a note on tickets at 1 percent per month on the unpaid balance. Also funds for the purchase of necessary items could be made available to the immigrants at their port of embarkation or at their arrival port of Galveston before their inland journey.[10] When the *Verein zum Schutze deutscher Einwanderer* (German Immigration Society) was organized in the 1840s by German capitalists to promote German immigration to Texas,[11] Edward Kauffman was appointed its fiscal agent, and it was in this capacity that he and Julius Kauffman arranged consignment of space aboard sailing vessels to emigrants.[12] In these early years the German emigrants were shipped from Bremen first to Galveston and then by smaller vessels to the nearby port of Indianola, Texas. It should also be pointed out that the Kauffmans and the *Verein* itself were taking advantage of laws passed by the Republic of Texas in 1841 and 1842 that sanctioned and encouraged the colonization of French, English, and German groups in Texas in order to discourage military intervention by Mexico over disputed borders.[13]

In the meantime another native of Bremen was beginning to take on a prominent role in the German immigration scheme. Henry Runge came to the United States through Baltimore in 1836, moved to New Orleans in 1841, and in 1845 pooled his resources with the *Verein* to support its Texas colony. In 1848 he established a shipping business and bank in Indianola—some claim it was the first bank in Texas.[14] Runge moved his base of operations to Galveston in 1868, and he formed a partnership with Kauffman in 1873, shortly before Runge's death. By that time the two Bremenites, both of whom had maintained political ties to Europe, held a near monopoly on the immigration business in Texas. As early as 1858, if not much earlier, Kauffman held the title of the foreign consul at Galveston for Austria, Saxony, Bremen, and the Netherlands.[15] Similarly Henry Runge had been appointed consul at Indianola, Texas, for the city of Hamburg in 1851.[16] Runge died in 1873, but his nephew and son-in-law Julius Runge was appointed consul for the German Empire at Galveston in 1875.[17] Julius Runge's unsuccessful attempt to corner the U.S.-European cotton market in 1884 was rumored to be backed by Kaiser Wilhelm II and the "Iron Chancellor," Bismarck, himself.[18] When Julius Kauffman died in 1880, his Austrian consular title was transferred to his son Julius Kauffman, Jr.

Several small groups that emigrated from northern Moravia in the 1850s were responsible for the initial settlements that established the population belt of Texas Czechs that stretches through Fayette, Lavaca, and Colorado counties. A group of Moravians arriving in 1860 established themselves in such communities as Sweet Home, Koerth, Mulberry (later Praha), Navidad (later Dubina), and Bluff (later Hostyn). However, the Civil War, with the Union blockade of Southern ports, effectively halted the flow of Czechs to Texas.[19] The last emigrant vessel from Bremen bound to New Orleans set sail on April 8, 1861, and no other emigrant ships took this route until the departure of the *Constantia* on September 4, 1865. Likewise the last emigrant ship from Bremen bound for Galveston departed on November 22, 1860. Not until October 5, 1865, did the bark *Fortuna* resume this service.

Largely because of this interruption, Czech immigration to Texas, though it began early, took place on a relatively small scale until about a decade after the war. According to U.S. Census data, only 780 foreign-born Czechs were residing in the state in 1870. By 1880 the number had risen dramatically to 2,669, and it reached its peak at more than 15,000 in 1910.[20] The *Missouri* incident is part of the history of the 1870s, when Czech immigration began to increase rapidly.

CHAPTER 6

The Emigrants

Sometime in 1871 a group of people living in neighboring villages in northern Moravia, like other small groups throughout the region, began to discuss the possibility of immigrating to Texas. By the fall of 1873, 36 individuals from eight different families had made the decision to leave.[1]

Three of the families came from the village of Fryčovice (see map 1). Among the first to commit themselves to emigration were the Láníks. Karel Láník, age 30, lived in house no. 142 with his wife Josefa, age 27, who was about five months pregnant. Josefa's mother, the widow Johanna Bujnoch (née Kublak), age 56, decided to accompany her daughter and son-in-law. Mrs. Bujnoch, who lived in house no. 59, would bring along three of her children: Františka, 24; Jiří, 22; and Mariana, 19. Mrs. Bujnoch's son Jan and his wife Mariana (née Olšovský) decided to remain behind in Fryčovice, but another family from the village joined the emigrants. From house no. 205 came Jiří Olšovský, 35; his wife Johana (née Nevlud), 32; and children František, 5; Agnes, 3; and Františka, 2. Johana was in the second month of pregnancy.

The village of Chlebovice lies less than one mile south of Fryčovice. Living in house no. 8 were František Šimek, age 38; his wife Mariana (née Kočích), 37; and their children Jan, 8; Josef, 6; Ferdinand, 2; and Cecilia, about ten months. According to Šimek family tradition, Cecilia had a twin sister named Julia who died during the voyage to Texas and was buried at sea; however, Julia's name was not listed on the document granting permission to emigrate.

František Šimek had been a soldier in the Austrian Imperial Army for about fourteen years. He had served in the war with Denmark (1864) and in Italy during the time of the Hungarian Rebellion (1866–67). Apparently his military experience helped to motivate Šimek in his plans to emigrate. According to his grandson, Šimek had premonitions of a "hell of a war" that was going to take place in Europe in the future and he did not want his sons to be soldiers. Šimek had several sisters, but none of them emigrated. His brother-in-law Jakub Bujnoch did eventually come to Texas at a later time.[2]

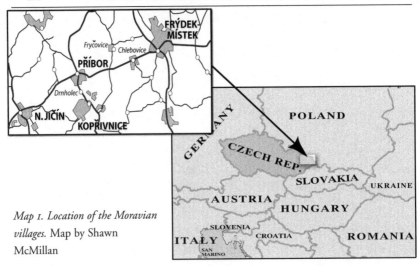

Map 1. Location of the Moravian villages. Map by Shawn McMillan

Also from Chlebovice came Ferdinand Moris, 24; his wife Clara (née Kuběna), 20; and their infant daughter Mariana.

Three more families came from Drnholec, a village located less than five miles southwest of Fryčovice. Jan Janča, age 32, was joined by his wife Mariana (née Liberda), 27, and their children Jan, 4, and Mariana, 2. Janča was a carpenter who specialized in making staves for the local winery. Mrs. Janča was in her seventh month of pregnancy. Her brother Joe Liberda, who had previously emigrated and was living at Sweet Home, a rural community in Lavaca County, Texas, provided financial assistance to pay for the Jančas' voyage.

Also in her seventh month of pregnancy was Rosalie Žárská (née Koláš, a surname that later became "Clos"), 37, accompanied by her husband Jakub Žárský, 37, and their children Mariana, 8; Jakub, 7; Jan, 3; and an infant daughter Tereza. Finally, there was Vincent Polášek, 37, with his wife Veronika (née Janča), 31; daughter Františka, 5; and infant son Josef.

In many ways this northern Moravian group was typical of Czech emigrants of the time, reacting to the push of economic hardship at home and the pull of perceived economic opportunity in Texas. Most important was the relative scarcity of good farmland in Moravia, contrasted with its relative availability in Texas. According to the last census prior to World War I in Bohemia and Moravia, more than one million small farming families each held five or fewer acres of land. However, more than 70 percent of all landowners owned only 6.5 percent of the land area.[3] As was typical, small landowners and craftsmen made up the *Missouri* group, which was ambitious for the economic security and prestige that would come with the acquisition of a sufficiently large plot of arable land. In Moravia, where political rights and social prestige were closely tied to the ownership of land, these ambitions were nearly hopeless, but the average holding of nearly one hundred acres for the typical early Texas Czech farmer was attractive indeed.[4]

The vast majority of Bohemian and Moravian emigrants at this time intended to work in agriculture, and their chief ambition was to own their own farms; furthermore most of them probably had a fairly realistic idea of the struggle that lay ahead. Since most immigrant families were poor and many went into debt in order to pay for their passage to Texas, it would not be easy to buy land there, though the land was relatively plentiful and inexpensive. Farm labor, their chief source of income once in Texas, paid little, and it was common for first-generation renters to work ten or twelve years before buying their own land. Information about these conditions was generally available, either directly from correspondence with friends or relatives who had previously immigrated, or indirectly from friends and neighbors who were in communication with previous immigrants. The *Missouri* group provides a typical example of "chain" migration: Jan and Mariana Janča, Karel and Josefa Láník, and perhaps other members of the group were in correspondence with relations in Texas. No doubt favorable reports in letters from Texas played a large part in convincing them to make their fateful decision, just as Bergman's letters had enticed the earliest groups two decades before.

According to the Bujnoch-Láník oral history,

> While still in [the Czech lands] the Karel Láník and Bujnoch families corresponded with the Chalupka and Janča families here in the States. As a result of the information from their friends here in the States, Karel and Josefa Láník and family decided to come to the New World. Great-grandmother Bujnoch and her family decided to come along to seek a different life than they had there in [the Czech lands].

Of course, the usual tendency in immigrant letters sent back to the homeland, beginning with the optimistic accounts of Bergman and Lešikar, was to emphasize (if not to exaggerate) the positive aspects of conditions in Texas, and potential emigrants, eager for a new and better life, no doubt were often all too ready to interpret these accounts in the most optimistic light.[5]

Added to the dominant economic motivations for emigrating were political and ideological ones. František Šimek, in spite of his military career, was typical of many Czechs in his wish that his sons not serve in the Austrian army.

Austria enforced a three-year compulsory military service for males, with few exceptions, but many Czechs considered themselves to be part of an oppressed national group and felt little loyalty toward the Austrian Empire or its emperor. A statement made by Valentin Haidušek gained the status of a proverb among the Texas Czechs: "I would rather live in this cabin as a free citizen than to live in a palace and be subject to the ruler of Austria.[6] And there were other sources of resentment towards the state and the nobility. Feudal institutions persisted in the Austrian lands longer than they did in the rest of Europe. Traditionally the most despised obligation owed by the Czech peasant to his lord, the noble landowner, was *robota,* a kind of forced labor. The peasant was required to work without pay for the lord a specified number of days a year. Although *robota* was officially abolished, along with serfdom, in 1848, it persisted in the popular memory. Josefa Láník, for example, told stories about the detested *robota* and other abuses to her grandchildren, stories which she must have heard from her own parents and grandparents.[7] According to her, at crucial times of the year, the peasants would have to work one day in the fields of the lord for each day spent in their own fields.

Even after the reforms of 1848, life remained difficult for the former peasants, the small landowners, and day laborers.[8] Apparently the members of the *Missouri* group, like most of the Moravian emigrants, belonged to these classes. The widow Johana Bujnoch later told her great-grandchildren about her struggle to make a living after her husband had died:

> Great-grandmother Bujnoch would walk about five miles to a salt mine for a block of salt (about five pounds) and carry it on her back to her home. She would grate and box it to sell on the streets at a price to include a profit of what would be a penny here in the States.[9]

After disposing of their property and personal possessions, some of the emigrants, such as the Šimeks, were able to pay for their own passage to America, while others, such as the Jančas, received financial aid from American relatives or agreed to be sponsored by prospective employers in Texas.

The Austrian Constitution of 1867 guaranteed the principle of free emigration, provided there was no conflict with military obligations or other complications. The state-subsidized railroads and the Ministry of Trade regarded emigration as a profitable business, and the government tended to view emigration as one means of relieving revolutionary pressures created by harsh economic and social conditions. Nevertheless, aside from the expense, the emigration process involved time-consuming technicalities.

The first step for the potential emigrant was to obtain a letter of character from a local official, granting permission to leave a particular area. Then a *křestní list,* or baptismal certificate, had to be obtained from the parish priest. This document contained the individual's birth date and birthplace and the names of his parents. The baptismal certificate, together with the letter of character, enabled the individual to apply for a *průvodní list* (permission to emigrate). This document was required in order to pass provincial checkpoints, border posts, and seaports. In addition men of conscription age had to have a certificate of military discharge.

The fourth step was to obtain a passport, which would allow passage first into Germany and then into the United States. If a family was traveling as a group, a family passport would be issued to the head of the family to cover all the members. This document contained the requested checkpoint route as well the names and ages of the individuals covered.

Records show that the Bujnoch, Olšovský, and Šimek families received their *průvodní list* documents, permitting emigration to America, on August 1, 1873. Similar documents indicate a date of August 8 for the Láník family and August 20 for the Moris family. Johana Bujnoch's status as a widow caused additional complications in obtaining permission for her minor-age children to emigrate. She was forced to appoint her brother-in-law Josef Bujnoch as their legal guardian, and he in turn gave his approval. In her letter of request, sent to "The Honorable Office of Government" in Místek, Moravia, she referred to Texas as a place "where I hope to find a livelihood."[10]

Finally the Bujnoch family, along with the other seven families, received its passport and traveling documents for the voyage. Like many others before them, members of this group must have felt complex and conflicting emotions: excitement, dread, hope, and regret. All worldly possessions that could not be packed into a single family trunk were sold or given away. Farewells were said to friends and loved ones who probably would never be seen again. Like the majority of Moravian emigrants, the members of this group were Catholic. In the last days before their journey it was common for Moravian Catholics to go to confession and attend a mass that included special prayers to bless their journey and their life in their new land. They visited family graves one last time. Final visits to the homes of friends preceded the customary village dance and celebration that would be held in their honor on the eve of the departure day. This party probably lasted until the wee hours of the morning, and no doubt some of the adult emigrants never slept during this momentous night.

The day of departure was well planned. Each group loaded its trunk on a cart pulled by oxen and traveled to the railhead at Místek. Unlike some emigrants who had to travel several days to reach a railhead, this group was fortunate: the station was only a few miles away. Nevertheless the distance must have seemed immense, as the steeple of the village church, that traditional symbol of security and home, faded into the distance. Upon their arrival at the station, the trunk was unloaded and checked with the station agent. The long wait for the train began.

Eventually a slight grayish column of smoke appeared in the distance, and the distinct sound of a steam locomotive was heard approaching. As the engine rolled by the platform, a hollow rattle dominoed back through the cars and sparks shot out from beneath the locomotive's wheels as the train jerked to a halt. This was a special train, one that would snake through the Austrian and German lands, picking up prerecruited emigrants destined for the steamship *Strassburg* at the north German port of Bremen. It was under the direction of an emigrant agent, who not only assisted the emigrants in their travel but who saw that all regulations were fulfilled. The cars resembled American cattle cars, similar to the ones that carried the Jews to the death camps in World War II, but of a more antique construction. Air brakes had been available for only a few years, and it is unlikely that a train in this service had such a luxury. The cars had practically no furnishings, only a few benches aligned along the walls, a water cask, and chamber pot.

After the agent checked and approved the papers of the eight families, the trunks were loaded into the cars, followed by the emigrants, with the provisions and baggage they had brought for the journey. The interiors were already crowded with emigrants picked up at previous stations. The water cask in each car was filled, and the chamber pot from a makeshift water closet in one corner was emptied before the door was slammed shut and locked from the outside.

The hollow rattle of the cars preceded the sudden jolt as the journey from Místek began. The train carried the emigrants northward through valleys, over mountains and past villages, and into the Moravian city of Olomouc, then turned northwest and then west toward the great city of Prague, which many of the passengers saw then for the first time. The continuous wind that whipped through the cars caused the trapped passengers to huddle in groups, hunkering down in their *peřiny*, traditional feather blankets. Many more emigrants were picked up along the way: some in Austria and many in Germany. Prague and Berlin were control points for these emigrant trains traveling from the Austrian Empire into the German Empire. At the control points the manifests held by the emigrant agent were checked against the passengers in each car and their corresponding documents before the train was allowed to proceed. Overcrowding was a common problem in the mass transportation of emigrants. The desire for greater profit margins by the transporters often superseded standards of common decency.

After several days of travel the emigrants arrived at Bremen, the German port used by North German Lloyd Lines. North German Lloyd was the main steamship line that carried Moravian immigrants to Texas, both indirectly and directly. At Bremen the immigrants were instructed by the agent about the procedures required before embarkation. They were to go through another customs inspection, a very thorough one. Vaccinations and medical checks were required, and the overall inspection was supervised by the American consul, who was concerned as much with the health of the travelers as with the legality of their documents.

In most instances health and travel documents had to be certified at least two days before departure. This procedure allowed time for all paperwork for the voyage to be completed and for the trunks and baggage of the travelers to be fumigated and loaded. The immigrants spent the days before departure at licensed boardinghouses and usually ate meager meals of soup or potatoes in order to conserve their money. Sometimes Moravian immigrants traveling to Texas under the direction of an Emigration Company or Immigration Society had lines of credit set up by an American sponsor for these incidentals.

The departure date was September 10, 1873. When the company officials were ready to load the immigrants aboard their ship, they transported them by rail to Bremerhaven, Bremen's outer seaport. The *Strassburg* was the first ship of the season to make the run from Bremen to New Orleans, with immigrants who were mostly destined for Texas. Shortly after the ship's embarkation from Bremen, a reporter for the New Orleans *Picayune* described the immigrants scheduled to land in his city:

> Departure of the Steamer *Strassburg* from Bremen with 710 German Emigrants Aboard—The Larger Portion of These Destined for Texas—How Many Are Expected for Louisiana—The Employment of Families.[11]

> We learn from the German Immigration Society that there is a brighter prospect ahead for the influx of stalwart laborers to our fields and plantations. The Secretary of this society, Mr. Karl Becker, yesterday informed a representative of the PICAYUNE that the steamer Strassburg had left Bremen on the 10th September [1873], with 710 German emigrants on board.

Of this number, Texas was to get 461, for whom passage had already been paid from Bremen to Galveston by the immigration societies of that State. The remainder, with the exception of five, were expected to be kept in our own State, and orders have already been sent in by planters engaging sixty of these.

Here are 250 laborers from Germany that are expected in on the Strassburg today. . . . the first large body of German emigrants that have left Germany for Louisiana for some time; but the agent states to us that, from information received direct from Bremen, he expects a large influx of such men in our State this winter, as three steamers per month will be plying between Bremen and this city, and many express the intention of coming here.

As to the manner of paying and refunding passage, steamship accommodations, work wages and satisfaction, the German society gives us the following information:

Many of the emigrants from Germany prepay their own passage. . . . Others get their passage bonded for them by responsible parties on either side, and refund these out of their work; some have their passage paid by the merchant of the employing planter and refund it out of their wages; others are brought over at the expense of various societies on both sides of the ocean.

The captains of the Bremen steamships have been liberal and accommodating in this matter of bringing over emigrants. The passage of these, for grown persons, is $40 (gold) and they are well fed and provided for on the trip.

After describing the practices of the Louisiana immigration societies, the reporter referred to "the more organized immigration societies of Texas, and the more successful results of their labors in bringing a large tide of immigration into that State."[12]

The *Strassburg* departed Bremen as scheduled; however, the thirty-six Moravians were not on board as planned. The reason seems to be legal complications regarding the status of Jiří Bujnoch. Germany had an agreement with Austria to detain all potential male emigrants of conscription age who did not hold a certificate of discharge or other form of release from their military obligation. Apparently Bujnoch possessed a valid passport and permission to emigrate. Also there is evidence that Bujnoch had indeed received an early release from his military obligation that, although legal, was not properly documented. In desperation Bujnoch sent a series of telegrams from

Bremen to military authorities in Místek, requesting an official statement that would allow him to be cleared for emigration. Bujnoch had to receive this statement by September 8 in order to qualify for the September 10 departure on the *Strassburg*.

Unfortunately he did not receive it in time, and the other members of the group would not leave without him. The Moravians, now stranded in Bremen, had two options: they could wait for about two weeks, by which time Bujnoch's documents would be in order, and leave on the *Hannover*, the next scheduled steamer to New Orleans; or they could choose an "alternate route" to Texas and leave immediately. This surreptitious or covert arrangement, designed to bypass the legal technicalities dogging Bujnoch, involved a voyage to New Orleans via Liverpool on the Mississippi and Dominion Line. With the help of an emigration agent, who had a pecuniary interest in the arrangement, the group was smuggled out of Bremen and on to Liverpool, probably on the ship *Gellert,* which arrived at Liverpool on September 10, 1873. From Liverpool they were to travel to New Orleans on board the steamship *Missouri*.

CHAPTER 7

The Ship

During the years 1855–56 two sister ships were built by the firm Caird and Company of Greenoch, Scotland, for the Hamburg America Line: the *Borussia* (Russia) and the *Hammonia* (Hamburg).[1] For the Hamburg American Line the two new ships represented the first serious attempt to convert from sail to steam in the increasingly competitive transatlantic shipping from Antwerp and Bremen. Each of the new steamers was constructed of iron and weighed about 2,025 tons, with one double-bladed screw and three masts.

The *Hammonia* was completed first. It was 280 feet in length, 38 feet in width, and 28 feet in depth. It had a draught of 16 feet in ballast and 21 feet fully loaded. Her power was supplied by geared oscillating engines, and she was rated at 10 knots. The *Borussia,* a little larger than its sister ship and powered by two 67–inch cylinders with a stroke of 6 feet, was sent to England shortly after the Crimean War to be used as a troop carrier.[2] In June, 1856, under Captain Schwensen, it commenced the Hamburg to New York service.[3]

The *Hammonia* was first sent to France as a troop carrier. Then in the summer of 1856, shortly after her sister ship had made her maiden transatlantic voyage, she traveled to New York for the first time, with merchandise and 394 passengers, under the command of Captain Hydtmann. Hydtmann, the commodore of the Hamburg America fleet, had vast experience in the company's sailing ships and had trained on steamers in the Mediterranean while the new ships were being built.

In 1858 the *Hammonia* made the crossing from Southhampton, England, to New York in thirteen days, one hour, and the return voyage in twelve days, six hours, twenty minutes. This extraordinarily rapid time was widely publicized.[4] Unfortunately the *Hammonia*'s favorable reputation was short-lived. Later in the same year, the ship had left Hamburg and was approaching the mouth of the Elbe River when the powder magazine in the rear of the chief cabin in the afterpart of the ship exploded. Although only one serious human injury was reported, damage to the ship was extensive.[5]

Photograph of a painting of the S.S. Hammonia, *commissioned in 1854 by the Hamburg-American Line with Caird and Company of Greenoch, Scotland. The* Hammonia *was sold to the Allan Line in 1864 and was subsequently renamed the* Belgian. *Later, in 1872, she was sold to the Mississippi and Dominion Steamship Company and renamed the* Missouri. *She was wrecked and a total loss after she ran aground on October 1, 1873, at Gingerbread Ground, Great Bahama Bank.* Photograph courtesy of the Peabody Essex Museum of Salem, Massachusetts

The *Hammonia* never fully recovered from this crippling injury. Her usefulness deteriorated through the years until she was no longer profitable for the Hamburg America Line to operate. In 1864 the vessel was sold to the Allan Line and renamed the *Belgian*.[6] Five years later the *Belgian* was reengineered by Laird Brothers with a 160-horsepower engine.[7] This change represented a great reduction in power as compared to her original engine and—given the increased competition in the shipping business at this time—it indicates that the vessel's tonnage rating had been lowered to such an extent that it was no longer profitable to operate a large engine that required huge amounts of coal for fuel and many men to service. In fact records show that by December, 1872, the *Belgian*'s rating had been lowered to 1,209 tons.

By this time the combined influences of the 1858 explosion and the stresses exerted by years of wear from heavy loads and rough seas had severely affected the structural integrity of the *Belgian*. Although the vessel was classified as an iron steamer, only the hull was actually constructed of iron. All of the beams and supporting structures were of wood construction and in a rotted condition.

The *Belgian* was sold to the Mississippi and Dominion Steamship Company in the late summer of 1872 and then, under the command of Capt. Henry Mathias, made two voyages from Liverpool to New Orleans and back. In February, 1873, the vessel, now renamed the *Missouri,* made a third voyage from Liverpool to New Orleans, but this time arrived under ominous circumstances. Before the court of Capt. Gaster in New Orleans's second precinct, Mathias charged six members of his crew with "treason on the high seas." The six sailors were arrested and brought before U.S. Commissioner Weller. Evidence indicates that the mutinous men were motivated by a fear that the *Missouri* was unseaworthy.[8]

Nevertheless the *Missouri* headed back to Liverpool on March 16, 1873, with a cargo of 3,292 bales of cotton, 1,077 sacks of oil cake, 6,000 staves, and 164 bales of hides.[9] After reaching Liverpool, the vessel was laid up for several months. About £15,000 was spent on repairs, apparently in an attempt to correct structural problems.[10] In the process the vessel's tonnage rating was increased to 1,818, still far below her original rating.

For unknown reasons Captain Mathias was dropped from the list of captains serving the line's Liverpool to New Orleans route. After several postings and replacements, Capt. Charles Edward Pearson, who had commanded the fleet's steamships *Mississippi* and *Vicksburg,* was chosen as the man who would command the *Missouri* in what was to be her last voyage in September, 1873.

One other curious fact about the *Missouri* should be noted. According to the London *Times,* at the time of her final voyage she was insured by Lloyds of London for half a million dollars.[11] This seems to be an extraordinarily large sum, especially when one considers the following statement on shipping disasters for the month of October 1873: "The number of vessels belonging to, or bound to or from ports in the United States, reported totally lost and missing during the last month is 50. . . . Their total value, exclusive of cargoes, is estimated at $718,000."[12]

CHAPTER 8

The Last Voyage of the Missouri

September 11–October 1, 1873

The *Missouri* was scheduled to steam from Liverpool to New Orleans under the command of Captain Pearson on September 10, 1873, but she did not leave until the following day. The Moravians were among 125 steerage passengers. There were also 3 cabin passengers and a crew of about 50.[1] The cargo included metal bands and bagging for cotton bales. The scheduled route was via Bordeaux, France; La Coruña, Spain; and Havana, Cuba. Havana was a regular stop for all immigrant vessels traveling to New Orleans and Galveston. The American consul at Havana inspected the ships and immigrants and wired his report by submarine cable to the appropriate port of destination.

England enforced the Passenger Act, which set certain requirements for the handling of steerage passengers by the steamship companies. The steerage passengers were required to supply their own bedding, which was supposed to be discarded before entering their destination port. Crudely made bunks were provided and regulations set a distance of 18 inches from the floor for the lowest bunk. People were to sleep side by side in these bunks. Although married men and women, single men, and single women were supposed to have separate quarters, this was seldom the case. The passengers were required to bring their own plates and eating utensils. The ship would provide food, but it was always recommended that the passengers bring extra supplies.[2]

There is no precise record of the accommodations and conditions for the steerage passengers of the *Missouri* on her last voyage; however, the following description of transatlantic conditions a few years later by a passenger on another steamer of the Mississippi and Dominion Steamship Company, the *Teutonia,* is suggestive:

Comfortable berths and good food were promised by the company and stipulated for in the contracts. The real facts are, that our berths were wet all the time, and not fit for animals to sleep in. The ship was kept in a frightfully dirty condition, the decks being swabbed only twice during the journey. The sanitary condition of the ship was abominable. Sham water closets were put up before leaving Liverpool, and taken down one day after leaving port. The chief complaints were, however, about the food. The beef served for the greater part of the voyage was absolutely rotten, the smell alone being sufficient to drive most of us on deck. The greater part of the passengers did not taste it during the voyage. Complaints were made to the stewards and captain. . . . The only eatable meals we received were while coming up the Mississippi, which were obtained from the captain by threats of legal proceedings.

There was no such thing as discipline on the ship, fights and drunken rows being quite common. Even the officers on the ship were aggressors in some cases. Steerage passengers could not get wines, liquor, or beer, even in sickness.[3]

We know of one passenger that never tasted food from Havana till entering the Mississippi. On offering to buy something to eat from the steward, he was refused.[4]

According to Janča family tradition,

many of the immigrants slept on deck as the ship was terribly overloaded and the heat was unbearable between decks . . . the ship had a powerful odor and they said it carried cattle [cow hides] before and was not sufficiently cleaned prior to the voyage. The route carried them close to the equator. During the voyage the ship took on a great deal of water due to leaks in the hull and the ship having only one operable bilge pump—the others were broken. The crew members were the only ones allowed to go down below to operate the pump and the crew had to guard the pump from the passengers. The Captain was afraid that the passengers would storm below and overwork the pump causing it to break. The Captain ordered only one sail to be raised, although the ship had three masts, as the crew reported that the timbers below were crumbling in their hands and he knew too much sail would create more stress on the badly leaking ship. This caused their travel time to be greatly extended and although they had plenty of normal staples of sauerkraut and biscuits,

their water supply ran very low, causing them to head for [Nassau].
. . . Before reaching the port a heavy rain fell upon the ship and after
spreading the sheets [sails] to capture the falling drops they were able
to fill all their barrels and did not enter the port. Instead they headed
[through the North Providence Channel] for Havana, Cuba.[5]

CHAPTER 9

From Shipwreck to Storm

When the *Missouri* passed Stirrup Cay and entered the Northwest Providence Channel at about one o'clock on the afternoon of October 1, the sea was calm and the sun was shining.[1] As the ship proceeded west, there was no sign of impending danger; on the contrary, the prevailing attitude on board was surprisingly casual. No depth measurements had been taken since the ship had left Liverpool, and experienced seamen among the passengers had remarked on the apparent carelessness of the officers. The tide was at its peak at about 2:18 P.M. and would not reach its low point for another six hours. Even as the ship approached the Gingerbread Ground, Great Bahama Bank, at about 4:00, some of the passengers were dancing on deck to the music provided by a small band.

Not a uniformed officer was to be seen on deck when, at about 4:15 P.M., the *Missouri* ran aground on a reef that made up part of the Gingerbread Ground.[2] The site was about 40 miles east-northeast of the Biminis and about 160 miles north of Nassau.

The passengers, who had no cause to expect an emergency, rushed about in confusion as Captain Pearson and his officers appeared on deck. Pearson attempted a series of maneuvers to free the ship, the fore section of which was raised above the water, hung up on the reef. Some of the ship's cargo and the passengers' baggage were thrown overboard in order to lighten the vessel, but efforts to dislodge the ship from the reef were unsuccessful.[3] Some of the Moravian immigrants lost nearly all of their belongings in this way, while others were able to save most of their possessions. Josefa Láník saved the family Bible by placing it in her bosom.

The sun set just before 6:00 P.M., leaving a gibbous moon to shine down on the unfolding drama. As low tide (8:35 P.M.) approached, it became apparent that Pearson's efforts to free the ship from the reef were in vain. He had begun to drink heavily after the accident, and his actions became increasingly irrational. Instead of taking measures to guarantee the safety of the passengers, Pearson abused them verbally, wishing them drowned.[4] Messrs. Chandley and

John Thorne, the first and second officers, finally decided to take charge, literally holding a gun to the head of the nearly incapacitated captain. They gave orders to send up signal rockets and attend to the lifeboats.

Rocket flares—intended to attract passing ships—shot up into the night sky.[5] The Mississippi and Dominion Line used rockets of red, white, and blue, which in normal night communication between passing ships would have been fired sequentially at intervals of one minute. The international distress signal consisted of three rockets of any color shot skyward at close intervals.

Under the command of Chandley and Thorne, passengers and crewmen worked together to lower the lifeboats, but that was no easy task. The davits seemed to be rusted in their sockets, and it appeared that the boats had not been removed in years. One of the six boats was swamped as it touched the water, but between the hours of 9:00 P.M. and midnight five boats were successfully lowered into the sea, some with passengers aboard.

About midnight, as the final lifeboat was being boarded, the stern of the ship began to settle rapidly into deep water and a breach opened up amidship, forward of the engine room. The main mast went over the side, carrying the mizzenmast with it. Now that all hope of saving the ship was lost, the crew released the steam from the boilers in order to prevent an explosion. As the ship continued to break in two, a large plume of steam rose skyward with a deafening blast.

At about the same time, orders were given to abandon ship, but the passengers remaining on board were terrified, and the scene was chaotic. Adding to their confusion was the mistaken notion—as the steam was blown off from the boilers—that the ship was burning. In the excitement of the moment some of the passengers, including Josefa Láník and her son Frank, jumped into the water. Mrs. Láník was saved by a black man who pulled her into one of the boats. Frank also was saved when one of the officers grabbed his hair and pulled him to safety.[6] It seems that Ferdinand Šimek, too, was pulled out of the water by his hair.[7]

Soon most of the passengers were distributed among the five boats. The weight in each boat was such that their gunnels were nearly level with the water, and the passengers were forced to bail water almost constantly. Each boat was provided with a sail and jib and stocked with a bag of bread and a container of water.

At about 1:00 A.M. the schooner *Jaspar,* under Capt. Joseph Saunders, arrived at the scene. Saunders, who had answered the *Missouri*'s distress signals, would assist in securing the stranded vessel for salvage and act as wreck master. By 3:00 A.M. the five lifeboats began to sail from the site of the wreck, but shortly thereafter one of the boats had to return to the *Missouri* to retrieve five crew members and three passengers who had inadvertently been left behind.

It was nearly 4:00 A.M. when the five boats, accompanied by the *Jaspar,* finally departed for the Biminis. They were joined en route by the schooners *Two Brothers* and *Admired.* The group of five lifeboats and three schooners arrived safely at Alice Town, North Bimini, at about 6:00 P.M., October 2.

The *Missouri* passengers and crew members were apparently treated very well. According to one passenger:

> The inhabitants of Bimini treated us with the utmost hospitality, killing pigs, chickens and every domestic animal they possessed to afford us something to eat, and affording us every accommodation at their disposal.[8]

On the next day, October 3, Captain Pearson, some of his officers, and about forty crew members boarded the *Admired* under Capt. James Sebastian Hanna and set out to the port of Nassau. Meanwhile Second Mate John Thorne returned to the wreck site aboard the *Two Brothers.*

As the rescued passengers were recovering from their ordeal, the salvage ships, operating out of Nassau, continued their work with the *Missouri.* Salvaging operations in the area were highly organized and commercially lucrative, although dangerous as well. The Bahamas area, or Baja Mar (low or shallow sea) as Christopher Columbus had named it, presented many navigational problems and was the site of frequent wrecks. Ancient sea law dictated that the captain of the first salvage vessel arriving at the scene of a wreck was designated the master, who would supervise the salvage operation. In this case Captain Saunders of the *Jaspar* was paid a fee of 15 pounds for serving in this capacity. In addition the owners, captains, and crews of the *Jaspar, Matchless,* and *Vanquish* shared a payment of 175 pounds per ship for aiding in the rescue of the *Missouri*'s passengers and crew, while the *Frolic* received 85 pounds for the same service. As usual many additional vessels would take part in the salvage of the *Missouri* in the coming days and weeks. After adjustments and the payment of special fees, the maritime courts of the time allowed for a division of the proceeds from the auctioned cargo among the owner and captain of each salvage vessel and its officers and crew members.[9] However, several vessels attempting to take part in the salvage of the *Missouri* during the week following the wreck were themselves destined to be wrecked by a powerful hurricane. The emigrants, temporarily housed on North Bimini, would have to contend with the storm as well.

The little group of Moravians, like the other stranded passengers from the *Missouri,* must have had mixed feelings about their adventures thus far. How unfortunate it had been to end up on the *Missouri,* a marginally safe ship under a seemingly inept command, run aground in broad daylight and calm seas, apparently through sheer negligence. On the other hand, it had not been a particularly tragic shipwreck: there had been no human casualties (one reason that insurance claims were not delayed by complicated investigations). An island in the Bahamas would seem to be a good place to recuperate from such an experience before resuming the voyage to the United States. Unfortunately the emigrants, like everyone else on the island, were almost immediately faced with a new crisis.

Early in the morning on October 6, the *Admired* reached Nassau, where Pearson would send telegrams reporting the wreck of the *Missouri* to company headquarters in Liverpool and meet with representatives of Messrs. T. Williams and Co., agents for the *Missouri*'s insurer, Lloyd's of London.[10] At about this time, squall winds began to hit the Biminis. By noon squalls were also blasting the wreck site, and they grew progressively stronger during the course of the afternoon.

Evidence suggests that in the first week of October, 1873, two hurricanes traveled from the Gulf of Mexico, across Florida, and into the Atlantic Ocean. The first one hit St. Thomas, West Indies, on the morning of September 28, destroying all the ships in the harbor. It caused heavy damage in Jamaica and Cuba before enlarging and sweeping over the Yucatan Peninsula.[11] Then it veered eastward, hitting the Florida Panhandle and causing record tides before it moved into the Atlantic and up to Charleston, South Carolina, where it caused one death and extensive property damage on the afternoon of October 6.[12]

While the first storm was wreaking havoc on northern Florida, a low pressure cell was forming west of Cuba near the Yucatan Peninsula. It is occasionally difficult to separate reports of this second storm from those of the first because they occurred so closely together in the same general area, but apparently the following reports refer to this second storm:

Havana: Oct. 6—A severe rain storm has been prevailing here for the last three days, and danger signals were hoisted at the United States Signal Office this morning. All steamers in the harbor are getting up steam in expectation of a hurricane. The wind is heavy . . . the water is rising and several streets are already flooded.[13]

The storm moved in a northeasterly direction and crossed between Key West and Punta Rossa, Florida, on the evening of October 6.

Havana: Oct. 7— . . . In the streets near the shores many houses were flooded, the sea breaking in the doors and washing the furniture away. Several persons were drowned. Most of the telegraph lines on the Island are down, and communication is much interrupted.[14]

Key West: It becomes our duty to record that on Monday last (October 6, 1873) we experienced one of those storms, which we citizens of these latitudes have yearly to prepare for and guard against.

The weather for several days previous had been boisterous and squally. Many of our vessels were already moored in Man-o-war harbour, waiting, as it were, for the worst.

A most destructive hurricane passed over our island . . . leaving desolation in its track. The approach of the terror was heralded eighteen hours in advance by decline and oscillation of the barometer, and the peculiarly portentous appearance of the clouds, and fresh easterly wind. At 6 o'clock A.M. of the 6th the wind had increased to a gale (forty miles per hour), and the barometer had fallen to 29.63.

At 9 A.M. it became evident that the hurricane was upon us. Barometer had fallen in 3 hours from 29.68 to 29.59. The first approach of high winds was from E. to S.E., veering from 2 to 3 points every 15 minutes. At 10 the tide was at its height—barometer still falling—the wind increases with violence and waves running very high. The old government wharf [gave] way with its timbers dashing along the beach. At 12 noon—the barometer at 29.40—wind hauling more to the southward, blowing with great violence.

At 4 P.M. the wind increased to sixty miles per hour; the barometer had fallen to 29.32. The barometer continued to fall until it reached 29.28 at 5 P.M., after which the mercury commenced going up slowly, the wind shifted to south-west, increasing to a hurricane at 7:30 P.M., when it reached its maximum velocity—eighty miles per hour—with barometer at 29.37. At 8 P.M. the instruments were carried away from the United States Signal Office.

The sea came surging in on the land with tremendous violence. Most of the inhabitants of the lower part of the city moved for the higher part of the island, many ladies wading through the water over 2 feet deep. The tide at 8:30 P.M. rose four feet above the rise of the highest spring tides, filling the streets in the business part of the city with boats, debris, &c., and perhaps the wind never blew with greater violence.

At 9 P.M. the wind commenced falling, and at midnight the wind was west-north-west, about 12 miles per hour, and the sky almost cloudless.

During the storm almost the entire island was flooded, the water from the Gulf rushed through the streets from two to four feet in depth, and salt spray filled the air killing vegetation and shrubbery as completely as a severe frost. The destruction to shipping in the harbor was great. Several buildings were blown down on the island, wharfs carried away, &c . . . Only one life lost. The storm center was some distance to the north and west of Key West. It did not extend as far south as Havana. At Punta Rossa, 100 miles north, it was more severe—the barometer falling to 29.00, and the signal station and telegraph office were almost entirely swept away. At Tortugas, sixty-five miles west, the wind blew terrific for twelve hours. Col. Langdon, in command at Fort Jefferson, states that a solid bar of iron weighing 1,800 pounds was carried 200 yards over the parapet of the fort. The mail steamer George W. Clyde, of the New York and Galveston Line, after having labored against severe gales and heavy seas for six days after leaving Galveston, was struck by the cyclone of the 6th about fifty miles to the westward of Tortugas. The staunch vessel withstood the beating of the storm until 6:40 P.M., when the pilothouse was swept away . . . She came out of the storm at 8 o'clock.[15]

The hurricane entered the Atlantic sometime after midnight on October 7, 1873. Its approach was noted at Bimini as early as daybreak on October 6 and at the wreck of the *Missouri* by midday. The weather gradually grew more boisterous on this day, causing the wreckers at the *Missouri* to seek shelter from the approaching storm. The schooner *Julia Howard* and sloop *Lady of the Lake* headed east to the lee of the Berry Islands, where they found safety. Other vessels headed west to the harbor at Bimini and the surrounding islands.[16]

The master of the sloop *Chili* . . . reports that his vessel experienced the gale of the 6th instant, while at anchor on the north side of Great Isaacs. The master and crew left their vessel at 4 o'clock in the afternoon, and she went to pieces in about six hours. The schooner *Fern* was also wrecked at the same time and place, but no lives were lost.[17]

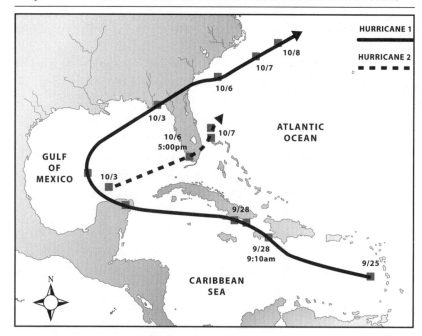

Map 2. The Hurricanes (1873). Map by Shawn McMillan

As the storm approached the Biminis, shelter was provided for the stranded travelers. Ferdinand Šimek, a child at the time, later told his son what he remembered about these preparations. The women and children were taken to a large log structure on a high point of the island. He recalled being carried on the back of a black woman. The men sought shelter in a second log structure that was nearer to the beach. During the storm, water rose up to waist level in the men's structure.[18]

One can only imagine the terror experienced by the Moravians during the height of the storm, which probably can be termed a relatively strong hurricane. As residents of landlocked Central Europe, most of them had never travelled far from their native villages, and most of them had never even seen the sea before they came to Bremen. In the log buildings, as the people trembled in the darkness of what must have seemed like a tropical hell, no doubt the words of the Lord's Prayer were often heard: *Otče naš, Jenž jsi na nebesích. . . .* At this point many among the group must have questioned their decision to leave their old and poor but relatively safe little corner of the world. Their journey must have seemed cursed, with one crisis following another.

Nevertheless, by morning the storm had spent its fury. The Moravians, like the other passengers, had much to be thankful for, because once again there had been no human casualties. Some of the families had lost nearly all of their

belongings in the shipwreck, while others had not. Jan Janča still had possession of his carpenter's tools, and several of the women had preserved their
feather blankets. In the wake of destruction left by the hurricane, food supplies
in general were low, but the approximately three hundred inhabitants of the
island shared their abundant stores of coconuts and bananas. Like other people
of the Bahamas, the people of Bimini boil coconut meat in water to make a
nutritious beverage, and this was probably consumed by the travelers.

While the erstwhile passengers of the *Missouri* were riding out the hurricane on Bimini, the storm was playing havoc with the salvage of the wrecked
ship itself, as the following reports from Nassau indicate:

Nassau: The schooner *Julia Howard* and sloop *Lady of the Lake*
arrived this morning [October 8, 1873] from the wreck. They experienced very heavy weather, having rode out a gale under the lee of
Berry Islands. They are partly laden with cargo saved from the ship
(*Missouri*), which the divers obtained with much difficulty owing to
her rolling motion. Two of the divers (Peter Russell and Richard
Clare), nearly lost their lives, the lines around their wrists having
while under water become entangled with the broken beams of the
ship. They were saved, however, by Sutherland Butler, who, not getting a signal from them for some time, dived into the vessel, cleared
the rope, and brought them up in an apparently lifeless state, and it
was with difficulty they were restored to animation.

An official investigation respecting the loss of the *Missouri* will be
held at the Police Office to-morrow [October 9].

The following vessels have left for the scene of the disaster: Schooners—*Bob, Ocean Monarch, Telegraph, Colonel Whitfield, Eliza
Catherine, Eagle, Mary, Scud, Julia, Twilight, Amazon, Handsome, Tip
Top, Confidence, George H. Eneas*, and *Dart*; Sloops—*Goodwill, Sylvia,*
and *Hennie*.[19]

Nassau: The schooner *Belle* (32 tons), of this port, which left on
Sunday last [October 5], for Key West, Florida, with a cargo of salt,
fruit, &c., experienced the gale and became a total wreck. Observing a
steamer (the *Missouri*) ashore on the Gingerbread Ground on Monday morning [October 6], the master brought his vessel up to the
scene, and the crew began to render assistance in saving the steamer's
cargo. After getting a boat load, the weather became so boisterous that
they were compelled to weigh anchor and seek shelter at the Biminis.

The wind blowing a hurricane at the time, and being unable to keep sails on the vessel, they found it necessary to run her ashore on the north point of the Biminis, near the east wells, in order to save the lives of the passengers and crew. Soon after they had left the schooner she bilged and drifted to sea, since which she has not been heard of.

The *Belle* was owned by Mr. J.W. Henry, of this island. Her master, with the passengers and crew, arrived here on Thursday [October 9] at noon. He reports that the wrecking schooner *Proof* had also been at the wreck of the *Missouri,* and had saved a load of general merchandise. In consequence of heavy weather on Monday [October 6], that vessel was also obliged to seek shelter, in company with the *Belle* and *Brothers,* at the Biminis, but was unable to enter the harbor. The *Proof* was therefore brought to anchor outside, off the east wells; but finding the weather becoming more boisterous, the master and crew (five men) were forced to leave in their boat for the shore, which they fortunately reached. The vessel soon after dragged her anchors and drifted to sea. On the approach of night she was lost sight of, and no intelligence has been received of her since.

News has just been received that the *Brothers* has unfortunately shared the fate of the *Belle* and *Proof.* She had the 2nd mate of the *Missouri* on board. We rejoice to add that all hands were saved.

The wrecking schooners *Vanderbilt, Achilles,* and *Wesleyan,* with the sloop *Quiver,* were at anchor near the wreck when the *Proof* left, and serious apprehensions are entertained as to their safety.

There has been more bustle in our streets within the last few days than for many months. The sale of the wrecked goods from the ill-fated steamship *Missouri* on Thursday last [October 9] realized, we believe, about one thousand pounds (£1,000), and from the spirited manner in which it was continued yesterday [October 10], we presume the result to have been similar. Cotton goods of various descriptions line the railings along Bay-street, and all its avenues team with wrecked property. Market-street, in particular, is all bustle and activity, and the run on one of the shops was so great that, after being filled with customers almost to repletion, so that its proprietor thought it advisable to close the doors, others effected an entrance through the windows. Fortunately the fine northerly wind which set in a few days ago has carried away, to a considerable extent, the effluvia arising from damp goods, therefore the health of the community has not been endangered. We regret to learn that several of the vessels which rendered assistance at the wreck have been lost in the late gale."[20]

On the evening of the day after the storm, October 8, the little British gunboat *Cherub,* under the command of Lieut. Commander Francis C. R. Baker, arrived at the island of North Bimini.[21] Early the next morning, the Moravians were among the 138 travelers who crowded aboard the vessel, which had come from Nassau for the purpose of transporting them to Key West. Several of the travelers later praised Baker and his executive officer Harry G. Hatch for their great courtesy and kindness. Captain Pearson of the *Missouri,* along with his first officer, was also aboard. After escorting the travelers to Key West, these men would have to return to Nassau and appear before a British commission that was investigating the loss of the vessel. Silas Weeks and Company of New Orleans served as agents for the steamship *Missouri.* On Saturday afternoon, October 11, 1873, their office received the following dispatch from Thomas A. Adams at Key West: "The steamship *Missouri* wrecked on October 1st on the Bahamas. The ship is broken in two. Crew and passengers here, all safe. They were landed at Bimini Island, and are now trying to get assistance to carry them to New Orleans."[22]

Another dispatch from the same messenger was received the following morning, Sunday, October 12, 1873: "Passengers leave here to-night in Steamer *Liberty.* The *Missouri* has entirely disappeared."[23]

The steamship *Liberty* (1,230 tons), with L. M. Hudgins commanding, had departed Baltimore on October 5, 1873.[24] It was scheduled to stop at Key West and Havana, then travel through the south pass up the Mississippi River to New Orleans. Its return trip was via the reverse route. As the *Baltimore Sun* reported, this voyage for the *Liberty* was of unusual interest:

> The steamship *Liberty,* of the Baltimore and Havana Steamship Company, Capt. L.M. Hudgins, commander, sailed from Baltimore at 8:00 A.M. yesterday for New Orleans, via Key West, for Havana. The steamship took out fifty-eight passengers, fifty-three of them being members of the Aimee French Opera Troupe, who came on from Philadelphia Saturday night, after their farewell performance in that city, reaching Baltimore before daylight Sunday morning, embarking immediately, and expecting to reach Havana in time to open the season in that city next Saturday evening according to engagement.[25]

Five of the 58 passengers were of a family named Baird and were traveling only as far as Key West. The steamer *Falcon* reported making contact with the *Liberty* on October 5, at Poplar Island, and the signal officer at Fort Monroe reported on October 6 that the *Liberty* put in for water at Norfolk due to a leak.[26]

> Nassau: [The *Cherub*] arrived [at Key West] at midday on the 11th [October 11, 1873], after a very fine passage. The steamer *Liberty*, of and from Baltimore, for New Orleans, via Havana, agreed to take the passengers to New Orleans for $20 a head, and left with them that evening. The *Cherub* sailed from Key West on the 13th, calling at the Biminis, and arrived here on Saturday night, 18th, experiencing strong head winds the whole voyage.
>
> Captain Pearson [and first officer Chandley], of the late steamship *Missouri*, who left in the *Cherub* to look after the passengers, returned in her.[27]

Although the *Liberty* normally carried only eight to twelve passengers, it now had 191 as it left Key West. In spite of the overcrowded conditions, the *Missouri* passengers were naturally pleased to be aboard and headed for Havana. According to one of them, "All the passengers speak in terms of the highest praise of the uniform kindness extended to them by the officers of the *Liberty*, especially Captain Hudgins and Purser N. Fitzpatrick. Also much praise is given to Mademoiselle Aimee and her troupe for the generosity in attending to the wants of the suffering passengers at Havana."[28]

But there was yet another emergency before they were safely delivered to Havana.[29] The ship entered Havana's harbor at night and at low tide, and the weather was squally. The captain misjudged the depth of the water at the entrance to the harbor, and the ship ran onto the bar. In light of their earlier experiences, it is not surprising that the passengers began to panic. Some ran from one end of the ship to the other, as it see-sawed back and forth. However, when the heavy rain abated and the lights of Havana became visible in the distance, the crew was able to calm the passengers, who then slept on deck until morning. Early the next day, small boats came out to the ship and took the people to shore.

Upon arrival at Havana the survivors of the *Missouri* had been through a shipwreck, a hurricane, and thirteen days of high adventure without a change of clothes. Their physical appearance must have fit the stereotype of the "filthy immigrant peasant," but they would long remember the humanitarianism of Mademoiselle Aimee and her group, who treated them kindly.

Even now, however, there were rumors of another kind of danger. According to the Bujnoch-Láník oral history, "After the passengers got to Havana—Grandma Láník talked about this when she lived with us—some of the German crew warned the immigrant men not to separate from their families to accept jobs for easy money . . . some immigrant men did [this in the past] and they were never heard from again—sold as slaves."[30] Nevertheless, after a short stop in Havana and apparently without further incidents, the immigrants continued their broken course to the United States. The *Liberty* arrived at her wharf at the foot of Calliope Street, First District, New Orleans, at 11:15 A.M., October 16, 1873, with 128 passengers and 10 crew members from the ill-fated *Missouri*.[31]

The *Liberty* was met by a large delegation as it reached the dock. As John Simpson and Mr. Paisly were interviewed by reporters of the New Orleans *Daily Picayune* and the New Orleans *Times,* the crew members of the *Missouri* were questioned by representatives of Silas Weeks and Company and the Crescent Mutual Insurance Company. The 36 Moravian immigrants were pleased to be greeted along with the Germans by Karl Becker, secretary of the German Immigration Society at New Orleans. His help in assisting them through U.S. Customs and in making arrangements for their transportation to Texas was greatly appreciated, although he did try to entice them to stay in Louisiana and be placed through his society. Herr Becker took charge of five of the German immigrants, including a woman who was very sick and needed immediate attention. He attended to their needs and conducted them to a respectable boardinghouse.

Flinn, Main, and Montgomery of Liverpool, the managing directors of the *Missouri,* received the official cable message confirming the loss of their vessel on Monday, October 13. On Friday of the same week, they declared the large dividend of 5 percent for the half of the fiscal year ending September 30, payable after October 23. This move, apparently made possible by claims on the unusually large insurance coverage that had been taken out on the *Missouri,* was especially conspicuous, considering the economic climate of the time. The eminent banking house of Jay Cooke and Company had failed in the previous month, igniting a chain reaction of business failures that was leading to an international financial crisis, and for the West the most severe depression of the century had begun.

Many wrecking vessels arrived at Nassau during the months of October and November, loaded with the recovered goods of the *Missouri* and the iron plating from her hull. When the wreckers were through with this lady of the seas, all that remained were her wooden ribs, perhaps the same wooden ribs that

Philip Janca discovered at the reported location of the wreck more than a century later.[32] Several auctions were held by Lloyds agents at Nassau, selling the cargo, iron plating, ship's materials, and rigging and even the five lifeboats that had carried the *Missouri* passengers to safety. As related earlier, Joseph Saunders was paid as wreck master, and several vessels were paid for their services in saving the lives of the passengers and crew. Other proceeds of the auctions were divided in Judge Taylor's decree: "That the expenses of wharfage, storage, and labour-hire be deducted from the appraised value of the dry cargo—such deduction has already been made from the gross proceeds of the sales of the property at auction. That from the net appraised value of the property thus ascertained, and from the net proceeds of the sale, the salvor's costs be further deducted; and then, as to the residue, that a salvage of 45 percent be paid on the goods and ship's materials."[33]

CHAPTER 10

End of the Journey

Galveston and Beyond

In October, 1873, the coastal areas of Texas and Louisiana were in the midst of a yellow fever epidemic. In spite of this, Galveston lifted its quarantine on October 1, and New Orleans followed on October 15. Although quarantines were not posted, most of the people arriving on ships and trains were afraid to remain long in these port cities.[1]

The newly arrived Moravian immigrants, having passed through New Orleans's customs, proceeded to the river ferry at the foot of St. Anne Street in Jackson Square. From this point they crossed the Mississippi River to Algiers on one of the ferries.[2] Charles Morgan's Louisiana and Texas Railroad depot was located on the south side of the river in Algiers. The immigrants continued by train westward to the end of the line at Brashear (also known as Morgan City), Louisiana.[3]

Charles Morgan had opened his rail-sea operation at Brashear on the Atchafalaya in 1872, after the channel had been dredged. By operating a hybrid (rail-sea) facility, Morgan took advantage of the commerce of New Orleans without incurring the expenses associated with pilots, towage, and wharfage.[4] Offering multiple services and subsidized by U.S. mail contracts, his was the only Gulf steamship line in 1873 with regularly scheduled steamers running from Brashear to Galveston. October, 1873, was, however, an off month for Morgan's business. During this period, only three steamers per week serviced the route.

Passage for the rail trip from Algiers to Brashear plus deck passage on the steamship from Brashear to Galveston cost four dollars per person.[5] On Saturday, October 18, the *Whitney* (built in 1871 and classified 1,338 tons), under the command of Captain Forbes, left Brashear with all the Moravian immigrants aboard. It was on this leg of the journey, according to Láník family tradition, that Josefa Láník's youngest son, Jiří, died of dysentery. Jiří, 18 months old, was the only member of the Moravian group who died en route

*View overlooking Charles Morgan's coastal steamship operation at
Central Wharf (21st Street) in Galveston, circa 1873.* Photograph courtesy of the
Rosenberg Library, Galveston, Texas

to Texas.[6] In later years Josefa Láník often spoke of how Jiří lay beside her, his cries gradually growing weaker. Succumbing to fatigue, Josefa drifted off to sleep, and when she awoke her little son was dead. She watched as he was wrapped in a sheet, tied, weighted, and lowered into the waters of the Gulf.[7]

The *Whitney* arrived at Central Wharf (21st Street) at the Port of Galveston on Sunday morning, October 19, bringing with her the mail, light freight, and the remaining 35 Moravian immigrants from the *Missouri*.[8]

The usual means of transportation from Galveston to the interior of the state for immigrants was by rail. The wagon bridge that later connected the island to Virginia Point was not built until 1893, and, although barge services were available, they were not commonly used in the transportation of immigrants from Galveston.

From Central Wharf the Moravians proceeded to one of the boarding-houses designed for the immigrant trade. There they spent the remainder of the day in preparation for departure on the morning train.

The rail depot was located at 24th Street near Water (Avenue A). From the depot the immigrants departed Galveston on Monday, October 20, taking the 6:15 A.M. train bound for Houston on the Galveston, Houston, and Henderson Railroad.[9] This line, built in 1857, was the only railroad that operated into Galveston at that period.[10]

At Harrisburg, a few miles south of present-day Houston, the immigrants made a connection with the Galveston, Harrisburg, and San Antonio Railroad (Sunset Road). Departure time for this train, which was bound for Columbus, was at 9:30 A.M.[11] The G.H.&S.A. line had tracks in place from Houston to Columbus by 1866, and it had tracks in place to Luling by the year 1874.[12] Although Columbus was the specified end of the line for the G.H.&S.A. in 1873, the railroad had at least seventeen miles of track beyond Columbus, extending to a point three or four miles beyond Jackson, a mile short of Weimar. This additional trackage had been completed by October 16, and the line would be opened all the way to Weimar on November 6, 1873.[13]

The trip by train was made in wooden passenger cars. Seating accommodations also were made of wood. If the temperature inside the cars became

GALVESTON, Texas.

The rail depot at Galveston located at 24th Street near Water (Avenue A).
Photograph courtesy of the Rosenberg Library, Galveston, Texas

uncomfortably warm, the windows were opened, but this allowed soot, dust, and smoke to enter the cars.

At Harrisburg, on the way to Columbus, the *Missouri* passengers were joined by another group of Moravian immigrants, and these new people shared their belongings with their less fortunate countrymen.[14] This second group of immigrants had had a much more conventional and comfortable passage, arriving at New Orleans on October 18, 1873, aboard the North German Lloyd steamship *Hannover*. Today Šimek descendants still tell the story of how "Grandpa Šimek" (František Šimek) and "Grandpa" (Josef) Blaha met on this train to Columbus.

The immigrants arrived in the vicinity of Columbus on Monday evening, October 20, 1873. This area, too, was experiencing the yellow fever epidemic, which had been spread by the coastal inhabitants fleeing inland for safety. By October 22 there were fifty active cases in the area, and several infected persons had already died.[15] The train rolled past the town of Columbus and unloaded its passengers at the end of the tracks.[16]

The final destinations of the individual Moravian families would lie along a route that led west from Columbus, Colorado County, skirting the southern border of Fayette County, and then down into Lavaca County. This last leg of their amazing journey was made in rented carts pulled by oxen, the women and children riding and the men walking alongside. Since the 1850s oxcarts such as these had provided the most common mode of transportation for groups of immigrants traveling from the rail heads to their places of settlement in the interior of the state.

The excruciatingly slow pace of this kind of travel at least had the advantage of providing the immigrants with a close-up view of their new homeland and plenty of time to think about the new life they had chosen for themselves. This would have been a highly emotional time for any such group, but in this case it was a time to reflect on the long series of hardships and disasters that had plagued them throughout their journey to the fabled land of Texas.

At this time of year, Central Texas did not much resemble the "promised land" described in the optimistic letters sent home by previous immigrants. They had arrived just in time for the first "cold snap" of winter, and the weather was bleak and dreary. It would be six months before they could witness the beautiful fields of wildflowers—the bluebonnets and Indian paintbrushes—they had heard so much about.

Nevertheless the Moravians were heading into the heart of Czech Texas. Fayette County had been the site of the first substantial Czech settlements, and groups of settlers soon moved from there into neighboring counties. In 1856 the first Czech settler, Matěj Novák, arrived near the community of Mulberry. Other Czechs followed during the next decade, and the town was renamed Praha (Prague), after the ancient capital of the Czech lands. About the same time that Novák came to Mulberry, Josef Janda and several other settlers from Trojanovice, Moravia, arrived in the community of Bluff. A Catholic church of logs was built in 1856 and a school in 1868. These settlers were followed by many others, and Bluff was renamed Hostyn, after a Moravian town. Similarly, the town of Navidad, on the banks of the Navidad Creek, became Dubina (Oak Grove), named by Valentin Haidušek, whose son was to become one of the most prominent Czech leaders in the state. By 1860 the Anglo and German settlement of Fayetteville already was becoming a Czech town, although Czechs remained a minority in La Grange, the county seat. Perhaps the first Czech Catholic elementary school in the United States was established in Bluff (Hostyn) with Terezie Kubálová as teacher in 1868, and several other such schools were built in the area in the following decades. Although Jan Habenicht's estimate of over one thousand Czech families in Fayette County by the turn of the century may be an exaggeration, Fayette very early became the Texas county with the largest Czech population and was the site of the early development of religious and social institutions, in particular the fraternal organizations.[17]

Neighboring Lavaca County also had been settled early. Alois Klimiček arrived in 1858, followed by a group of fellow Moravians two years later. The first Czech to settle in what became the community of Moravia was Václav Matula, in 1872. The county had other settlements with Czech names, including Novohrad, Komensky, Bila Hora, and Vsetin. By the 1890s Hallettsville, the county seat, would be the home of two important Czech-language newspapers—*Nový domov* and *Obzor*.[18]

František Šimek and his family were the first members of the group to end their journey. The Šimeks took refuge under a large live oak tree located on the Navidad River near Weimer, Colorado County, just across the line from Fayette County. This tree provided shelter from the wind and rain that accompanied a cold front on the evening of October 22, 1873. Initially they cooked their evening meals with coals provided by the fireman of the train that had brought them inland. These meals were little more than broth made from a jar of zásmažka (rue) and the water of the Navidad. Later the Šimeks acquired a house with a dog run near this location and lived there with their cousin Adolf Šimek and his family for several years.

The Olšovský family settled in northern Lavaca County, just across the line from Mulberry (Praha), Fayette County. Johana Nevlud-Olšovský gave birth

The Janča family, circa early 1890s. In the back row are (from left to right) *Frances, John A., Josef, and Karolina. In the middle row are Mary, Jan, and Marie Liberda Janča. Johanna is sitting in front.* Photograph courtesy of Virginia Startz Bockholt

to her daughter Paulina on April 25, 1874. Paulina was baptized on May 10, 1874, and her godparents were John and Teresa Pargač. The Janča, Žárský, Bujnoch, Láník, Polášek, and Moris families all settled in the vicinity of Sweet Home, located a few miles southwest of Hallettsville, in Lavaca County. The Janča family was initially provided for by Joseph Liberda and wife Agnes Jalufka-Liberda. Mariana Liberda-Janča gave birth to Františka Janča on November 4, 1873. This child was baptized on the following November 18, and the godparents were Joseph and Victoria Kutač. Josef Liberda, a carpenter, built a church at Koerth with the help of Jan Janča and his son Jan. Rosalie Clos (Koláš)-Žárský gave birth to Cecelia Žárský, on November 1, 1873. She was baptized the same day as Františka Janča, and her godparents were Frank and Magdalena Buček.

The Bujnoch and Láník families took refuge in a barn on the Dyer (or Dryer) farm. It was at this barn that Josefa Bujnoch-Láník gave birth to Agnes Láník, on January 14, 1874. As in the case of the Žárský girl, her godparents

The family of Jiří and Anna Bujnoch, circa 1897. In the back row are (from left to right) Charles Mizera (step-son), and Joe, Cecelia, and Frances Bujnoch. In the center are Frank Kahanek (step-son) and his wife, Veronica. In the front row (standing) are George, Jr., John, and Jim Bujnoch. Seated are Jiří Bujnoch and his wife Anna, holding their son Peter.
Photograph courtesy of George and Dorothy Bujnoch

at baptism were Frank and Magdalena Buček. The first birth of a child in the Polášek family after arriving in Texas came on January 14, 1876. Rudolph and Agnes Kozelsky-Steffek were the godparents. After the death of his wife Agnes, Rudolph Steffek later married Mariana Bujnoch. It is not known whether the Moris family produced children in Texas.

Like most previous groups, the agriculturally oriented Moravians had planned their big journey in between harvest time in the old homeland and spring planting in the new. They were eager to build a prosperous new life in rural Central Texas. However, most of them found life there to be far from easy. Although they had plenty of wild game to eat, the Šimek family could not afford to buy white flour for about seven years. Their first barrel was purchased jointly with another family for a Christmas celebration in 1880.[19]

When the Janča family wrote letters back to relations in their native village of Drnholec, telling of the hard economic times in America, they were ridiculed for being foolish enough to emigrate. In later years, when times were better in Texas, Jan sent letters offering to pay passage to America for other family members; however, they declined his offer, saying, "Do not send passage tickets, send money."[20]

But their more adventurous relations in Texas, the future-oriented survivors of shipwreck and hurricane, must have known that the greatest benefits of immigration are not immediate: they come to the second, third, and later generations—generations that can repay their forbears only by remembering the past.

Excerpts from Texas co cíl stěhování (Texas as a Destination for Emigration, 1882)

The following excerpts, translated into English, are taken from August Siemering's 1882 Czech-language pamphlet entitled *Texas co cíl stěhování* (Texas as a Destination for Emigration).[1] Also in 1882 the G.H.&S.A. Railroad published a German-language pamphlet by Siemering entitled *Texas als Ziel deutscher Auswanderung* (Texas as a Destination of German Emigration). As pointed out in the General Introduction, both the German and the Czech pamphlets are similar in content and arrangement to Kingsbury's original and contain introductory remarks by him, but there are attempts to appeal to the specialized audience in each case. At any rate, it is clear that Siemering was collaborating closely with Kingsbury, and his primary roles seem to be those of editor and translator.[2]

In addition to introductory sections by Kingsbury, it is useful to examine testimonials from Czech and German immigrants already living in Texas and an essay on Slavic (Czech, Polish, Serbian) immigrants in Texas written by Augustin Hajdušek. Haidušek, as his name was usually spelled, immigrated to Texas with his Moravian family as a young man and became one of the first Czech immigrants to practice law in the United States. In 1880 he was elected to the Texas state legislature, the first Czech-American to hold an elective office of this kind, and his short essay in Siemering's pamphlet—reprinted from the *Galveston News* of September 9, 1882—was written during his first term. Later, as judge of Fayette County and as editor of the Czech-language newspaper *Svoboda* (Freedom), he solidified his position as one of the most influential Czech-Americans in Texas.[3] Like Kingsbury and Siemering, Haidušek was a promoter of European immigration to Texas in the decades following the American Civil War.

TEXAS

As a Destination for Emigration: A conscientious description of the largest state of the United States of North America, its economic and political conditions, its climate and health, with a special focus on West Texas, settlement and life.

FOR THE BENEFIT AND USE OF TRAVELLERS
Written by
A. Siemering in San Antonio, Texas
Published by the railroad company
Galveston, Harrisburg & San Antonio,

TEXAS

Preface

It is my solemn duty while publishing this document to add some changes that have occurred in 1881 and during the first six months of the year 1882.

The most important change I am supposed to mention here is the completion of the railroad from New Orleans and Galveston to San Francisco in California, for which this book is dedicated and distributed, carrying the permanent name "Southern Pacific Railroad" or "Sunset Route." This railroad is 2,500 English miles long, and when all connections that are now under construction are finished, the company will count up to 8,000 miles all together of its own rails. Everything will be under one management. On August 1, the first train will leave for San Francisco. Also, this company will open a new steamboat line with 24 steamboats, 5,000 tons each. On this line the company will transport wheat and other agricultural products from California and Texas to Europe; and from Europe to America the company will be able to transport passengers at a low price. The railroad cars are designed in such a way that as soon as they are emptied out, the cars can be adjusted into comfortable sleeping cars. When this steamboat line will start is not yet set, but in any case it will happen soon. This is the wealthiest and the most powerful company in the world, and therefore it is obvious that the first settlers of this company also will be wealthy very soon. First, because of the increasing price of land and, second, through a convenient access to the market where one can sell his own products. All different types of climate and soil can be found along the railroad. The land is good for agriculture, raising livestock, and also mining.

The company intends to leave the choice of land up to the immigrants and wants to sell the land for an ordinary price. The company owns and offers millions of acres of land of different types, and it is much better for immigrants if they contact the company, which is well established and secure, rather than doing business with persons who can at any time go bankrupt or disappear. Railroad companies must keep business alive, and therefore they offer better possibilities and long-term loans with smaller interest payments. Last year the export of wheat from California was 66 million bushels, and this will now be transported exclusively by this railroad company. I have to let you know that the price of land in Texas in one year has increased by 100 percent, but there is still cheap land available, and the company finances it with long-term loans. The price of livestock has increased by 50 percent, and a good cow with a calf sells for 25 dollars. Also the population is rapidly increasing; over the past 10 years the population was increased by 773,142 new immigrants, and more people are coming to Texas than ever before. The development of railroad connections and agriculture is fantastic. From September, 1880, till September, 1881, 1,634 miles of new railroad tracks were laid. Today, there are 4,389 miles that are open for business, whereas only ten years ago barely 300 miles had been built. The railroads now being built will cost $27,850,000 by September 1, 1882, and maintenance costs must be added to that figure. There is plenty of money in Texas, and, where there is a lot of money, there is also a chance for everybody to gain something. In 1881 the cotton harvest produced 1,258,742 bales, 500 lbs. each. Every bale was worth 200 [German] marks. This year's predictions [1882] are even more promising, and anyone who arrives in Texas anytime from August to Christmas can find a well-paid job. Oats were 70 bushels per acre, though wheat, which suffered this year, was only 18 bushels. The corn harvest is expected to be great.

Last year Texas began to build a state capitol, which will cost 3 million dollars when completed. It will be the largest and the most beautiful building in all of America. Also, the State University is being established, and, once finished, this university will be comparable to any in the world. Almost 3 million dollars was put aside for this university, and education will be free of charge. The educational fund holds 40 million acres at the moment, worth 100 million dollars. This sum is larger than that held by any other land fund in all of America, and, therefore, education in Texas will be of the highest quality that money can buy.

Everything mentioned above, together with the rich soil and mild and healthy climate, indicates that Texas is most suitable for poor and rich alike in America. Those who purchase land now act more wisely than those who wait: for just as in Europe, it will go into someone else's hands.

W. G. Kingsbury

41 Finsbury Pavement, London E.C.

Galveston, Harrisburg, and San Antonio Railroad

This little brochure has been written by one of the most famous citizens of Northwest Texas and it has been supplemented with contributions from his friends with the intention of providing their fellow-countrymen with pleasurable reading.[4] This brochure is sponsored by the previously mentioned railroad company to be published and distributed in Europe. The railroad company owns three million acres of land and wishes that this land be inhabited and cultivated soon so that business can flourish.

The previously mentioned company offers its own land to settlers at very low prices on credit. It owns choice land, two to five English miles distant from the railroad station, selling at twelve marks, i.e., six gold coins, per acre. If entrepreneurs wish to buy land of larger proportions, they can contact the main office—H.B. Andrews, Chief of Land Department, San Antonio, Texas, USA—where they will be offered the best prices available. A labor shortage is predominant at this moment in Texas; more than 3,000 miles of railroad are now under construction, and all possible means are being used to finish this project.

Last year 20,000 new farms were built, and 40,000 will be added this year. No other state in America is making such rapid progress as Texas. In 1865 there were 350 miles of rail in Texas, today there are 3,000 miles and just as many are under construction. In 1870 there were 812,000 inhabitants in Texas, today there are 1,600,000, and if growth continues in this way, in 1890 there will be 3,000,000, and in 1900, 6,000,000 inhabitants in Texas. Nowadays, economically, the state of Texas leads all American states in growing cotton and raising livestock; it is second in the wool industry, which is growing fast. No other place in America beats Texas in growing wheat, corn, and other agricultural products, including vegetables and fruits. Cotton is, however, the most profitable agricultural product because one can plant three times more than he can harvest. Moreover, women and children can pick cotton alongside men.

Many of those who immigrated to the company's land during the past few years were already employed in the cotton fields at sunrise on the day after their arrival. This work provided them with wages until Christmas, and then they, in turn, would buy or rent land. Last year there was a huge demand for workers: more than 1 million dollars worth of cotton was not harvested. We have large houses for immigrants, where, at the beginning, they can live for free. People in charge of these houses provide the immigrants with work on nearby farms, or they find land for those who want to buy. The conditions under which the land can be bought or rented are very advantageous: the land-owner offers the tenant an improved, well-fenced farm, living quarters and fuel, a team and feed, all seeds and tools, a garden in which the settler can plant potatoes, and two cows. Tenants work the land and give half of the harvest to the owner. The owner also offers to a needy tenant the basic necessities for living, like bread and meat, on credit until the tenant is able to sell his crops. Those who want to come to Texas during the cotton harvest have to do so in September. The undersigned, who has lived in Texas for 36 years, will answer all the questions you might have.

W. G. Kingsbury

European Agent G.H.&S.A.R.R.

41 Finsbury Pavement, London.

Introduction

America is the destination of emigrants from Austria, Germany, Switzerland, etc. By the term America we usually mean the states of North America. The U.S. republic, however, represents a territory that is larger than all of Europe; it is composed of 38 states, each of them with its own government. As far as the climate, customs, agricultural products and conditions are concerned, they are as different as they are in different European countries. The difference between Norway and Italy cannot be greater than that between Minnesota in the north and Texas, the most southern state of the American union. The distance between them is 2,000 English miles or 500 geographical miles. Whereas Michigan is rich with coniferous forest, there are palm trees in the state of Florida. Therefore, one must be very careful when choosing the destination of emigration. Those who travel blindly, just to get to America, and who think that by arriving in New York, Baltimore, or New Orleans, they have reached their destination, often waste time and money unnecessarily, traveling hundreds of additional miles before finding a place they like and which is well-suited to them.

There are still many places for immigrants throughout the states of the American union, and every hard-working and thrifty settler can find adequate subsistence for himself in every state. The United States had 50 million inhabitants in 1880, while there is enough space and sustenance for a hundred million people. According to the American census, some of the states are already sufficiently populated; for example, in the state of New York there are 93 inhabitants per square mile. In Florida, on the other hand, there are 4 and in Texas 6 inhabitants per square mile.

Even though there are still many places for immigrants, some of the states have big advantages over others, and for that reason they are particularly recommended for settlers. Those who are looking for a place to live want to find the state that would suit them best: they would like to enjoy the climate, location, social conditions; they want a state where there are many of their fellow-countrymen and where they can follow their vocations. Texas is such a state.

The writer has lived in Texas for 30 years and has spent the longest and best part of his life there. Therefore he feels somewhat qualified to offer his observations about the land and the people of Texas, unbiased judgments more reliable than those based on the superficial first impressions of a traveller.

The following is an accurate and conscientious description of Texas, its inhabitants, development and social conditions. The writer will make an effort to avoid all extremes and to stick to the truth. Texas has both good and bad sides; the former, however, prevails over the latter to such an extent that this land can be called a good target for emigration.

At the beginning we have to discourage everyone who wants to immigrate to Texas but cannot or does not want to work, unless he has enough money and property to sustain him without having to work. Very few roasted pigeons have been flying in the air here, and, also, just as in other countries around the world, we don't pick up money from the ground. Those who want to work will never be sorry that they immigrated to Texas. Moreover, if they have a little money at the beginning, it is amazing how they can put it to good use. There is no other place where capital can be used so well as in Texas, as you will see from the following information. This is the great advantage that this land has over all European countries: that diligent and thrifty workers can achieve an independent and secure existence in the course of time. This is impossible in Europe, even with the greatest diligence and economy.

Immigrants' Housing

The company has built large buildings near the railroad stations where the immigrants can live for a certain period of time for free. However, they have to provide food for themselves.[5] In each of these buildings there are agents who find jobs for immigrants or show land to those who are interested in buying. The cotton crop will be plentiful this year, and high wages are guaranteed for everybody: men, women and children. All agents have maps to distribute among the immigrants. These maps are a good source of information regarding the above-mentioned buildings, available jobs, etc.

Those who travel to Texas via New York can consult the "Texas Farm Association" bureau on 17 State Street, New York, where they will get the best advice. As for land immigrants, they can consult H. B. Andrews, San Antonio.

If anybody wants to know about something that he did not find in this brochure, he can contact me, and I will provide him with the required information.

W. G. Kingsbury,

41 Finsbury Pavement, London E. C. England.

Testimonials

I, Jan Pfeil, was living in Rockshagen, Prussia, and in order to immigrate to Texas in 1873 I had to borrow money from my friends. When I arrived in Galveston, I did not have any money. I went to Schulenburg and leased a piece of land that I cultivated for 5 years. Then I bought 241 acres of land with woods, 60–70 acres of which I am now cultivating. Last summer my crops consisted of cotton worth 800 dollars and 500 bushels of corn worth 300 dollars. Also I have a good dwelling place, barns, 4 horses, 8 milch cows, 19 head of smaller stock, and 6 pigs. I live here happily and I would not like to go back.

Jan Pfeil

I, Frant. Štancl, was living in Poloná, in the district of Hranice in Moravia, and moved to Texas in 1871 with 1,000 dollars on me. I bought a lot in Schulenburg, but I lost everything due to bad speculation with money, an illness, etc. Now, after 10 years of work, I have a farm near Schulenburg, 150 acres in size, which is worth at least 400 dollars. I have houses, barns, 15 horses, 15 cows, and a larger number of pigs. Last year my crops included 27 round bales of cotton worth 1,420 dollars, 1,000 bushels of corn worth 600 dollars, 10 carts of oats worth 50 dollars, and 10 carts of hay worth 50 dollars. Besides that, I sold milk worth 150 dollars in Schulenburg. In Lavaca County I own 400 acres of land, worth 3,200 dollars, out of which 70 acres has been cultivated.

Fr. Štancl

I, Jakub Gerlic, was living in Litschel, Moravia, and I left in 1874. I traveled to New York and from New York to Texas. I settled in Schulenburg. I arrived there penniless; I took a piece of land on lease and worked on it for five years. In this way I saved 600 dollars. Now I have a farm 100 acres large, 80 acres of which has been cultivated. I have 4 horses, 23 cows, and 3 pigs. Last year I harvested 15 round bales of cotton worth 1,000 dollars, 300 bushels of corn worth 150 dollars. I am completely satisfied, and I plan never to return to Europe.

Jakub Gerlic

I, Karel Zellner, was living in Halden in Westphalia, and I moved away in 1860. I arrived in Brenham where I married a widow who owned 55 acres of land. I came to Texas without money and served in the army during the war. I stayed in Brenham till 1870 and then went to Schulenburg. Today, I have a farm of 194 acres, 164 acres of which is cultivated. Last year my crops consisted of 16 round bales of cotton worth 800 dollars, 300 bushels of corn worth 150 dollars. I have 6 horses, 25 cows, and 10 pigs. Besides that, I have a cutting machine, ploughs, harrows, and other agricultural tools.

E. K. Zellner

I, Frant. Pohl, was living in Nové Město near Friedland, and in 1855 I moved to Texas. I brought 700 dollars with me, and I bought a farm near Fayetteville, 45 acres large, for 600 dollars. Now I live near Schulenburg, and I have a farm 310 acres large and 200 acres of which is cultivated. Last year I harvested 22 round bales of cotton worth 1,200 dollars, 1,000 bushels of corn worth 400 dollars, and 50 bushels of potatoes for domestic use and 25 bushels of sweet potatoes.[6] I have 7 horses, 30 cows, and 8 pigs. In addition, I have all the agricultural tools, besides 600 acres of good land that I have bequeathed to my children. From my forest land I sell wood for an annual profit of 200 dollars.

Fr. Pohl

I, Isidor Fecht, was living in Coblenc on the Rhine, and in 1864 I moved to New York. From New York I traveled to Matamoros in Mexico, stayed for three years there, and then moved to Galveston. In Galveston I worked as a merchant; I had 1,110 dollars then. Currently I work for a mercantile company, Leon Blum & Co. I own a house in Galveston and have an annual income of 3,600 dollars.

I. Fecht

I, Josef Dobrola, had lived in Frenštát, Moravia, and I moved to Texas in 1860. When I arrived with my father in Texas, we did not have any money. At first we rented a farm on the Comal [River], then we rented other farms and lived that way for 20 years before I could buy a farm of my own in Fayette [County]. Currently I have a farm 59 and ½ acres large, 35 acres cultivated. Last summer I harvested 7 round bales of cotton worth 350 dollars and 300 bushels of corn worth 150 dollars. I have 9 cows, 3 horses, and a pig. I came to Texas with my father, who returned home when I was 9 years old. I stayed here and I am satisfied with my living conditions. I am 29 years old now.

Josef Dobrola

I, Bedřich Windel, was living in Opendorf, Prussia, and I moved to Texas in 1860. When I arrived in Washington County, I was 17 years old, and I had 12 dollars on me. I took a job on a farm for 80 dollars a year, food, and shelter. I then served in the army until 1864. After that I returned to Texas, went to Mexico, and then went on to New Orleans, where I worked on steamers. In 1866 I went back to Texas again. At first I worked in Washington County, in the fields, until I saved 400 dollars. Then I settled in Fayette County. I married and bought 217 acres of land, out of which I have cultivated 100 acres. This summer, I harvested 10 round bales of cotton on 14 acres; the previous summer I harvested 16 round bales of cotton worth 800 dollars on 16 acres and 1000 bushels of corn on 26 acres that brought me 450 dollars. Besides that I have 200 acres of land, out of which 100 acres is cultivated. I have 15 cows and two big mules. The capital that I saved up to now amounts to 1500 dollars.

Bedř. Windel

I, Jiří Knipr, was living in Buchenwald in Silesia, and I moved away to Texas in 1854. When I arrived in Texas with my parents, I was 17 years old, and I had no money. First, I worked for two years at the mill in New Ulm for 10 dollars a month with food and shelter provided. Then I went to Fayette County, and I worked partly for my father and partly for other farmers. Then I rented one farm on which I worked for 5 years and another one where I worked for 4 years. As soon as I had saved 5,000 dollars, I bought 170 acres of land. Now I have 640 acres of land, 80 acres of which is cultivated and the remainder of which consists of fenced meadows. I have 50 or 60 cows, 8 horses, and 8 pigs. Last year I harvested 26 round bales of cotton worth 1,430 dollars, 1,000 bushels of corn worth 450 dollars; also rye, potatoes, and vegetables for my own use. In addition, I have saved up 3,000 dollars.

Jiří Knipr

The State of Texas, Fayette County

The undersigned notary public in Fayette County, Texas, certifies that the persons who gave the above statements, are known personally to him and that their statements to the best of his knowledge are truthful.

H. Hendersen,
Notary Public.

A Short Outline of the Slavic Race in Texas
(written by A. Haidušek, La Grange, Texas)

In Texas there are about 50,000 people of this race. Many of them have lived here since 1850, but most of them have moved into Texas later. Mainly, they are Czechs and Moravians; there is no significant difference between them, just that Czechs come from Bohemia and Moravians from Moravia.[7] Both are subject to Austria, and they have a common language. Besides Czechs and Moravians, there are also Poles and Serbs, and, as mentioned above, altogether there are about 50,000 Slavs in Texas: 35,000 Czechs and Moravians and 15,000 Poles and Serbs. Czechs and Moravians reside in Fayette County (about 8,000), in Austin County (5,000), in Lavaca County (4,500), in Colorado County (3,500), in Washington County (3,000), 24,000 altogether. The remaining 11,000 reside in various other counties and districts. Poles and Serbs settled especially in the counties of Bandera, Bexar, Karnes, DeWitt, Robertson, and Lee.

The first immigrants came in 1850, and since then their number grew larger, up to the outbreak of the last war. The first immigrants settled near Cat Spring, Austin County, but there are only a few of them alive now. The second wave of immigrants, who came in 1854, settled in Fayette County—on the buffalo and horse prairies. Altogether, there were seven families, and the family of this writer was among them. These families were the first that settled west of the Colorado River, and they bought land there. This happened in December, 1856. The following year 500 people settled in Fayette County, and they made up the largest group of immigrants before the war. Soon after the war, their number started growing, and it has been growing ever since.

As a rule, all the immigrants, or at least most of them, are farmers, and they stay together in a group as long as possible, that is, as long as they are leasing land. However, as soon as they can pay their first installment, they buy a piece of land. And if they want to settle down permanently and cannot find a suitable place nearby, then they leave the group of fellow immigrants. When they settle in a certain place and furnish their dwellings, they make sure that a church and school are built right away because it is around these two buildings that a settlement grows and flourishes.

It is possible to call them a nation of farmers; they cultivate land well, and they almost always reach the point where they can pay for all their own needs. They generally consider themselves the best farmers in Texas. Only a few of them are exclusively merchants or mechanics, even though it must be said that most of them excel in mechanics. On the whole they are thrifty and hardworking, and even women work in the fields. They are honest and polite, too, and they carry out their duties diligently. They are sociable, and so they really like to enjoy themselves, and some of them—as it happens everywhere—overindulge themselves a little; however, they are very polite, and they obey the laws. All of them are Christians, and they belong to either the Catholic or a Protestant church.

In Texas most of them are Catholics, but Moravian and Czech Protestant sects are growing in number, too.

As far as their material and spiritual growth is concerned, this writer can only comment on those in Fayette County. Although most immigrants came here without money, more than ¾ out of the 8,000 here are settled, independent farmers who own their own homes. Some of them have up to 35,000 dollars of capital. After the end of the war they built several attractive churches, and then they began to collect money with plans to build another three; these churches are notable for their beautiful design. Our fellow countrymen take good care of their children; they have 10 schools that are always full and good teachers who run them. The school year usually lasts 8–10 months, and English and German are taught in addition to Czech.

"Slovan," an 8–page Czech periodical, comes out weekly in La Grange, Texas. It was founded in 1879, and it is the only Czech periodical south of St. Louis, not a small benefit for the Czechs in Texas.[8]

("Galveston News")

September 9, 1882

Conclusion

The detailed information in this volume can lead the reader to a deeper understanding of European immigration to Texas in the 1870s—from the point of view of the immigrants themselves and from that of the agents who sought to lure them from their Old World homelands. The nineteenth-century pamphlets by Kingsbury and Siemering, contemporaneous newspaper accounts, the first-hand account by Wright, and the oral legacy of immigrant stories passed down to the second, third, and fourth generations, all of these help to contextualize the narratives of the immigrants: their historically specific and primarily agrarian vision is one that most readers today can only imagine.

Interesting but previously unknown historical characters, the courageous Moravian pioneers left descendants who continue to live in Texas, and the intrepid explorer and close observer Wright left for posterity a record of his first impressions of the state. The thirty-six Moravians from Chlebovice, Fryčovice, and Drnholec are representative of those individuals and groups who found out about this distant land of opportunity through a fortuitous chain of personal contacts and communications, while the Englishman Wright was attracted directly by the railroad's—and Kingsbury's—promotions, though Wright was an individualist with a healthy skepticism who was eager to see the fabled land for himself and investigate its potential in his own way.

Each of the two case studies documented in this volume for the first time is of interest in itself, in addition to providing insight into the magnitude and complexity of the interlocking systems of transportation and communications that characterized the Europe-to-Texas immigration trade in the 1870s and early 1880s. The Mississippi and Dominion steamship line, recommended by Kingsbury at this stage of his career to English immigrants and used both by Wright and the Moravians, was indeed a problematic enterprise, with its old and battered ships—converted and renamed time after time—and unenviable safety record, illustrated by the personal experience of Wright, shipwrecked off the coast of Spain in his initial attempt to cross the Atlantic, and, of course, that of the Moravians, as described in this volume.

The Moravians' streak of bad luck began when it was discovered that Jiří Bujnoch did not possess the papers he needed to document his release from the Austrian army, and, in order to circumvent the German authorities who required them, they passed up their opportunity to sail on the North German Lloyd's *Strassburg* from Bremen and then found their way to the *Hammonia-Belgian-Missouri* in Liverpool. Most obvious was the bad luck to encounter a hurricane en route to America, but, as previously noted, other factors, related not to chance but to the mismanagement of the Mississippi and Dominion steamship line, may have played a large part in this tragedy: in addition to the overall bad safety record, there is the dismissal of the troubled Captain Mathias under mysterious circumstances and his replacement by the apparently incompetent Captain Pearson, the suspicious "overinsurance" of the steamship, and the peculiar circumstances of the wreck itself in broad daylight and calm water. Although neither Wright's nor the Moravians' wreck resulted in loss of life, the wreck of *Borussia,* the *Missouri*'s sister ship—about a month after Wright's wreck, and only few days after embarking from La Coruña, the site of the Wright shipwreck, on its way to Havana—cost 169 lives. It is beyond the scope of this book to analyze the Mississippi and Dominion safety record relative to the transatlantic transportation industry as a whole during this period; however, this would seem to be a worthwhile topic for future historical research.

Finally, it seems clear that such figures as W. G. Kingsbury, August Siemering, and Augustin Haidušek—each of whom was an adventurer and pioneer in his own right—deserve further study by historians and other scholars interested in the political, economic, and cultural development of Texas in the second half of the nineteenth century.

Notes

General Introduction

1. See chapter 6, note 1.
2. See the *Eleventh Census of the United States, 1890,* vol. 1 (Washington, D.C.: Government Printing Office, 1892), 508.
3. In 1890, there were 100,763 Texans who had been born in Alabama and 106,678 who had been born in Tennessee. *Eleventh Census, 1890,* vol. 2, 14–19.
4. *Eleventh Census, 1890,* vol. 1, 508.
5. There were also 8,201 immigrants from Ireland, 2,172 from Scotland, and 321 from Wales. *Eleventh Census, 1890,* vol. 2, 600–603.
6. For the Moravians this route was somewhat out of the ordinary, as explained in the text below. The usual route for Czech immigrants to Texas at this time was directly from the German port of Bremen to Galveston.
7. "The Loss of the Borussia," *Times* (London), Dec. 29, 1879, sec. D, p. 5.
8. A fuller historical account of the *Borussia* and the *Hammonia* is given in chapter 7. The seaworthiness of each ship was questioned prior to the time it was wrecked. Such vessels were not equipped to compete in the brisker trade of the northern routes; on the other hand, they were able to utilize southern ports where the harbor was too shallow to accommodate the newer steamships.

    When it arrived in Galveston in 1881, the *Gutenberg* was the last emigrant sailing vessel from Bremen to arrive at the North American continent. Letter from Dr. Adolf Hoffmeister, Staatsarchiv Bremen, to Lawrence H. Konecny (henceforth L. H. K.), Jan. 11, 1994.
9. Clinton Machann and James W. Mendl, *Krásná Amerika: A Study of the Texas Czechs* (Austin: Eakin Press, 1983), 75.
10. Ibid., 71–86; and Robert L. Skrabanek, *We're Czechs* (College Station: Texas A&M University Press, 1988).
11. Machann and Mendl, *Krásná Amerika,* 72–81.

Part I. W. G. Kingsbury and His Pamphlet for the Galveston, Harrisburg, and San Antonio Railroad

Chapter 1. Introduction

1. A biographical sketch of Kingsbury appears in John Henry Brown, *Indian Wars and Pioneers of Texas* (Austin: Daniell, 1880; rpt. Easley, S.C.: Southern Historical Press, 1978). His obituary can be found in the *San Antonio Express,* Sept. 12, 1896.
2. The practice was temporarily suspended during the years 1869–73 by the Texas Constitution

of 1869. Unlike other states, Texas had been allowed to keep its public land, and large tracts of this land was used to finance the school system as well as railroad construction. In addition a homestead law modeled after that of the United States was used to encourage immigration. Railroad companies were issued land script, and this could in turn be sold to individuals wishing to locate on the land. During the period 1854–82 more than 32 million acres of land were granted to railroad companies. See S. G. Reed, *A History of the Texas Railroads, and of Transportation Conditions under Spain and Mexico and the Republic and the State* (Houston: St. Clair, 1941; rpt., New York: Arno, 1981), 155.

3. Henry V. Poor, *Manual of the Railroads of the United States for 1877–78* (New York: H. V. and H. W. Poor, 1877), 848.

4. Ibid., 848.

5. R. B. Hubbard, *Centennial Oration of Gov. R. B. Hubbard of Texas, Delivered at the National Exposition, September 11, 1876* (St. Louis, 1876); James L. Rock and W. I. Smith, *Southern and Western Texas Guide for 1878* (St. Louis: Granger, 1878). Hubbard became governor in 1876, and served until 1879. In his oration, addressing the president of the United States and the U.S. Centennial Commission, he emphasizes the enormous natural resources of Texas, defends the moral character of Texans against the "myth of lawlessness," and calls for a healing of the wounds left by the Civil War.

6. The figures are based on articles published in the *Galveston Daily News;* see Lawrence H. Konecny and Clinton Machann, "German and Czech Immigration to Texas: The Bremen to Galveston Route, 1880–86," *Nebraska History* 74 (Fall/Winter 1993): 136–41.

7. "German Immigrants Coming," *Galveston Daily News,* September 26, 1880, p. 4, col. 2.

8. From Kingsbury's letter to the *Galveston Daily News,* dated London, October 23, 1880, "Immigration at Work," *Galveston Daily News,* Nov. 11, 1880, p. 4, col. 2; see also "Texas," *Galveston Daily News,* Sept. 8, 1882, p. 7, col. 1.

9. A pamphlet titled *Immigrants Guide to Western Texas Sunset Route* had been published the previous year by the Boston office of the G.H.&S.A. Railway Co., then located at 58 Sears Building, Boston. Kingsbury is not mentioned in the pamphlet, which lists Dr. Ammi Brown as the company's Eastern Land and Immigration Agent. A second edition of Kingsbury's pamphlet was published, with some editorial revisions, in 1878 by the London publisher Langley & Son.

Chapter 2. A Description of South-Western and Middle Texas *(1877)*

1. In the original, White misspells his name as T. W. Pierce. For an account of Peirce's aggressive leadership of the G.H.&S.A. Railroad, see S. G. Reed, *A History of the Texas Railroads,* 71, 137, 192–98, 205–206, 226, 243, 261, and 666.

2. Kingsbury's prose has not been edited for grammar or style, and deviations from Standard English have been allowed to stand. In a few instances, as noted, Kingsbury's spelling of certain words has been standardized to prevent confusion.

3. Kingsbury has "spinnage."

4. Kingsbury has "mezquit."

5. Istle—or ystle, as it is spelled in the first edition—is a Mexican-Spanish word for the pita plant or its fiber.

6. Kingsbury writes "Uvalda" for Uvalde.

7. In Kingsbury's text—both in the letters he quotes and in his own commentary—the word "ranch" is sometimes spelled "ranche." The spelling has been standardized here.

8. In the elaborate table omitted here, Kingsbury estimates that total profits over a ten-year period for a sheep raiser in Texas would be $99,011.90.

9. The original text has "itinaracy."

10. At this point Kingsbury inserts a table titled "Health of Columbus, Colorado Co., Texas," prefaced as follows: "The following novel but certainly very convincing table is taken from a pamphlet descriptive of Colorado county, by Rowan Green, Esq. of Columbus. Mr. Green is in the Real Estate business, and will send his pamphlet to all who write for it. Enclose a three-penny piece for postage." The caption on the table reads: "The following are the names of persons (white) living in the Corporate limits of Columbus over 50 years of age, and the year they came to Texas. For a city of 4,000 inhabitants (2,500 white) we defy any town or city in Texas, or out of it, to exhibit such a record of health. There are 56 names and the average age is 61 years, and the average number of years they have lived in Texas is about twenty-five. This record will convince any person that Columbus is one of the most healthy locations in Texas, and certainly one of the most beautiful." This table is followed by one "Showing Mortality, Mean Temperature, and Relative Humidity of the Air, at San Antonio, Texas, during the year 1876, by Dr. Fred Petersen, City Physician of San Antonio. . . ."

    In the second edition, these charts are followed by a short section titled "A 100 Acre Farm at £15 a Year":

    > As Englishmen seem to be more accustomed to renting, than to buying land, and have a great horror of interest, I make the following proposition: —I will measure off 100 acres of as good land as the average in England, and the purchaser shall make a first payment of £15—In 1880 £15; in 1881 £15; in 1882 £15; in 1883 £15—and with this last payment, I will make him and his heirs a clear free-hold title to the land, no interest and no other charges of any kind. This will be equal to paying an annual rental of 3/- [3 shillings] per acre for five years, and then becoming the owner of the farm with all improvements. To farmers who have been accustomed to paying from two to three *pounds* per acre as rent, with no hope of ever becoming the owner of the soil, this extraordinary offer must be apparent. The cultivation of only *three* acres of this land in cotton, will always meet the £15, and generally double that sum. Should there be a failure in crops, as sometimes happens in all countries, we would let the payment stand over a year on payment of ten per cent. interest, and all this shall be stated in the title bond. I have sold nearly five thousand acres in the last ninety days, and as this Second Edition of my book goes to press September 3rd, 1878, I am selling almost daily, and may be instructed to advance the price at any time, for I am only an Agent subject to orders.

11. Kingsbury goes on to mention the Guion Line of steamships from Liverpool to New York; however, in the second edition he drops this reference and instead includes a detailed description of the fares offered by three other steamship lines:

    > There are three routes to Texas:

No.1. *Mississippi and Dominion Line,* sailing from Liverpool about every 15 days, with privilege of calling at Coruna and Havana.

FARE for Adults to New Orleans . . . . £ 6 6 0

Thence to Galveston by Morgan Steamships 1 4 0

Thence to Houston by Morgan Steamship or Rail 0 5 0

Thence to San Antonio or any station on G.H.& S.A.R. . . 1 0 0

£ 8 15 0

Children under 8 years, half-fare to New Orleans; Infants, £1 1 0. From New Orleans to Galveston, over three and under 12, half-fare; under three, free; from Galveston to San Antonio, over five and under 12, half-fare; under five, free. Ten cubic feet of Luggage free to New Orleans and two hundred pounds from there on. Sailing time on this route about 20 to 25 days, delays in calling at other ports extra. See advertisement on inside of wrapper.

Route No. 2. From Liverpool to New York by the *National* and *White Star Lines,* also by the National from London, sailing weekly from each port.

FARE—Cabin, from twelve to seventeen guineas, according to position of berth, all having the same saloon accommodations. Steerage to New York, £6 0 0, children under 8, half-fare, infants, £1 1 0; thence by the Mallory Line of Steamships to Galveston, £4 4 0 each adult, thence to San Antonio, as mentioned in route No. 1, £1 5 0. From New York to Galveston, children from 5 to 12, half-fare, from 3 to 5, quarter-fare, and under 3, free. Total, for adults £11 5 0; children, between five and twelve, £5 12 6; under five, £4 0 0; under three and over one, £3 0 0; infants, £1 1 0. At present the Mallory Steamers sail but once a week, Saturdays, but passengers are accommodated at very low rates, and the Mallory Line pays one-half the expense for transferring luggage. Time by this route, from Liverpool or London to San Antonio, about eighteen to nineteen days not counting delays at New York. Ten cubic feet of luggage free. These steamers also connect at New York with the various Lines of Railroads, and are too well known throughout Europe to need any encomiums from me. See advertisements. [However, a notice at the end of the second edition points to a few errors in this section. "NOTICE. —The attention of the reader is called to the errors contained on page 42, viz.: —Fare by Mallory Steamers, from New York to Galveston, should read £4 for adults and half fare for children between 12 and 5, and quarter fare for children between the ages of 5 and 2, and under 2 free. In route No. 2 it should have been specified that the Steerage rate of the White Star Line from Liverpool to New York is £6 6 0. The Cabin fares of White Star Line from Liverpool to New York are from 15 to 21 guineas."]

Route No. 3. From Liverpool to Philadelphia by the *American Line,* sailing weekly and making direct connection with the Pennsylvania Railroad through to San Antonio.

Cabin fare, from Liverpool to Philadelphia, from 15 to 21 guineas, and Intermediate (a special feature of this Line) £8 8 0; first-class from there to San Antonio, £14 3 0.

Steerage, Liverpool to Philadelphia, £6 0 0, and second-class thence to San Antonio
by rail, £7 19 10. Children under eight, half-fare on steamer, and from five to twelve,
half-fare on the railway; under five, free. Time from Liverpool to San Antonio about 15
days. This is said to be the quickest possible route by which the trip can be made, and
no better line of steamers sails the Atlantic than the American Line. This line transfers
passengers from Philadelphia to New York by rail, for connection with the Mallory
Line free of charge. See advertisement.

I may get some reduction on these rates, and if so passengers shall have every advantage. I book passengers on all these Lines, but the local Agents of either can do the
same and at the same rate, and where they are giving information about Texas it is but
right that, you book by them. Address—

W. G. KINGSBURY, 5, Euston Grove, London, N.W.

At this point in both editions Kingsbury inserts three tables: "Monthly and Annual
Mean Temperatures—in degrees and hundredths—at San Antonio, Texas," "Amount of
Rain—in inches and hundreths," and "Maxima and Minima Temperature of Western
Texas." Each table covers monthly measurements from 1858 through the first five months of
1875. The third table is attributed to the "Station at Institution for Deaf and Dumb, Austin,
Texas. J. Van Nostrand, Observer," and Kingsbury comments:

The above is an exceedingly interesting table and I regret not having the data for the
last three years, though they are not materially different. It is hotter than in England
(it is about like France), and well for us that it is, for want of sunshine is the great
objection to this climate. With rich land, moisture, and heat, crops grow like magic
and ripen early, while with continual cold wet weather they linger and often perish. In
some places in this country wheat often stands upon the ground from ten to twelve
months subject to all the vicissitudes; too much rain rusts it, a drought kills it, storms
blow it down, birds prey upon it, and the weeds, having full time, seed and foul the
lands. In Texas, our wheat is safe in the mill by the tenth of May, and I have known it
to be harvested, thrashed, ground, and on the table as bread, in the month of April.
None but practical farmers can appreciate this truly great advantage.

12. An advertisement for the "Dominion Line" was inserted into the pamphlet. In the second
    edition, Kingsbury refers the reader to full-page advertisements for three lines: the White
    Star Line, the National Line, and the Dominion Line. The White Star and National both
    ran from Liverpool to New York rather than to Galveston (see note 11 above). In addition,
    the second edition of the pamphlet carried smaller advertisements for three Liverpool hotels.
    Two "temperance hotels," the John Fry—affiliated with the Dominion Line—and the Phila-
    delphia, offered special rates for Texas-bound travelers. The St. Nicholas Hotel, specializing
    in immigrants intending to sail for "Texas, Brazil, Australia," offered the comforts of an
    "English Home," along with "good *French* Cooking" [emphasis added].

13. At this point Kingsbury inserts a short note on an erratum pertaining to a chart that had
    appeared earlier in the text but that was omitted in this edition.

Part II. The Texas Diary of William Wright,
February 13–July 1, 1879

Chapter 3. Introduction

1. Thomas W. Cutrer, *The English Texans* (San Antonio: University of Texas Institute of Texan Cultures at San Antonio, 1985), 14.

2. See Cutrer, 79, 82.

3. The following is from an article entitled "British Immigrants," that appeared in the *Daily Picayune* (New Orleans), Nov. 5, 1879, p. 2, cols. 4 and 5:

> The great majority of emigrants to this country, from all parts of Europe, have hereto-fore been farm laborers, but the arrivals during the past year or two, and more espe-cially during the last few months, have shown a great increase of machinists, cutlers, painters, carpenters, joiners and other trades, factory workers, coal miners and shop-keepers' assistants. The reason for this is assigned from a general stagnation in business for years past, whereby tens and hundreds of thousands of persons engaged in these pursuits have been either thrown out of employment or compelled to work for the bare necessaries of life. In Great Britain a marked improvement has for some time past been evident in the iron districts, but other businesses are still stagnant and suffering, and emigration or starvation is the question that is now agitating the masses thus situated.

4. "Lone Star" Coyle himself crossed over from Liverpool to New Orleans aboard the steam-ship *Teutonia,* on the same crossing with Wright, in October, 1879, when Wright returned with his family to settle in Texas, as described below. In a letter dated November 3 that was published under the title "On Board an Emigrant Ship," in the *Daily Picayune* (New Or-leans), Nov. 7, 1879, p. 8, col. 5., Coyle refers to Texas as the "new El Dorado," but his chief purpose is to advertise the supposedly ideal conditions on board the *Teutonia:*

> The steerage is scrupulously cleaned every morning, and examined by the captain, doctor and chief steward. The sanitary arrangements are perfect, and the discipline of the ship seems to be governed by that golden rule, "a time and place for everything, and everything in its proper time and place." Great care is taken to protect the moral-ity and safety of the female passengers.
>
> The food served in the steerage is of the best quality, and served with cleanliness and liberality.
>
> The stewardess and stewards are polite and attentive, especially to the children and sick. In the discharge of his onerous duties the chief steward, Mr. Owens, won the esteem of all. The doctor was zealous and attentive, and the state of our passengers' health during the voyage is his best recommendation.

As noted below, Wright's four-year-old son, who apparently had become ill during the voyage, died about one week after reaching the United States. Coyle was en route to New Philadelphia, the Anglo-American settlement established about sixty miles west of Houston by Kingsbury and the Galveston, Harrisburg, and San Antonio Railway. In his diary Wright offers an unfavorable description of this settlement.

5. "Emigration to Texas," *Times* (London), Nov. 13, 1879, p. 10, col. 1.

6. Biographical data concerning William Wright and his family was supplied by Wright's grandson William L. Wright of Portland, Oregon, in private letters to L. H. K.

7. William L. Wright was uncertain as to his grandfather's motives for emigration. Economic hardship does not seem to be one of them, although Wright no doubt was seeking economic opportunities abroad. Letter from W. L. W. to L. H. K., 19 May 19, 1992.

8. The passenger list for this voyage of the *Teutonia* has not survived, but evidence from various sources, including the newspaper article referring to the death of Wright's son, cited in note 9 below, supports the chronology given here.

9. The boy's death was reported in the *Galveston Daily News,* Nov. 12, 1879, p. 4, col. 1.

Chapter 4. The Diary

1. Three indecipherable words have been deleted from the heading.

2. La Coruña is a seaport on the northwest coat of Spain.

3. William Harris, referred to as W. H. in the original text, is the father of Wright's wife Agnes.

4. Wright refers to his wife Agnes as "A" throughout the diary.

5. Wright consistently refers to his brother Frank Wright as "F."

6. The photographs probably pertained to the shipwreck.

7. Beginning at this point, Wright occasionally notes the number of miles traveled by the *Teutonia* in a single day.

8. Wright records his brother's birthday.

9. Wright made no entry for April 6; however, it appears that he intentionally left a blank space, perhaps intending to fill it in later.

10. Wright habitually refers to W. G. Kingsbury, immigration agent of the Galveston, Harrisburg, and San Antonio (Sunset Road) Railroad, as "K."

11. There are extensive references to Williams and to Lavaca County in the text below. Moulton, Sweet Home, and Hallettsville are located in Lavaca County; Schulenburg and Flatonia are located in neighboring Fayette County.

12. Apparently this is the man identified in the entry for April 21 as Wright's friend and traveling companion Charles Smith and to whom multiple references are made in the following pages. There is also an additional reference to the man named Harley in the entry for April 17.

13. This is the first of several references to David Brown, a sheep rancher who lives near Pleasanton and to whom Kingsbury refers repeatedly in his pamphlet. Wright also refers to a C. Brown, who also raises sheep, in the entry for May 14.

14. The following was written vertically across the April 15 entry: "Received a letter from Agnes and one from Tom."

15. Wright writes "Edinbro.'"

16. Wright writes "Harely."

17. The Central Hotel in the city of San Antonio.

18. Unidentified.

19. A tent covering.

20. Not included in Kingsbury's pamphlet reprinted in Part 1.

21. The Guadalupe River.
22. At this point Wright inserts "a rough sketch of 2 sections for sale and one other which he would let at a nominal rent as he could not prove title" that is not reproduced here.
23. A hamlet in South Essex, England.
24. Wright does not give the name of the woman.
25. Unidentified.
26. Thomas Hawkins Wright, Wright's brother, to whom he also refers as "Tom."
27. Alsop and Caldwell are unidentified.
28. Unidentified.
29. Wright writes "Rock Creek."
30. Not identified.
31. Wright wrote "12:30 A.M."
32. Vigo is a city on the northwest coast of Spain.
33. See note 7 above regarding miles per day traveled.
34. Unidentified.
35. This is the final entry in the diary portion of Wright's notebook. Following the diary are nineteen pages of various lists of items, addresses, and other notations, most of which apparently relate to Wright's stay in Texas.

Part III. The Wreck of the *Missouri* and Czech Immigration to Texas in 1873

Chapter 5. Introduction

1. Bimini, or the Biminis, is a group of small islands, about nine square miles in total area, located in the Bahamas, east of Miami, Florida. The largest of the islands are North Bimini and South Bimini; it was on North Bimini that the Moravian immigrants took shelter after the wreck of the *Missouri* in 1873.
2. Ironically the description of the wreck given here is based on an account by Philip Janča, a specialist in the salvage of antique ships, who happens to be the great-grandson of Jan and Mariana Janča. At the time he investigated this site, he did not know that it was located at the precise coordinates reported for the wreck of the *Missouri* on October 1, 1873. Telephone conversation with L. H. K.
3. L. H. K., who is distantly related to the Bujnoch family through his great-grandmother Josefa and to the Olšovský family through his great-great-grandmother Mariana, first heard a version of the story involving the Moravian immigrants and their adventures in a series of telephone conversations in the fall of 1987 with Leo Baca, a specialist in Czech history and genealogy in Texas who is known for his transcripts of passenger lists of Czech immigrants who passed through the ports of Galveston, New Orleans, New York, and Baltimore. These conversations inspired the original research that eventually led to the writing of this section of the book.
4. The figures given for Austrian and Czech emigration are taken from Josef Polišenský, *Začiatky Českej a slovenskej emigrácie do USA* (Bratislava, 1970), 48.
5. For an overview of Czech immigration to Texas and a bibliography of specialized sources see Machann and Mendl, *Krásná Amerika*, 9–38.

6. The history of railroad construction in the Czech lands, particularly Moravia, during the period 1836–1906 is given in Josef Hons et al., *Čtení o severní dráze Ferdinandově* [Readings about Ferdinand's Northern Railroads] (Prague, 1990). The description of developments in railroad construction given in the text is based on this work.

7. German immigration to Texas already had become a big business by 1850. See Chester W. and Ethel H. Geue, *A New Land Beckoned* (Baltimore: Genealogical Publishing Co., 1966); Ethel H. Geue, *New Homes in a New Land* (Baltimore: Genealogical Publishing Co., 1970); and Terry G. Jordan, *German Seed in Texas Soil: Immigrant Farmers in Nineteenth-Century Texas* (Austin: University of Texas Press, 1975), and *Immigration to Texas* (Boston: American Press, 1980).

8. Rosenberg Library manuscript (78–0035), personal diary of Joseph Franklin, bk. 1, 80; and Galveston County Probate Cause #1255, bk. 10, 414, 444, 475–88, 589, 631.

9. "Kauffman & Runge," *Galveston Daily News,* Jan. 2, 1882, p. 2, col. 3. The Kauffman House provided information to the Republic of Texas in assisting the establishment of the Bremen-to-Galveston trade. See Anson Jones, *Memoranda and Official Correspondence Relating to the Republic of Texas—Its History and Annexation 1836 to 1846* (Chicago: Rio Grande Press, 1966), 207, 208.

10. Rosenberg Library, Galveston, Texas, Manuscript #56–0005.

11. This organization was incorporated in Texas as the German Immigration Co. German immigration to Texas already had become a big business by 1850. The *Verein* held its first meeting at Biebrich on the Rhine in 1842 and was formally organized in 1844. Galveston's Kauffman House was involved in the shipment of emigrants from Bremen to Galveston from the beginning of the *Verein*'s first shipments in 1844 through the charter steamship era, which ended in 1886.

12. Chester W. and Ethel H. Geue, *A New Land Beckoned,* 52. Solms says that he appointed Klainer as agent, and he implies that Fischer appointed E. Kauffman as agent without Solms's permission; however, Solms states that he appointed E. Kauffman as agent at Carlshafen (Indianola). According to newspaper accounts of the time, the first two ships were consigned to Kauffman, as were the vast majority of the ships that followed. Other historians refer to this arrangement as "Kauffman and Klainer," yet this partnership did not exist at this time. See Jones, *Memoranda and Official Correspondence Relating to the Republic of Texas,* 326, 327.

13. In 1841 and 1842 the Congress of the Republic of Texas passed laws that authorized the president to make contracts for the purpose of settling vacant lands in the Republic.

14. Rosenberg Library, Galveston, Texas, Manuscript #56–0005; and Henry J. Hauschild, *The Runge Chronicle—A German Saga of Success* (Victoria, Tex.: Privately printed, 1990), *passim.*

15. W. and D. Richardson, *Galveston City Directory,* 1859–60.

16. "Galvestonian Figured in Fight against Low Price of Cotton 50 Years Ago," *Galveston Daily News,* Sept. 10, 1931, p. 6.

17. Hauschild, 163, 164.

18. "Gigantic Attempt to Corner Cotton Market Once Made by Julius Runge, Merchant King," *Galveston Daily News,* Feb. 17, 1935, p. 5.

19. Machann and Mendl, *Krásná Amerika,* 35.

20. United States Department of Commerce, Bureau of the Census, *Thirteenth Census of the United States, 1910,* vol. 1 (Washington, D.C.: Department of Commerce, Bureau of the Census, 1910–14), 978, especially "General Report and Analysis, table 13."

Chapter 6. The Emigrants

1. Information about the Moravian emigrants is largely derived from oral histories contributed to L. H. K. during the period 1987–1993 by descendants of some of the families living in Texas. Some original audiotapes and additional documentation of the oral histories are in the possession of L. H. K.

   The Bujnoch-Láník oral history was contributed by Maj. Magdalene Drozd, U.S. Army Retired, daughter of Agnes Láník-Drozd and granddaughter of Karel and Josefa Láník, as it was relayed to her by Mrs. Annie (Baros) Láník-Wallace. Mrs. Wallace, now deceased, was the wife of František Láník, a youthful member of the emigrant group. Her information was received from her husband and his mother, Josefa Bujnoch-Láník, also a member of the original group. Portions of this history have been published in Dorothy Bujnoch, *The Bujnoch Family: Our Czech-American Heritage* (Halletsville, Tex.: private printing, 1986).

   The Simek oral history was preserved by Josef, Ferdinand, and Vlasta Simek, children of Ferdinand Simek and grandchildren of František and Mariana Šimek, the latter three being members of the emigrant group. As part of the research for this book, L. H. K. conducted an interview with Ferdinand and Vlasta at the family farm near Old Dime Box, Texas.

   The Janča oral history consists of a series of telephone interviews conducted by L. H. K. with Rudolph Janca, son of Jan Janca and grandson of Jan and Mariana Janča, the latter three being part of the emigrant group.

   Occasionally the oral histories as transcribed by L. H. K. are cited to document specific points of information, but it can be assumed that, when newspapers or other printed sources are not cited, the incidents as described in this book are based on the oral histories.
2. Šimek oral history.
3. Cited in Edgar E. Young, *Czechoslovakia: Keystone of Peace and Democracy* (London, 1938), 137.
4. Machann and Mendl, *Krásná Amerika,* 74–75.
5. See for examples the autobiographical accounts of Czech immigrants in *Czech Voices: Stories from Texas in the Amerikán Národní Kalendář,* ed. by Clinton Machann and James W. Mendl (College Station: Texas A&M University Press, 1991).
6. Quoted in Machann and Mendl, *Krásná Amerika,* 206. Valentin Haidušek is the father of Augustin Haidušek, whose article "A Short Outline of the Slavic Race in Texas" is included as an excerpt from the Siemering pamphlet in chapter 11.
7. Bujnoch-Láník oral history.
8. See Machann and Mendl, *Krásná Amerika,* 9–18.
9. Bujnoch-Láník oral history.
10. Bujnoch family history.
11. The Moravians were classified among the "710 German immigrants." U.S. newspapers routinely described Czech emigrants arriving from the Austrian Empire as "Germans."
12. "Immigration," *Daily Picayune* (New Orleans), Oct. 3, 1873, p. 1, col. 7; p. 8, col. 1.

Chapter 7. The Ship

1. "The Shipwreck of the Missouri," *Times* (London), Oct. 14, 1873, p. 5, col. 3; see also "Loss of the Steamship Missouri," *Daily Picayune* (New Orleans), Oct. 12, 1873, p. 4, col. 2.
2. The initial service of both the *Hammonia* and the *Borussia* as troop carriers was considered desirable because, in addition to the generous payments received, it gave the German sailing

crews the opportunity to gain experience in the operation of the steamships. See Frank C.
Bowen, *A Century of Atlantic Travel 1830–1930* (Boston: Little, Brown, 1930), 79–80; see also
David Budlong Tyler, *Steam Conquers the Atlantic* (New York: Arno Press, 1972), 253.

Fitted for passengers, each steamer was designed for 54 first-class and 146 second-class
passengers, with an additional 310 in steerage. They were both fine ships and were clocked at
twelve knots under good conditions (Bowen, 79–80).

3. The subsequent history of the *Borussia* is not unlike that of the *Hammonia* but more tragic.
Eventually it too was purchased by the Mississippi and Dominion Line and used on the
Liverpool-to-New Orleans route. On one such voyage in December, 1879, it sank during a
storm at sea with considerable loss of life, as discussed in the General Introduction above.
Like her sister ship, the *Borussia* had deteriorated through the years, and the circumstances
of her sinking suggested "structural weakness" as a contributing cause of the disaster. See
"The Loss of the Borussia," *Times* (London), Dec. 25, 1879, sec. A, B, p. 8. In this case, of
course, there is no hint of intentionality in the cause of the wreck. According to the *Times*
report, the *Borussia* was insured for only £20,000, while her cargo alone was estimated to be
worth £30,000. The ship's captain was among the 169 casualties.

4. Bowen, 102.

5. "Explosion on Board a Hamburg Steamer," *Times* (London), Sept. 8, 1858, p. 9, col. 6; see
also "Hamburg," *Times* (London), Sept. 20, 1858, p. 8, col. 5.

6. Bowen, 124.

7. "The Shipwreck of the Missouri," *Times* (London), Oct. 14, 1873, p. 5, col. 3.

8. "Mutiny," *Daily Picayune* (New Orleans), Mar. 10, 1873, p. 8, cols. 1–2.

9. "Marine News—Exports," *Daily Picayune* (New Orleans), Mar. 16, 1873, p. 9, col. 6.

10. "Loss of the Steamship Missouri," *Daily Picayune* (New Orleans), Oct. 12, 1873, p. 4, col. 2;
see also "Loss of a Steamer," *New York Times*, Oct. 12, 1873, p. 8, col. 5.

11. "Latest Intelligence," *Times* (London), Oct. 13, 1873, p. 5, col. 3; see also "Sabbath Flashes,"
Atlanta Constitution, Oct. 14, 1873, p. 1, col. 2; and "Loss of a Steamer," *New York Times*,
Oct. 12, 1873, p. 8, col. 5.

12. "October Disasters," *Galveston Daily News*, Nov. 7, 1873, p. 3, col. 6.

Chapter 8. The Last Voyage of the Missouri

1. "Sailings," *Times* (London), Sept. 12, 1873, p. 7, col. 6; see also "The Shipwreck of the Missouri," *Times* (London), Oct. 14, 1873, p. 5, col. 3.

2. Bowen, 89–90; see also, Melvin Maddocks, *Atlantic Crossing* (Alexandria, Va.: Time-Life
Books, 1981), 143–57.

3. Wines, liquor, and beer were used as sedatives by steerage passengers suffering from sea sickness. They were also commonly given to children suffering from nausea and dysentery
aboard ships, inadvertently compounding the common problem of dehydration. This practice accounts for the fact that during this period many children died on ocean voyages due
to alcohol poisoning.

4. "Grave Charges," *Daily Picayune* (New Orleans), Jan. 12, 1881, p. 2, col. 3. William Wright
also crossed over in the *Teutonia*, in March, 1879. See his comments in his diary, chapter 4,
beginning with the entry for March 15.

5. Janča oral history.

Chapter 9. From Shipwreck to Storm

1. Capt. John S. Simpson of Baltimore and a Mr. Paisly were passengers of the *Missouri* on her last voyage. After their arrival in New Orleans, they gave detailed statements concerning the wreck of the *Missouri* and the succeeding events: "The Wrecked Steamer Missouri," *Galveston Daily News,* Oct. 17, 1873, p. 2, col. 5; "Loss of the Steamship Missouri," *Times* (London), Oct. 18, 1873, p. 10, col. 6; Simpson's presence disputed, "The United States," *Times* (London), Oct. 18, 1873, p. 5, col. 3. The following account is reconstructed from Captain Simpson's and Mr. Paisly's statements, along with the statement given by Captain Pearson at Nassau, the decree of the Vice-Admiralty Court at Nassau by Acting Judge E. B. A. Taylor, and the Láník-Bujnoch, Janča, and Šimek oral histories. See "Wreck of an English Steamer on the Gingerbread Ground," *Nassau Guardian,* Oct. 8, 1873, p. 2, cols. 1, 2; this article does not claim that Pearson himself was the source of the information attributed to him; and see "In the Vice-Admirality Court of the Bahamas," *Nassau Guardian,* Dec. 6, 1873, p. 2, col. 2 (court decree); "Loss of the Steamship Missouri," *Times* (London), Oct. 18, 1873, p. 10, col. 6 (managing directors dispute the presence of a master mariner as a passenger). In response to Simpson's and Paisly's statements, the managing owners of the *Missouri* made a statement attesting that there was no master mariner who was a cabin passenger on board the *Missouri* and they were doubtful that there could have been among the steerage passengers anyone competent to criticize the conduct of the officers. It should be noted that parts of Captain Pearson's statement conflict with the information given by the other sources mentioned.

2. According to Simpson, "There was no apparent cause for the ship being wrecked at that time, and I believe that it was through carelessness or ignorance of the officers in charge. There was not an officer on deck at the time of the disaster. Nobody was in charge. . . ." See "The Wrecked Steamer Missouri," *Galveston Daily News,* Oct. 17, 1873, p. 2, col. 5. The oral histories often refer to "the captain"; however, it appears they are sometimes referring only to a uniformed officer. See Dorothy Bujnoch, *Bujnoch Family History* (Halletsville, Tex: private printing, 1986).

3. "The Wrecked Steamer Missouri," *Galveston Daily News,* Oct. 17, 1873, p. 2, col. 5.

4. According to Paisly, "The only service rendered by the captain, in saving life or property was by getting stupidly drunk. I did not notice that he drank until then. He made no exertion to lower away the boats or to do anything to relieve the distress of the passengers, but added insult to injury by wishing that most of the unfortunate passengers had been drowned." See "The Wreck of the Missouri," *New Orleans Times,* Oct. 17, 1873, p. 3, col. 1.

5. The Šimek oral history describes the stranded crew of the *Missouri* shooting pistol flares into the night sky to attract passing ships. In reality the signaling devices of the era were rockets. See "Lights on the Atlantic," *Times* (London), Sept. 16, 1873, p. 8, col. 4.

6. Bujnoch-Láník oral history.

7. Šimek oral history.

8. "The Wreck of the Missouri," *New Orleans Times,* Oct. 17, 1873, p. 3, col. 1.

9. James P. Baughman, *Mallorys of Mystic* (Middletown, Conn.: Wesleyan University Press, 1972), 58–59.

10. "Sabbath Flashes," *Atlanta Constitution,* Oct. 14, 1873, p. 1, col. 2; also supported by "New Orleans, Oct. 13," *Daily Houston Telegraph,* Oct. 14, 1873, p. 2, cols. 2–3; and "Loss of a Steamer," *New York Times,* Oct. 12, 1873, p. 8, col. 5.

11. "The October Storm," *Galveston Daily News,* Dec. 12, 1873, p. 1, col. 3.

12. "The Florida Cyclone," *Galveston Daily News,* Oct. 8, 1873, p. 1, col. 3; "The Florida Cyclone," *Galveston Tri-Weekly News,* Oct. 10, 1873, p. 1, col. 8; "Havana," *Daily Picayune* (New Orleans), Oct. 12, 1873, p. 1, col. 3; "The Storm," *Galveston Daily News,* Oct. 17, 1873, p. 2, col. 1.

13. "Havana, Oct. 6," *Daily Picayune* (New Orleans), Oct. 12, 1873, p. 1, col. 3.

14. "Havana, Oct. 7," *Daily Picayune* (New Orleans), Oct. 12, 1873, p. 1, col. 3.

15. See "Hurricane at Key West," *Nassau Guardian,* Oct. 22, 1873, p. 2, cols. 2–3, quoting the *Key West Dispatch,* Oct. 11, 1873.

16. "Wreck of an English Steamer," *Nassau Guardian,* Oct. 8, 1873, p. 2, cols. 1–2; and "Effects of the Gale," *Nassau Guardian,* Oct. 11, 1873, p. 2, cols. 1–2.

17. "[Untitled]," *Nassau Guardian,* Oct. 18, 1873, p. 2, col. 1.

18. Šimek oral history.

19. "Wreck of an English Steamer on the Gingerbread Ground," *Nassau Guardian,* Oct. 8, 1873, p. 2, cols. 1–2.

20. "[Untitled]," *Nassau Guardian,* Oct. 11, 1873, p. 2, col. 1; and "Effects of the Gale," *Nassau Guardian,* Oct. 11, 1873, p. 2, cols. 1–2.

21. "The Wrecked Steamer Missouri," *Galveston Daily News,* Oct. 17, 1873, p. 2, col. 5.

22. "Loss of the Steamship Missouri," *Daily Picayune* (New Orleans), Oct. 12, 1873, p. 4, col. 2; and clarified by "In Our Report of the Missouri," *Daily Picayune* (New Orleans), Oct. 14, 1873, p. 4, col. 4.

23. "Further from the Missouri," *Daily Picayune* (New Orleans), Oct. 13, 1873, p. 1, col. 3.

24. "List of Vessels," *Daily Picayune* (New Orleans), Oct. 14, 1873, p. 6, col. 2.

25. "Sailing of the Steamship Liberty," *Baltimore Sun,* Oct. 6, 1873, p. 4, col. 3.

26. "Arrival of the Steamship Falcon," *Baltimore Sun,* Oct. 6, 1873, p. 4, col. 2; and "Ship News—by Telegraph," *Baltimore Sun,* Oct. 7, 1873, p. 4, col. 6.

27. "H.M.S. Cherub," *Nassau Guardian,* Oct. 22, 1873, p. 2, col. 1.

28. "Arrival of the Liberty," *Daily Picayune* (New Orleans), Oct. 17, 1873, p. 8, col. 1.

29. Janča oral history.

30. We have been unable to document this rumor concerning immigrants sold into slavery.

31. "The Wrecked Steamer Missouri," *Galveston Daily News,* Oct. 17, 1873, p. 2, col. 5; see also "Baltimore, Havana & Key West," *Daily Picayune* (New Orleans), Oct. 20, 1873, p. 7, col. 6.

32. See chapter 5, note 2.

33. "In the Vice-Admirality Court of the Bahamas," *Nassau Guardian,* Dec. 6, 1873, p. 2, col. 2 [court decree].

Chapter 10. End of the Journey

1. "Galveston Quarantine Removed," *Daily Picayune* (New Orleans), Oct. 3, 1873, p. 8, cols. 1–2; see also "Board of Health," *Daily Picayune* (New Orleans), Oct. 4, 1873, p. 8, col. 2.

2. James P. Baughman, *Charles Morgan and the Development of Southern Transportation* (Nashville: Vanderbilt University Press, 1968), 103, 157–59, 241. The ferries at the time were the *Porter,* the *Lucretia,* and the *Sarah.*

3. Baughman, *Charles Morgan,* 103, 155–56.

4. Ibid., 103, 149, 155–56.

5. Ibid., 179–80.

6. However, note the reference in chapter 5 to "Julia Šimek," supposedly the twin sister of Cecilia Šimek.

7. Bujnoch-Láník oral history.

8. "Marine," *Galveston Daily News,* Oct. 21, 1873, p. 4, col. 2.

9. "Galveston, Houston & Henderson Railroad Schedule," *Galveston Daily News,* volumes in October, 1873.

10. Charles P. Zlatkovich, *Texas Railroads: A Record of Construction and Abandonment* (Austin: University of Texas Bureau of Business Research, 1981), 69–70.

11. "Galveston, Houston & Henderson Railroad Schedule," *Galveston Daily News,* volumes in October, 1873.

12. Zlatkovich, 63, 69.

13. "The Citizen," *Galveston Daily News,* Oct. 22, 1873, p. 4, col. 1; see also "Gone Forward," *Galveston Daily News,* Nov. 8, 1873, p. 3, col. 2. The Galveston, Harrisburg, and San Antonio Railroad, which aggressively promoted immigration to Texas, is discussed more fully in chapter 1. In 1877 the company justified its name by completing track all the way to San Antonio.

14. Šimek oral history.

15. "From Columbus," *Galveston Daily News,* Oct. 23, 1873, p. 2, col. 3; see also "Changing Their Base," *Galveston Daily News,* Oct. 22, 1873, p. 3, col. 1.

16. Šimek oral history.

17. See Machann and Mendl, 46.

18. Machann and Mendl, 46–47.

19. Šimek oral history.

20. Janča oral history.

Chapter 11. Excerpts from Texas co cíl stěhování (Texas as a Destination for Emigration, 1882)

1. Portions of Siemering's pamphlet were translated from the Czech for this edition by Daniela Kukrechtová.

2. As pointed out in the General Introduction, however, Siemering had established a reputation as a German-American writer. His novel *Ein verfehltes Leben,* published by the Druck der freien Presse für Texas in San Antonio in 1876, was translated and adapted as *The Hermit of the Cavern,* by May E. Francis, and published by the Naylor Printing Company of San Antonio in 1932. A journalist and novelist of considerable ability, Siemering continued to write in German until his death in 1883, shortly after he had lent his talents to the Galveston, Harrisburg, and San Antonio Railroad and its master propagandist and recruiter of immigrants, W. G. Kingsbury.

3. For more on Haidušek, see Machann and Mendl, *Krásná Amerika,* 86–89, 171–86, 221–27.

4. This reference is confusing, since Siemering—like Kingsbury, before he moved to England—was a resident of San Antonio.

5. These excerpts are taken from an appendix to the brochure. "Immigrants' Housing" is part of a section under the heading "Texas in the Year 1882."

6. Pohl refers to a vegetable he calls "batata," which we conjecture is a Czech slang term for the American sweet potato.

7. The Czech Republic today is made up of two major geographical and administrative regions, Bohemia and Moravia, that have closely related but in some ways distinctive histories. Both Bohemians and Moravians speak the Czech language (although there are distinctive

Moravian dialects in the spoken language) and are generally referred to as "Czechs." However, the Czech name for geographical Bohemia is *Čechy*, for Moravia, *Morava*, and, strictly speaking, the majority of Czechs who settled in Texas originated from Moravia and were not Bohemians at all; some of them resented being called Czechs rather than Moravians. On the distinctively Moravian identity of Czech immigrants in Texas, see Machann and Mendl, *Krásná Amerika*, 169–70, and Machann and Mendl, eds., *Czech Voices*, 113–33.

8. Haidušek published this short article three years before launching his own highly successful Czech-language journal *Svoboda* (also in the city of La Grange), as mentioned above. Haidušek's reference to the Czech-American newspaper *Slovan* is ironic in that he later became a bitter rival of its editor, Josef S. Čada. See Machann and Mendl, *Krásná Amerika*, 181–84.

Index

Pages with illustrations are indicated by
italic typeface.

Abbotts, Lancelot (letter by), 23–24, 58
Achilles (ship), 132
Adams, Thomas A., 133
Adamson, Elizabeth, 8
Adamson, William, 8
Admired (ship), 125–26, 127
Agincourt (ship), 76
Aimee French Opera Troupe, 133–34
Allan Line, 119
Allen, W. R., 57
Alleyton and area, 96
Allis, Mr., 93, 94
American Line, 161–63n11
America (ship), 16
Andrews, Mr., 96
Arch, Joseph, 21–22
Atascosa County, 43, 63
Atlantic travels. *See* ocean voyages
Austin, Moses, 73
Austin County, 154
Austrian army, 109, 111–12

Baca, Leo, 166n3
Baker, Francis C. R., 133
Ball, Hutchins, and Co., 58
Baltimore and Havana Steamship
    Company, 133
Baring, Brothers, and Co., 58
Becker, Karl, 115, 135
Bee County, 43, 48–51, 49
beekeeping, 26
Beeville, Texas, 43, 49, 50
Belgian (ship), 119–20. *See also Missouri*
    (ship)

Belle (ship), 131–32
Benjamin, J. P., 58
Bergman, Josef Ernst, 105–106
Bexar County, 43
Bimini (islands), 105, 125, 127–33, 166n1
Blaha, Josef, 140
Blanco and area, 88–89
Blue Jacket (ship), 100
Bluff, Texas, 141
Blum & Co., 152
Boerne and area, 51–52, 65, 84–85
Bohemia, 105–106, 154, 172–73n7
Borden, Texas, 81
Borussia (ship), 7–8, 118, 157, 168–69n2,
    168n3
Bourne, Stephen, 29
Bracketville, Texas, 43
Bradfield, Mr., 94
Brashear, Louisiana (Morgan City), 76,
    77, 137
Brazos River and area, 35–36, 98
Bremen, Germany, 16, 106, 107, 115
Bright, Mr., 94–95
Brother, Mr. (Bracketville), 58
Brothers, Mr. (London), 43
Brothers, Mr. (San Antonio), 58
Brothers (ship), 132
Brown, C., 90
Brown, David, 43, 46, 75, 82–83, 165n13
Buček, Frank, 143–44
Buček, Magdalena, 143–44
Bujnoch, Anna, *143*
Bujnoch, Cecelia, *143*
Bujnoch, Frances, *143*
Bujnoch, Františka, 109
Bujnoch, George, Jr., *143*
Bujnoch, Jakub, 109

Bujnoch, Jan, 109
Bujnoch, Jim, *143*
Bujnoch, Jiří, 109, 116–17, 143
Bujnoch, Joe, *143*
Bujnoch, Johanna (born Kublak), 109,
    112, 113
Bujnoch, John, *143*
Bujnoch, Josef, 113
Bujnoch, Josefa (later Láník), 109, 112,
    124, 125, 137–38, 143, 168*n*1
Bujnoch, Mariana, 109, 144
Bujnoch, Mariana (born Olšovský), 109
Bujnoch, Peter, *143*
Bujnoch family, 109, 111, 112, 113, 116–17,
    143–44, 168*n*1
Burr, Charles, 51
Burr, F. E., 43, 48–52
Butler, Sutherland, 131

Caird and Co., 7, 118
Caldwell County, 8
capital. *See* expenses/revenues
Caribbean voyages, 80–81, 99–100, 133–35
Cartwright, Dr., 62
Castroville and area, 26, 43, 86–87
Castroville Era, 65
Cat Spring, 105–106
cattle ranching, 33–37, 49, 67, 147
Chamber of Commerce, Galveston, 57
Chandley, Mr., 124–25, 134
Cherub (gunboat), 133, 134
Chili (ship), 129
Chlebovice, Moravia, 109–10
churches: built by Moravian immigrants,
    141, 143; Haidušek's description, 155;
    testimonials, 50, 54, 55; Wright's
    descriptions, 88, 93, 96
Cibolo Creek, 89
Civil War, 95, 108
Clare, Richard, 131
Clarke, Mr., 99–100
Cling (German farmer), 85
Clinton, Texas, 81
Clos (Koláš), Rosalie (later Žárský), 110,
    143

coal, 60–61
Coal Creek and area, 87
Colorado Citizen, 65
Colorado County, 141, 154, 161*n*10
Colorado River, 35–36
Columbus and area, 95–96, 139, 140,
    160*n*10
Comal County, 24
Constantia (ship), 108
Content and area, 95
Cooke, Mr., 97–98
Cooper, Mr., 58
copper, 60–61
corn crops: Kingsbury's descriptions, 24–
    25, 27, 32; testimonials, 151–53;
    Wright's descriptions, 88, 91, 92, 93
costs. *See* expenses/revenues
cotton crops: Kingsbury's descriptions,
    24–25, 27, 32, 35–36, 147, 148;
    testimonials, 151–53; Wright's
    descriptions, 85–86, 88, 91
Cotton Factors, 58
Coyle, J. C., 74, 164–65*n*4
Crane, Mr., 94, 95
Crane, Mrs., 95
Crescent Mutual Insurance Company, 135
crops. *See* farming/ranching, crops/
    livestock
Cuba, 80, 100, 121, 134–35
Curtis, Edward P., 58
Cutrer, Thomas, 73
Czecho-Saxonian Railroad Company, 106

dairy farming, 66, 151
Darden, Stephen H. (letter by), 57
death rates, England/Texas compared, 64
debt protection, 67–68
Dobrola, Josef, 152–53
Drnholec, Moravia, 110
droughts, 27, 54, 81, 82, 84
Drozd, Magdalene, 168*n*1
Dubina, Texas, 141

Eagle Lake, Texas, 81, 96–97
Eagle Pass, Texas, 43

Edward Kauffman and Co., 107

Edwards County, 91

England, emigration to Texas, 7, 73

English peas, 60

expenses/revenues: debt protection, 67–68; farming, 29–33, 58–59, 61–63; immigration travel, 67, 68, 107, 110, 116, 161–63n11; lodging, 99; salvage operations, 126, 132, 135–36; testimonials, 151–53; timber, 152; wagon rental, 82. *See also* land prices

expenses/revenues, livestock: cattle, 33–37, 147; dairy cows, 66; goats, 90; hogs, 59–60, 67; horses, 41, 42, 83; sheep, 42–43, 44, 45, 46, 47–48, 50, 90, 161n8

fares, passenger, 68, 160–62n11

farming/ranching, crops/livestock: cattle, 33–37, 49, 67, 147; dairy cows, 66, 151; fruit, 26, 67, 96; hogs, 59–60, 67, 151–53; horses, 37–42, 67, 151–53; oats, 25, 27, 151–53; sugar, 24–25, 47, 59–60, 61–63; vegetables, 26, 67, 152, 153; wheat, 25, 32, 81, 85, 88, 91, 147. *See also* corn crops; cotton crops; sheep ranching

farming/ranching, generally: Haidušek's portrayal, 154–55; Kingsbury's descriptions, 19, 24–33, 66–67; tenant arrangements, 63–64, 149, 151–53; testimonials, 51–55, 150–53; Wright's descriptions, 81, 88

Fayette County, 8, 140–41, 153, 154–55, 165n11

Fayette County Record, 65

Fayetteville, Texas, 141

Fecht, Isidor, 152

fences, 31–32, 34

Fern (ship), 129

Finsterne (ship), 49

fishing, 85, 86

Fitzpatrick, N., 134

Flatonia, Texas, 165n11

Flinn, Main, and Montgomery, 135

Florida, 150

Forbes, Captain, 137

Ford, E. A., 57

forests. *See* timber/forests

Fortuna (ship), 108

Francis, May E., 172n2

Fredericksburg and area, 31, 86, 87–88

Frolic (ship), 126

fruit crops, 26, 67, 96

Fryčovice, Moravia, 109

Galveston, Harrisburg, and San Antonio Railroad: criticisms of, 74–75, 97–98; Kingsbury's promotion, 8, 19–20; Moravian emigrant travels, 139–40; role in immigration, 8, 15–17, 73–74, 145, 159n9; testimonials for, 20–24

Galveston, Houston, and Henderson Railroad, 138–39

Galveston, Texas, 19, 57, 106, 107–108, 137–38, 152

Galveston News, 65

Gaster, Captain, 120

Gay, R. K. (letter by), 61–63

geography, descriptions: Kingsbury's, 19, 63; Siemering's, 149; Wright's, 81, 84, 89, 93–94

geology/minerals, 60–61

George W. Clyde (ship), 129

Gerlic, Jakub, 151–52

German colony, Fredericksburg area, 31

German Immigration Society, 107, 115–16, 135, 167nn11, 12

Gillespie County, 31

Gingerbread Ground, 124

goats, 90

Godden, Mr., 92

Goldie (Verde Creek man), 85

Gonzales and area, 65, 92–93

Gonzales County, 24

grasshoppers, 26–27

Green, Rowan, 161n10

Griner, Hulet, 43

Grinshaw, C., 58

Guadalupe County, 24

Guadalupe River and area, 24, 67, 84, 91–92
Guion Line, 161*n*11
Gullet, Mr., 91, 92
guns, 65
Gutenberg (ship), 159*n*8

Habenicht, Jan, 141
Hackberry and area, 94–95
Haidušek, Augustin, 5, 145, 154–55
Haidušek, Valentin, 112, 141
Hall, Mr., 58
Hallettsville and area, 8, 94–95, 141, 165*n*11
Hamburg America Line, 118–19
Hammonia (ship), 7, 118–19, 168–69*n*2. *See also Missouri* (ship)
Hanna, James Sebastian, 126
Hannover (ship), 117, 140
Harley (Wright's companion), 82, 83
Harris, Ann Agnes (later Wright), 76–77, 90, 99, 101
Harris, William, 76
Harrisburg, Texas, 139–40
Harris County, 8
Hatch, Harry G., 133
Havana, Cuba, 80, 100, 121, 134–35
Hayden, Peter, 87
Hays County, 65
health conditions: Kingsbury's descriptions, 64, 66; testimonials, 50, 52, 55, 161*n*10; Wright's descriptions, 81, 93; yellow fever epidemic, 137, 140
Henry, J. W., 132
Hobby, A. M., 57
hog raising, 59–60, 67, 151–53
honey crops, 26
horse ranching, 37–42, 67, 85, 151–53
Hostyn, Texas, 141
houses, 29–31, 149, 150–51
Houston, Texas, 81, 98–99
Hubbard, R. B., 56–57, 160*n*5
Hudgins, L. M., 133–34
Huggins and Co., 57–58
hunting, 82, 85–86

hurricanes, 127–33
Hutchins, Mr., 58
Hutchinson (ship), 99
Hydtmann, Captain, 118

Immigrants Guide to Western Texas Sunset Route, 15–17, 160*n*9
immigration/immigrants (generally): arrival/early years, 9–11; dreams/expectations, 5–7, 9, 110–11; information sources, 3–4, 5–6, 16–17, 74, 105–6, 111, 145, 160*n*9; statistics, 7, 16, 105, 108, 147, 154, 159*n*5; Texas legislative incentives, 107, 159–60*n*2, 167*n*13; travel routes, 7–8, 64–65, 106–107, 161–63*n*11
Indianola, Texas, 107, 108
The Inquirer, 65
insect pests, 26–27
Ireland, emigration statistics, 159*n*5
iron, 60–61
istle (pita plant), 37, 160*n*5

Jackson, Texas, 139
Jacob, R., 49, 51
Jalufka, Agnes (later Liberda), 143
James, John: background, 43–44; on sheep raising, 44–48
Janča, Frances, *142*
Janča, Františka, 143
Janča, Jan, 110, 131, *142*, 143, 168*n*1
Janča, Jan (John A.), 110, *142*, 143, 168*n*1
Janča, Johanna, *142*
Janča, Josef, *142*
Janča, Karolina, *142*
Janča, Mariana, 110
Janča, Mariana (born Liberda), 110, 143
Janča, Marie (born Liberda), *142*
Janča, Mary, *142*
Janca, Philip, 136, 166*n*2
Janca, Rudolph, 168*n*1
Janča, Veronika (later Polášek), 110
Janča family, 110, 122–23, *142*, 143, 144, 168*n*1
Janda, Josef, 141

Jaspar (ship), 125–26
John Fry Hotel, 163*n*12
Johnson, Thomas J. (letter by), 55–56
Judson, George H., 43
Julia Howard (ship), 129, 131

Kahanek, Frank, *143*
Kahanek, Veronica, *143*
Kauffman, Edward, 107, 167*n*12
Kauffman, Julius, 107–108
Kauffman, Julius, Jr., 108
Kauffman House, 107, 167*n*11
Kendall County, 65
Kerrville and area, 85
Kingsbury, William Gilliam: background,
    15; criticisms of, 74–75, 81, 83–84, 97;
    role in immigration, 16–17, 73–74;
    testimonials for, 53, 56–57
Kinney County, 43
kinship ties and immigration (generally),
    9–10
Klimiček, Alois, 141
Knipr, Jiří, 153
Kočích, Mariana (later Šimek), 109, 168*n*1
Koerth, Texas, 143
Koláš, Rosalie (later Žárský), 110, 143
Kozelsky, Agnes (later Steffek), 144
Kubálová, Terezie, 141
Kuběna, Clara (later Moris), 110
Kublak, Johanna (later Bujnoch), 109,
    112, 113
Kutač, Joseph, 143
Kutač, Victoria, 143

Lady of the Lake (ship), 129, 131
La Grange, Texas, 141
La Grange New Era, 65
Laird Brothers, 119
land: credit buying, 161*n*10; as emigration
    incentive, 5–6, 9, 28, 68–70, 110–11;
    rental arrangements, 63–64, 66, 149,
    151–53
land grants, 15, 159–60*n*2
land prices: Kingsbury's statements, 30,

32–33, 47, 147, 148; testimonials, 49–
    50, 52, 53; Wright's statements, 87, 89,
    94, 96
Langdon, Colonel, 129
Langley & Son, 15–17, 160*n*9
Láník, Agnes (later Drozd), 143–44, 168*n*1
Láník, Annie (later Wallace), 168*n*1
Láník, Frank, 125
Láník, František, 168*n*1
Láník, Jiří, 137–38
Láník, Josefa (born Bujnoch), 109, 112,
    124, 125, 137–38, 143, 168*n*1
Láník, Karel, 109, 168*n*1
Láník family, 107, 111, 113, 143–44, 168*n*1
Lavaca County, 90, 141, 143, 154, 165*n*11
law enforcement, 55, 65
law schools, 66
lead, 60–61
Leal and Brothers, 43
Lemonias and Co., 58
Leon Blum & Co., 152
Leon Springs, 43, 84, 89
Lešikar, Josef L., 106
Liberda, Agnes (born Jalufka), 143
Liberda, Joe, 110, 143
Liberda Janča, Marie, *142*
Liberty (ship), 133–35
limestone, 60–61
livestock. *See* farming/ranching *entries*
Lloyds of London, 120, 127, 135
Londonge, F., 83
Louisiana and Texas Railroad, 137
Lubbock, F. R., 58
Luling and area, 81–82, 92, 97
Lytle, Samuel, 43

Manchaca, Captain, 27
Matchless (ship), 126
Mathias, Henry, 120
Matula, Václav, 141
Maverick County, 43
McCulloch and Co., 58
McGowans, Mr., 94–95
Medina County, 43, 65
Memphis (ship), 76

Merino sheep. *See* sheep ranching
mesquite, 27
minerals/geology, 60–61
Mississippi and Dominion Line, 7–8, 16, 76, 120, 161–62n11, 169n3. *See also* *Missouri* (ship)
Missouri (ship): background, 7, 119–20; grounding/wrecking, 105, 124–26, 170nn1, 2, 4; last voyage, 121–23; salvage operations, 126, 131–33, 135–36
Místek, Moravia, 114
Mitchell, Mr., 95
Mizera, Charles, *143*
Moravia, Czech Republic, 172–73n7
Moravia, Texas, 141
Moravian emigrants: Bimini to New Orleans journey, 133–35; departure process, 112–16; families summarized, 109–10; hurricanes, 127–31; incentives for leaving, 105–106, 110–12; New Orleans to Texas journey, 137–41; ocean voyage, 121–23; shipwreck/ rescue, 124–26, 133; statistics, 154
Morgan, Charles, 137
Morgan, J. S, 58
Morgan City, Louisiana, 76, 77, 81, 137
Moris, Clara (born Kubena), 110
Moris, Ferdinand, 110
Moris, Mariana, 110
Moris family, 110, 113, 143, 144
Morris, Francis, 87
Morryce, Mr., 43
Moulton and area, 8, 93–94, 165n11
Mulberry, Texas, 141
mustangs, 38–39

National Bank, Missouri, 58
National Line, 161–62n11, 163n12
Navidad, Texas, 141
Naylor Printing Company, 172n2
Nelson, Dr., 90
Nevlud, Johana (later Olšovský), 109, 141–43
New Braunfels and area, 91
New Orleans, 80–81, 99, 135, 137

New Philadelphia, Texas, 81, 97–98
newspapers, 65–66, 135, 141, 145, 155, 173n8
Newton, Henry, 40
New York, 150
New York and Galveston Line, 129
North Bimini, 105, 125, 166n1
Northern Railroad of Emperor Ferdinand (KFNB), 106
Northern State Railroad, 106
North German Lloyd Line, 16, 106–107, 115
Novák, Matěj, 141

Oakland, Texas, 95
oat crops, 25, 27, 151–53
ocean voyages: general immigration routes, 64, 106–107, 161–63n11; Moravian emigrants, 121–23; Wright's, 76–77, 79–81, 99–101
Olšovský, Agnes, 109
Olšovský, František, 109
Olšovský, Františka, 109
Olšovský, Jiří, 109
Olšovský, Johana (born Nevlud), 109, 141, 143
Olšovský, Mariana (later Bujnoch), 109
Olšovský, Paulina, 141, 143
Olšovský family, 109, 113, 141, 143
oxcart journey, 140–41

Paisly, Mr., 135, 170nn1, 4
Pargač, John, 143
Pargač, Teresa, 143
Parrish, W. D., 43
Passenger Act, 121
Pearson, Charles Edward, 120, 124–25, 127, 133, 134, 170nn1, 4
Pedernales Creek and area, 85–87
Peirce, Thomas W., 16, 74, 97
Petersen, Fred, 161n10
Pfeil, Jan, 151
pita plant (istle), 37, 160n5
Pleasanton, Texas, 43, 82
Pohl, Frant., 152

Polášek, Františka, 110
Polášek, Josef, 110
Polášek, Veronika (born Janča), 110
Polášek, Vincent, 110
Polášek family, 110, 143, 144
Polish colony, Wilson County, 30–31
Pontefract, Mr., 97
population statistics: immigrant, 7, 16, 105, 108, 147, 154, 159n5; Texas generally, 7, 8, 148, 159n3; U.S., 149–50
potato crops, 26, 152, 153
Pothonier, Hall and Co., 58
Praha, Texas, 141
Proof (ship), 132

Quiver (ship), 132

railroads: Czech, 106, 114–15; fares, 161–63n11; immigrant routes, 64–65, 114–15, 138–40; land grants/sales, 15, 146–47, 159–60n2; Morgan's operation, 137; and ranching, 35, 36, 59, 147; strikes, 66; transnational, 146; Wright's travels, 77, 81–82. *See also* Galveston, Harrisburg, and San Antonio Railroad
rain. *See* weather/climate
Ralph, F. H., 49
ranching. *See* farming/ranching *entries*
Reid, Captain, 99
rental arrangements, 63–64, 66, 149, 151–53
revenues/expenses. *See* expenses/revenues
ribbon cane crops, 62
Richardson, Mr., 92
Richardson, W. R. (letter by), 53–54
Richmond and area, 98
Riepl, Franz, 106
rivers, descriptions: Kingsbury's, 19, 24, 35–36, 67; Wright's, 84, 91–92. *See also* water, descriptions
robota, 112
Rock, James L., 16
Rocky Creek and area, 94
Rodgers, Mr., 96

Runge, Henry, 107–108
Runge, Julius, 108
Rusk County, 8
Russell, Peter, 131
Rutland County, England, 64

Saluda Creek, 89
San Antonio and area: clergyman testimonial, 55; Kingsbury's statements, 20, 24–25, 26, 35, 64; Richardson's statements, 53; sheep ranching, 42, 43; Wright's observations, 82, 83–84, 90–91
San Antonio Express, 65
San Antonio Herald, 65
San Marcos and area, 91–92
San Marcos Free Press, 65
San Saba News, 66
Saunders, Joseph, 125–26, 136
scab disease, 43, 44
schools, 20, 66, 92, 141, 147, 155
Schulenburg, Texas, 151–52, 165n11
Schwensen, Captain, 118
Scotland, emigration statistics, 159n5
Scott, B. J., 51
Scott, James M., 25
Searcy, J. G. (letter by), 57
Seguin Times, 65
Selma and area, 91
sheep ranching: Burr's letter, 48–52; James' article on, 43–48; Kingsbury's descriptions, 42–43, 48, 66, 67, 161n8; Wright's descriptions, 82–83, 86, 90
shipwrecks, 7–8, 76, 105, 124–26, 170nn1, 2, 4
Siemering, August, 5, 145, 171n2
Šilar, Josef, 106
Silas Weeks and Co., 133, 135
silver, 60–61
Šimek, Adolf, 141
Šimek, Cecilia, 109
Šimek, Ferdinand, 109, 125, 130, 168n1
Šimek, Ferdinand, Jr., 168n1
Šimek, František, 109
Šimek, Jan, 109

Šimek, Josef, 109, 167*n1*
Šimek, Julia, 109
Šimek, Mariana (born Kočích), 109,
    168*n1*
Šimek, Vlasta, 167*n1*
Šimek family, 109, 113, 125, 130, 141, 144,
    168*n1*
Simpson, John S., 135, 170*nn1, 2*
slavery, 95
Slavic groups: emigration statistics, 7, 16,
    105, 108, 154; Haidušek's history, 154–
    55
Slovan (newspaper), 155
Smith, Charles, 82, 84, 86, 89–90, 165*n12*
Smith, Jarnes, 58
Smith, Mr., 58
Smith, W. I., 16
snakes, 65
Solms, Mr., 167*n12*
Soper, A. W., 57
sorghum crops, 59–60, 62–63
Southern and Western Texas Guide for 1878
    (Rock and Smith), 16
Southern Pacific Railroad, 20, 146–47
St. Louis Iron Mountain and Southern
    Railroad, 57
St. Louis (ship), 99–101
St. Nicholas Hotel, 163*n12*
Štancl, Frant., 151
Startin, George, 51
Steffek, Agnes (born Kozelsky), 144
Steffek, Rudolph, 144
Stephenson, James D. (letter by), 51–52
Stone, William, 43
Strassburg (ship), 115–16
strawberry crops, 26
sugar crops, 24–25, 47, 59–60, 61–63
Sunset Road. *See* Galveston, Harrisburg,
    and San Antonio Railroad
Sutherland Springs, Texas, 65
Suwa (ship), 100
Svoboda (newspaper), 145, 172*n8*
Sweet Home and area, 8, 94, 110, 143,
    165*n11*

Tapscott, Smith, and Co., 58
taxes, 67, 87
Taylor, E. B. A., 136, 170*n1*
Taylor, Old Man, 86
temperatures. *See* weather/climate
Temple, Captain, 86
tenant farming arrangements, 63–64, 66,
    149, 151–53
testimonials: clergymen, 53–56; farmers,
    51–52, 150–53; Kingsbury's list of, 57–
    58; sheep ranchers, 44–51; for Texas/
    immigration generally, 20–24, 53–56;
    Texas state officials, 56–57
Teutonia (ship), 76–77, 79–80, 121–22,
    164–65*n4*
Texas Farm and Freehold Union of
    England, 73–74
Thorne, John, 125, 126
timber/forests: Kingsbury's descriptions,
    19, 31–32, 49, 55; testimonials, 152;
    Wright's descriptions, 81–82, 85, 88,
    89, 92, 93
Todd, Elizabeth, 7
Todd, William, 7
tradesmen/professionals, 68–69, 163*n3*
Two Brothers (ship), 125–26

Union Land Register, 65
Uvalde County, 43, 47

Vanderbilt (ship), 132
Vanquish (ship), 126
vegetable crops, 26, 67, 152, 153
Verde Creek, 85
Verein zum Schutze . . . (German
    Immigration Society), 107, 135,
    167*nn11, 12*

wages. *See* expenses/revenues
Wales, emigration statistics, 159*n5*
Walker, Samuel Hamilton, 15
Wallace, Annie (earlier Láník), 168*n1*
Walthew and Co., 58
Washington County, 8, 154

water, descriptions: Kingsbury's, 19, 45, 49, 51, 55; Wright's, 87, 88, 89, 92. *See also* rivers, descriptions

weather/climate: Kingsbury's descriptions, 19, 20, 27–28, 59, 163*n*11; testimonials, 45–46, 50, 52, 53, 54, 55; Wright's descriptions, 81, 82, 84, 87, 90, 93, 95

Weeks and Co., 133

Weimar, Texas, 139

Weller, Commissioner, 120

Wesleyan (ship), 132

wheat crops, descriptions: Kingsbury's, 25, 32, 147; Wright's, 81, 85, 88, 91

White, James (testimonial), 20–22, 68

White Star Line, 161–62*n*11, 163*n*12

Whitney (steamer), 77, 137–38

wildlife, 39, 65, 82, 84–85

Wilkinson, Mr., 96

Williams, John, 82

Williams, Mr., 94–95

Wilson, Mr., 96

Wilson County, 30–31

Wilson County Chronicle, 65–66

Windel, Bedřich, 153

Witff, Sebastion, 26

Wolsey, Mr., 62–63

wool. *See* sheep ranching

Wright, Ann Agnes (born Harris), 76–77, 90, 99, 101

Wright, Percy Walker, 77

Wright, Thomas Hawkins, 80

Wright, William, *75*; biographical highlights, 10, 75–77; commonalities with Moravian immigrants, 6–8

Wright's diary: horseback travels, 84–90, 91–99; ocean voyages, 79–81, 99–101; railroad journey, 81–82; San Antonio stays, 82, 83–84, 90–91; wagon trip, 82–83

Wurzbach, Dan, 87, 88

yellow fever epidemic, 137, 140

Žárský, Cecilia, 143

Žárský, Jakub (junior), 110

Žárský, Jakub (senior), 110

Žárský, Jan, 110

Žárský, Mariana, 110

Žárský, Rosalie (born Koláš), 110, 143

Žárský, Tereza, 110

Žárský family, 110, 143

Zeller, Karel, 152

ISBN 1-58544-317-4

90000

9 781585 443178